Classroom pedagogy and prim...

In this provocative book, David McNamara looks at primary education as it struggles to create for itself a post-Plowden ideology. He argues first of all that a 'teacher-centred' approach to teaching in the primary school, especially in the later years, is actually in the best interests of the children. The teacher must be seen to have ultimate responsibility for what and how children learn, and at the heart of the complex relation between teaching and learning is the subject matter of teaching defined in the broadest sense. The upshot of debates about teaching methods, matching, and curriculum organisation should be to focus upon the tasks provided for children so as to foster their learning. Second, McNamara attempts to define the distinctive professional expertise of the primary teacher – the application of subject knowledge within the special circumstances of the classroom – and to show how this expertise can be articulated and codified to establish a body of educational knowledge which is both derived from practice and practically useful to others.

At a time when primary education is at the top of the political agenda, this book takes a refreshingly unbiased look at the educational issues involved. It will help teachers at all levels to define their own role in the creation of educational knowledge.

David McNamara taught in primary schools before his university career and has researched and published widely in the fields of teacher education and educational practice. He is currently Professor of Primary Education at the University of Hull.

Classroom pedagogy and primary practice

David McNamara

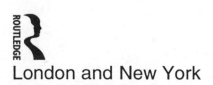

London and New York

First published 1994
by Routledge
11 New Fetter Lane, London EC4P 4EE

Simultaneously published in the USA and Canada
by Routledge
29 West 35th Street, New York, NY 10001

© 1994 David McNamara

Typeset in Palatino by LaserScript, Mitcham, Surrey
Printed and bound in Great Britain by
TJ Press (Padstow) Ltd, Padstow, Cornwall

British Library Cataloguing in Publication Data
A catalogue record for this book is available from the British Library

Library of Congress Cataloging in Publication Data
has been applied for.

ISBN 0–415–08311–7
ISBN 0–415–08312–5 (pbk)

To my mother and father

Contents

List of figures   ix
Acknowledgements   x

Introduction   1

1 **On teaching**   8
  Teaching as a familiar activity   9
  The inherent stability of teaching   14
  The classroom context for teaching and learning   21

2 **On learning**   24
  The psychological contribution   25
  The sociological contribution   28
  The child's disposition to learn   32

3 **The teacher's responsibility for learning**   38
  Learning as a practical activity   43

4 **Relating teaching to children's aptitudes**   46
  Matching teaching to learning   46
  The evidence   47
  Assessing the evidence   51
  Closeness of match   54
  What can and cannot be seen   59
  Summary   61

5 **Organising teaching to promote learning**   63
  Maximising the time and opportunity for learning   63
  To group or not to group   64
  Teaching as practical pedagogy   67
  Demonstrating to children the importance of work   71
  Learning as work   72
  Summary   78

6 Organising subject matter for learning   80
   The organisation of knowledge   82
   Knowledge of subject matter and its application   89
   How is the teacher's knowledge to be acquired?   91
   The application of subject matter knowledge   92
   Summary   97

7 Pedagogy in practice: the case of subtraction   99
   The research evidence   100
   Practical considerations   105

8 Teachers' pedagogic expertise   109
   Teachers' practical pedagogy   109
   Acquiring vernacular pedagogy   113
   The method   117
   Interpreting vernacular pedagogy   120
   Vernacular pedagogy by proxy   122
   Summary   123
   Appendix   123

9 The professional authority of the teacher   129
   Professionals and professional authority   130
   Thinking about thinking about teaching   134
   Towards a professional knowledge base   137
   The establishment of teachers' knowledge   140
   Towards professional authority   144

   Notes and references   146
   Index   162

Figures

1 Flow chart for a project on the theme of 'The Sea'   87
2 Flow chart for a school's topic work   88
3 A structure for pedagogical content knowledge in fifth grade
  equivalence of fractions   94

Acknowledgements

Some of the themes in the text have been introduced in previously published papers, namely: 'Research on teachers' thinking; its contribution to educating student teachers to think critically', *Journal of Education for Teaching* (1990) 16; 'Subject knowledge and its application: problems and possibilities for teacher educators', *Journal of Education for Teaching* (1990) 17; 'Vernacular pedagogy', *British Journal of Educational Studies* (1991) 29. Chapter 7 is based upon D. McNamara and D. Pettitt 'Can research inform classroom practice? The particular case of buggy algorithms and subtraction errors', in *Teaching and Teacher Education* (1991) 7, reproduced with the permission of the publisher, Pergamon Press. Figures 1, 2 and 3 are reproduced with permission from respectively: Methuen & Company, Methuen Educational, and the *Journal of Teacher Education*. The two lines from T.S. Eliot's 'East Coker', *The Four Quartets*, are quoted by permission of Faber & Faber Limited.

Grateful thanks are due to: my erstwhile secretary, Betty Fairley, who interpreted early drafts and developed a remarkable capacity for converting my scrawl into coherent typescript with only the occasional 'Are you deliberately trying to confuse me?', and latterly to Audrey Rusling for coping with me patiently and efficiently; to my colleague, David Waugh, who contributed to the ideas contained in Chapter 5, and especially to Deirdre Pettitt whose direct scrutiny improved some preliminary drafts and who co-authored the paper upon which Chapter 7 is based; Mari Shullaw whose pointed editorial advice has caused me to rewrite and I hope improve much of the text; and Anne whose practical experience in the infant classroom and sceptical attitude towards educationists has kept my academic feet in reasonably close contact with the ground with the odd 'Are we off to write our story then?'.

Introduction

Primary education has been subject to intense scrutiny and debate during recent years. The foundations in literacy and numeracy established in primary schools are regarded as necessary prerequisites for later success both within the educational system itself and beyond in the world of work. It is hardly surprising, therefore, that people hold strong views about how young children should be educated during the vital primary years. The debates about primary schooling are often couched in broad terms between, say, those who advocate 'traditional' or 'formal' approaches to education, and those who favour 'progressive' or 'informal' methods. All too easily the arguments take on a political flavour, as when 'progressive' educationists are cast as left wingers or wishy-washy liberals and 'traditionalists' are regarded as conservatives or reactionary bigots. All parties to the primary debate claim, of course, to have the child's best interests at heart and to know how to teach children so as to foster their learning.

The reality which has to be faced is that no one has the golden key to learning in the primary school. After all, if we actually had reasonably secure and verifiable knowledge about how children learn in response to the teaching we provide for them, that would go a long way towards silencing the debate about how we ought to teach. In a sense it is unfortunate (in that it illustrates how muddy the waters are) that children can be sent to highly didactic infant schools and because of or despite of what is given them in the name of education they learn, while their friends may attend child-centred schools and still manage to learn. The debate cannot be easily decided and attempts to do so always push discussion back into issues such as 'What do we mean by learning?' or 'What is education for?' One approach to resolving the question about how best to educate children during the primary years is to seek to reconcile the strengths of both 'progressive/child-centred' and 'traditional/subject centred' approaches.[1] In practice it is more likely that primary schools will need to adopt solutions which place an emphasis upon either 'formal' or 'informal' methods.

One important lesson to learn from the controversy surrounding primary education is that the study and practice of education are not dispassionate or disinterested endeavours. All attempts to analyse teaching and learning, make suggestions for policy and practice, and engage in teaching itself are informed by values and beliefs. These may be covert and taken for granted or overt and based upon informed reflection. Our concerns for matters such as the relationships between schools and society, the content of the curriculum, or the layout of the classroom are influenced by our values and experiences and what we consider education is for and about. Teaching and learning in classrooms are of intense interest to politicians, pundits, parents, employers, educationists and others who have a legitimate and vested stake in children's education. Interest groups represent the broad range of political, ideological, and educational points of view and, because of the vast corpus of literature and research evidence addressing educational issues in all their varieties, any proposals for classroom practice can be buttressed by reference to some authority or body of information. The grounds for policy proposals and recommendations for practice may range from appeals to theory, research evidence, rational argument, experience, common sense, or the operation of the free market. These do not confer an element of objectivity or special authority upon the proposers or their proposals since what is appealed to is itself infused with beliefs and assumptions. A fault with much discussion about educational practice is that commentators offer their observations with authority and confidence leaving it to the audience to tease out the assumptions which have informed the analysis and proposals. It is preferable at the outset to make my position clear and articulate the educational beliefs upon which this book is based.

Teaching and learning in classrooms should be teacher centred. Embodied within this notion of teaching is a recognition that the teacher knows more than her pupils and that her mandate is to pass on to them knowledge, understanding, and skills which heretofore they were ignorant of. The teacher is the central figure in the classroom who is responsible for children's learning. A corollary is that those parties who have a legitimate interest in education should respect the teacher's authority and expertise in matters concerning learning in the classroom. If society places a special burden upon teachers to be responsible for children's learning, then teachers should not be regarded as the passive receivers of lay opinion or political precept. Teachers should be actively involved in the development of professional knowledge and because they have responsibility for children's education they should be equal parties in any discussions concerning the conduct of teaching and learning in the classroom.

The Plowden Report articulated a clear vision for primary education and proclaimed that, 'At the heart of the educational process lies the child.'[2] I wish to switch the emphasis and suggest that at the heart of the educational process lies the teacher. Consider Plowden's premise in other contexts: at the heart of the play lies the audience; at the heart of the operation lies the patient; or at the heart of the charter flight lies the passenger. There can be no question that the audience, the patient, or the passengers are a necessary and crucial part of the activity and that their needs must be attended to. But the essential reason why they are involved at all is because of the knowledge and expertise of the actor, surgeon, or pilot. It is the expert's competence which provides the rationale for and determines the success or failure of the enterprise. Equally, it is the teacher who is at the heart of the educational process. It is, of course, part of the teacher's professional responsibility to attend to the needs of her children and to have an appreciation of their characters, aptitudes, qualities, and dispositions but to shift the central focus from the teacher to the child does no service to either children or teachers. One of the reasons why child-centred and discovery orientated views of teaching are attractive is that they carry the connotation of enthusiastic children enjoying their work under the eye of a caring teacher. The teacher-centred, subject-centred view, on the other hand, is often associated with an image of a harsh authoritarian Gradgrind who demands that children engage in enervating learning in a sterile environment. There is no necessary or logical reason why this should be so. The so called 'subject-centred' teacher can be just as caring, friendly and sensitive to her children's needs and circumstances as the 'child-centred' teacher. Indeed the subject-focused teacher may be more aware of her pupils' needs since she recognises that in the longer term it is by doing everything possible to maximise children's learning that she best enhances their aspirations, educational opportunities and chances in life. The onus should be upon the teacher to take responsibility for organising the classroom for learning and for adopting a prescriptive stance towards what and how children learn.

Teachers must, of course, care for children and be sensitive to their personal circumstances and in this sense they may be regarded as 'child centred'. Nevertheless, because of the nature of their professional responsibility, their concern for children's learning must have a cutting edge. The term 'sharp compassion'[3] has been used to illustrate the point that within the caring professions there is little room for sentimentality. The professional must have compassion for her clients but it must be a hard headed compassion whereby she acts in their best interests. This contrasts with the romantic image which often characterises much primary education.[4] All teachers should be caring and sensitive folk but since their mandate is to be responsible for children's learning their compassion should be tempered with a sharpness which always seeks to promote children's learning. The predicament which teachers must accept is that formal schooling is an imposition upon the child and seeks to change him.

I wish to place the teacher centre stage and assert that

- The teacher is the crucial authority in the classroom who is responsible for children's learning. While the teacher cannot legislate for children to learn or teach so as to make them learn it is her responsibility to do all that can reasonably be expected and teach intentionally so as to foster children's acquisition of knowledge, skill, and understanding.
- The teacher is responsible for organising teaching and learning within her classroom so as to optimise the opportunities for children to engage in learning activities and tasks.
- The teacher should focus upon the subject matter of lessons (however defined) and consider how best to represent and communicate content, rather than speculate about the nature of the child's mental processes and aptitudes which are conjectured to shape the child's capacity and disposition to learn.
- When children fail to learn the teacher should be disposed to examine the content of lessons and how material is represented and conveyed to children rather than seek accounts or reasons (such as lack of intelligence or poor home environment) which provide explanations for children's failure to learn but which may remove the onus from the teacher and offer no advice about how to remedy the situation.
- The way in which the teacher can do most to improve children's life chances and educational opportunities and help them overcome any adverse biographical circumstances is by doing everything possible to foster their acquisition of knowledge, understanding, and skill.

By placing the teacher at the centre of the educational process I also wish to establish her as a professional whose practical endeavours to promote children's learning are based upon judgement and reflection informed by a body of professional knowledge. Unfortunately, much of the knowledge base which teachers have had presented to them does not and cannot underpin their classroom practice. Rather than be the receivers of inappropriate information teachers should contribute to the development of a corpus of knowledge which is rigorous, subjected to critical analysis, and also directly relevant to classroom practice. In short, to assist in the development of usable professional knowledge. This may seem an unrealistic aspiration but when we locate teachers within the context of current educational debate and policy making and note the way in which the teacher's authority and credibility is being eroded it is evident that a strategy must be found to re-establish teachers' professionalism in a way which ensures that their expertise is attended to by those people and groups who wish to influence teaching and learning in the classroom. As society has elevated the importance of education it has intruded more into the processes of teaching and learning. In the postwar era and increasingly during the past two decades schools have become more exposed to the scrutiny of inspectors, advisers and parents and subject to audit and appraisal. Much of this interest and activity is to be welcomed in so far as concerned parties think clearly and sympathetically about education and expose professional practice to examination. There is a sense, however, in which education has been appropriated by policy makers, reformers, politicians, academics, researchers, inspectors, advisers and administrators and taken out of the hands of practitioners. The teachers not only support a huge workforce of 'experts' but in doing so their own authority, experience and status is questioned and devalued. New languages are devised by academics, educational psychologists and designers of new curricula. These can be imposed upon teachers (by, for example, the National Curriculum Council or the School Examinations and Assessment Council) or be promoted as avenues to a new enlighten-ment and professional advancement (by academic educationists). The teacher is always on the receiving end. George Steiner has expressed concern about the dominance of the secondary and the parasitic in our culture and explored the way in which the practitioner's performance or creative act becomes subject to an ever-growing body of analysis and criticism generated by critics and commentators which becomes an end in itself. He asks whether there is anything in what they say and argues for the removal of the 'interpositions of academic journalistic paraphrase, commentary, adjudication'[5] and the need to recognise that the per-formance, of itself, is and should be the critical act; in his telling phrase, 'our master intellegencers are the performers'.[6]

In this spirit I articulate what it is that constitutes the essence of the teacher's expertise and authority and explore how teachers may contri-bute to the process of developing a corpus of professional knowledge which will establish teachers' authority and underpin their right to be fully and equally involved in educational discussions and decision mak-ing. My analysis addresses the central function of schools which provides the rationale for their establishment, namely teaching and learning in classrooms. Schools have many other worthwhile functions; for instance they care for children, they seek to foster standards of behaviour and values, and they act as focal centres within the community. These import-ant dimensions of the school's work are associated with its primary function but a school which does not take teaching and learning as its essential task fails in its responsibility to children and becomes redundant since the school's other valuable activities can be undertaken within other institutions. Many factors impinge upon the classroom but I refer to them only in so far as it is necessary to address my central theme. Hence I do not become extensively involved with discussions about the content of the curriculum and what children ought to know since the reality facing the teacher is that there is, currently, a statutory requirement to teach the Basic Curriculum (this does not preclude thinking critically about the curriculum and appraising its 'teachability' and suitability). Similarly I do not become involved with matters of school policy and the general organisation of teaching and learning within the school as a whole. I concentrate upon the educational process in the classroom, bearing in mind that events without will have an influence upon what takes place within.

For the most part I have in mind teaching and learning in primary schools, especially during the junior (KS2) years but I hope that my analysis has a wider relevance and may inform discussion concerning teaching and learning during the infant and secondary phases.

Why *Classroom Pedagogy*? The *Shorter Oxford English Dictionary* notes that nowadays the notion of pedagogy has a hostile tone with implications for pedantry, dogmatism, or severity and the *Longman Dictionary of the English Language* notes that pedagogy is usually used in a derogatory sense. It is worrying that the word traditionally employed to signify the art and science of teaching and to convey the notion that the teacher is responsible for learning should carry such negative associations. It suggests that we have shifted too far from the idea that the teacher is an authority who should be responsible for learning. Pedagogy is important and needs re-establishing within educational discourse. It will not be suggested that pedagogic practice can be based upon scientific principles drawn from theory and research in the social sciences but I will propose that we have a substantial body of knowledge relating to pedagogy which identifies certain themes and issues which have clear implications for classroom practice and which should at least be considered by teachers before deciding to teach in one way rather than another. There is no consensus as to what constitutes 'good' primary[7] practice and teachers should be wary of those who seek to impose models of 'good' practice upon them.

Professional conduct requires informed discussion about good practice and a recognition that judgements have to be made between alternatives. All teaching decisions entail making choices and at the very least pedagogical knowledge addresses the nature of these choices and identifies possible benefits and costs associated with making them. Teaching and learning are fundamental ways of behaving which pervade activities within many settings such as the church, the parade ground, or the sales convention. Hence *Classroom Pedagogy* to denote the distinctive nature of teaching and learning within classrooms. The essence of the teacher's task is not that she teaches, *per se*, but that she does so within a particular institutional environment characterised by distinctive factors which make class teaching a demanding challenge which requires special professional expertise and training.

Chapter 1, 'On teaching', and Chapter 2, 'On learning', articulate the case for an alternative way of regarding teaching and learning within the contexts of primary classrooms. My aim is to suggest that teaching and learning are not incredibly difficult notions to understand, requiring an arcane and complicated vocabulary. In passing I seek to remind readers why much of the recent 'theorising' about teaching and learning has, justifiably in my view, been subject to criticism. I also aim to show that a more 'traditional' approach to primary teaching is appropriate because it reflects the way in which most primary teachers are disposed to teach when left to their own devices. Chapter 3, 'The teacher's responsibility for learning', argues that in so far as is reasonable the teacher should be held responsible for children's learning but this must be tempered with the recognition that to some degree learning must also be seen as the independent achievement of the child. Each of Chapters 4, 5, and 6 'Relating teaching to pupils' aptitudes', 'Organising teaching to promote learning', and 'Organising subject matter for learning', focuses upon a central aspect of primary education and makes suggestions as to how the class teacher should cope with the problems of matching learning tasks to children's abilities; organising and managing children for group or whole class teaching; and teaching through subjects or topics. Chapter 7, 'Pedagogy in practice', illustrates the case articulated in the previous chapters with reference to the specific problem of teaching subtraction, diagnosing children's learning difficulties, and thereby deciding how to teach so as to aid their learning and understanding. Chapters 8 and 9, 'Teachers' pedagogic expertise', and 'The professional authority of the teacher', shift the emphasis. I demonstrate how it is possible for the practising class teacher to make a worthwhile contribution to the knowledge base for teaching and in so doing contribute to a process of re-establishing the professional expertise and authority of primary teachers and, thereby, ensuring that their voice is listened to in educational decision making and policy discussion.

I attempt to avoid partiality and achieve consistency in the use of personal pronouns by using she or her when referring to teachers (since the majority of primary teachers are women) and he or him in all other cases.

Chapter 1

On teaching

If we ask, 'What is an accountant or a surgeon and what is the basis for their authority and expertise?' the approach to finding an answer is reasonably clear-cut. We describe their work in terms of the activities and tasks they undertake and identify the body of formal knowledge which underpins and informs their professional expertise. The accountant must know tax law and the surgeon anatomy. There is an agreed body of knowledge and skill which must be acquired and demonstrated before anyone can claim to be practising as an accountant or surgeon. Teachers, too, are professionals whose work requires training and expertise but it is misleading and unhelpful to compare teachers with other occupations. To consider school teaching in the same manner as, say, the accountant and surgeon does not permit such a straightforward response. This is because teaching is a general form of behaviour which all sorts and conditions of people engage in from time to time. The accountant will teach his client how to organise his affairs for his financial advantage; the surgeon who devises a new operating technique may invite colleagues into his theatre so that he can teach it to them. In what follows I argue that teaching is one of the familiar ways in which people behave in various social contexts and then go on to ask what is distinctive about school teaching and what is the basis for the school teacher's professional expertise? Another way to approach the question, 'What is teaching?' is to ascertain what teachers actually do in their classrooms. Thus in order to gain an appreciation of what constitutes professional practice it is necessary to attend to the ways in which the majority of teachers teach for most of their time because there appear to be some enduring characteristics of classroom practice which suggest that they are intelligent ways of coping with the demands of teaching in classroom environments. If we wish to consider how teachers ought to teach or make suggestions for improving the quality of teaching and learning it is prudent to establish how, in practice, teachers go about their teaching and why they behave as they do, rather than start with an ideal view of how teachers ought to teach based upon educational philosophy or psychological conjecture about how children learn.

TEACHING AS A FAMILIAR ACTIVITY

In all walks of life and in a variety of circumstances human beings teach and they do so without the benefit of training or the layering on of expert knowledge. Parents, doctors, preachers, sergeant-majors, insurance sales-men, journalists, and professors are among those who seek to teach and instruct and they manage, for the most part, without the benefit of lengthy professional training in teaching. It is hardly surprising, there-fore, that there is a distinctive tradition within English educational thought which takes the view that teaching may be considered as an 'amateur' or 'natural' activity[1] whereby it may be claimed that most people engage in forms of teaching on various occasions throughout their lives and that they do so in a comparatively natural and spontaneous manner without prior training in the practice of teaching. In this context the notion of 'natural' is used to suggest that teaching can be thought of as a normal or ordinary activity which may be adopted readily by people who are placed in situations where they are required to take on the role of 'teacher'. It does not embrace the notion that the ability to teach is gene-tically programmed or a physiological necessity, like the ability to breathe, and it is not intended to be prescriptive by implying that what is natural is preferable to that which is artificial. The advocates of this view of teaching argue that the distinctive quality of the school teacher is not that she has an arcane skill or that she has spent many years mastering a repertoire of methods and techniques but that she undertakes the commonplace activity of teaching within the particular framework of the school. What distinguishes the primary school teacher from the generality of teachers is that she must teach in special and peculiar circumstances where one teacher is responsible for teaching thirty-odd individual children who may or may not be disposed to learn. She must undertake this task over a long period of time with the same group of learners, usually for a year, all day and every day and in a closely confined space with only limited resources of time, energy and material at her disposal.[2] These circumstances impose a distinctive burden upon the class teacher and she will need professional training in order to acquire the expertise which will enable her to optimise her pupils' learning. It is not the case that the beginner needs professional preparation in order to become a teacher, *per se*; it is rather that she needs distinctive training to become a teacher in a primary classroom. This view of teaching continues, often in covert ways, to influence deliberations about the nature of teaching, what constitutes 'good' or 'effective' teaching, and how teachers should be trained. For instance attention is often paid to the character or personality of the teacher. Intangible qualities such as 'enthusiasm', 'commitment', 'dedication', 'sense of proportion', 'ability to form relationships', 'able to work with children', and so on, must, so it is claimed, be demonstrated by potential entrants to the teaching profession and by those who are rated as good teachers. Indeed the personal qualities of the teacher are often judged more highly than her distinctive pedagogic skills[3] and a recurring theme in the voluminous research into teacher effectiveness is that teachers who are rated highly on their general characteristics as people are often thought to be effective teachers.[4] Personable qualities are difficult to disentangle from skill, technique, and knowledge of subject matter. Teacher training institutions have always been interested in the personal qualities of their entrants and the old training colleges were communities which sought to exemplify established values such as concern for others[5] and educationists continue to stress the importance of developing the personal qualities of student teachers.[6]

The proposition that many human beings have a natural disposition to behave as teachers may be illustrated in a number of ways. On one occasion my 7-year-old daughter spent Sunday morning teaching her dolls arithmetic. At lunchtime she announced that they would be ready to go on to 'takes' and possibly 'shares' in the afternoon. Having the misfortune of an educationist for a father she was asked how she knew that the dolls were ready for takes and shares. This presented her with no problem. She had spent the morning teaching 'adds' and had given the dolls a test. They all scored at least twenty out of twenty-five, so they could go on to the takes. For her it was simply common sense to test the dolls' competency in what they knew before proceeding to teach more difficult material. In New Zealand teacher trainers were faced with the problem of recruiting and training native Maori-speaking teachers because of the demand for bilingual education. It thus became necessary to encourage Maori speakers from various walks of life who had never considered becoming teachers to change their careers. At one university[7] the inhibitions of prospective mature Maori student teachers were overcome by inviting them to a session where they listened to a tape recording of a teacher teaching a child to read. They then discussed the contents of the tape and considered how the methods used by the teacher could be incorporated into their own teaching. They were then asked if they would like to see a video recording of the same lesson to see what they could learn from that. This revealed an older child teaching her sister to read and the point is made that members of the audience will have often acted as teachers and that they have natural abilities which can be developed in the classroom. At the national level Cuba[8] offers an instructive example. In January 1961 Castro declared to the United Nations that he would, within a year, eliminate adult illiteracy in Cuba which was then running at 20 per cent. To do this he mobilised the youth of the country during the summer months and together with available teachers over 100,000 young people were given at most eight days' training before being dispatched to poor, isolated, rural areas (which we would immediately define as 'deprived') in order to teach adult illiterates to read and write. According to independent UNESCO evidence, Cuba's adult illiteracy rate was reduced to 4 per cent by December 1961 and eventually fell to 2 per cent.

While we may accept that teaching may be a form of natural behaviour that people engage in from time to time, it does not follow that they will all be good at it. The psychologist Stephens[9] has developed a masterly thesis seeking to explain teaching and learning in terms of natural propensities. (Possibly because his analysis offers such a threat to the academic education community his work has been studiously ignored, even though he reworks a massive corpus of information drawn from educational research as evidence to support his case.) As part of his endeavour Stephens elucidated the characteristics of those people who are disposed to become good teachers. Teachers must have a knowledge of subject matter (history, algebra or whatever) which other people approve of but have only a passing concern for. That is, the teacher must know the subjects she is to teach in school; these are likely to be subjects which other people in society consider important but not to the extent that they, themselves, would wish to teach them. The teacher must have a willingness, an urge, or even a compulsion to communicate knowledge to others and be the sort of person who is prepared to linger over her subject and if necessary go over material repeatedly. The teacher must care about her subject to the extent that she spontaneously reinforces appropriate responses by non-verbal and verbal gestures and be a person who is so concerned about knowing the subject correctly that she rapidly ensures that mistakes are remedied. What is required is prompt reinforcement arising from a genuine commitment to the subject rather than deliberate or postponed reinforcement undertaken as a matter of duty or because it is seen by some psychological theory as the correct way to proceed. In order that the teacher may motivate her pupils and for her expressions of approval or disapproval to have an effect upon them she must be a person who through her demeanour is taken seriously. She may be loved, admired, or feared, but she must count and not be disregarded. Teachers, argues Stephens, are more likely to have an impact upon pupils' learning if they have a genuine concern for the material they teach and that children should learn it. He goes so far as to utter the heresy that teachers do not necessarily have to be kind or pleasant people, they may not even like children but they must care deeply that what is taught is learned correctly. A common Chinese model of teaching and teacher training, bears a striking resemblance to Stephens's analysis.[10] It is based upon a view of the teacher as a virtuoso performer who plays a leading role in the transmission of knowledge to pupils. Knowledge is placed at the core of teaching and its possession is regarded as the most important requirement for the teacher. Teachers are expected to operate under the belief that all children can learn. While teachers must be expert in their field and possess deep knowledge they must, when teaching, put on a performance which requires giving of oneself and having 'heart'. During practice sessions student teachers spend much time observing and taking instruction from master teachers who are themselves practising teachers. Students are required to devote time to developing their critical skills by reflecting upon their own teaching and discussing it with experienced teachers who have observed their practice; in a manner rather like the critique of an artistic performance.

To summarise thus far; there can be no doubt that the knowledge which we teach to children changes dramatically over time but there is considerable merit in the proposition that the teacher's ability to convey that knowledge may be seen as a natural disposition which is acquired to a greater or lesser degree by all human beings. I have a geography and astronomy textbook for use in schools which was in its third edition in 1810.[11] Among the fascinating gems of information is a comment about the moon to the effect that, 'the inhabitants of the opposite hemisphere . . . will never see the earth; unless prompted by curiosity, they make a voyage to behold the extraordinary phenomenon'.[12] Yet in the intro-ductory pages much sound advice on teaching is offered such as:

> At the beginning of each section is given an abstract of the problems contained in that section, together with the principles upon which they are founded. This will serve as a sort of connecting chain, and enable the learner easily to review the whole of the problems contained in the work.[13]

This was some two hundred and fifty-odd years before psychologists introduced the notion of 'advanced organisers' into educational discourse!

The proposition that teaching is a 'natural' mode of behaviour and that people have a disposition to engage in teaching acts is the basis for my proposal that teaching should be viewed as a familiar, practical activity. The notion that teachers may be 'born and not made' has much to commend it as a starting point, but its limitations must be recognised. These include

- A failure to recognise that while most people may have a disposition or propensity to teach they are not all equally good at it. People in other walks of life may be required to teach but we are all likely to have been on the receiving end of awful or bungled 'teaching' when someone has sought to teach us but lacks the skill and sensitivity to do so. We may have a natural propensity to aid the sick but it would be dangerous to permit everyone to practise medicine. Successful professional per-formance requires identifying tyros who may be better than others as performers and then providing appropriate training.

- A failure to appreciate the particular circumstances in which lay people usually teach. The sergeant-major may be a remarkably effective teacher on the parade ground, but what he is teaching is comparatively straightforward and he has enormous power to ensure that his learners attend to him and execute his instructions exactly. The driving instructor has only one highly motivated learner, and there is much evidence that parents can be particularly effective teachers, precisely because they can engage in one-to-one interaction with a 'pupil' with whom they have an affective bond.[14] The circumstances in the school classroom are, of course, quite different; one teacher is responsible for the instruction of many pupils of varying abilities and aptitudes within the constraints of scarce time and resources.
- Teachers in other occupations will typically spend only a limited proportion of their time teaching and it will be only one part of their professional responsibilities. They are, moreover, unlikely to be in a situation where they are also responsible for the conduct of those whom they teach. Crucial to the task of primary school teaching, on the other hand, is the requirement that teaching is the whole job – it lasts all day – and, moreover, it is an unusual form of teaching in that it also demands that teachers ensure the orderly behaviour of their charges while teaching.

These points are not so much fundamental flaws that undermine the notion of the 'natural' teacher but are issues that must be addressed in developing the notion of teaching as a familiar practical activity because the idea of the natural teacher has much to commend it for three reasons. First, regarding teaching as a 'natural' or 'ordinary' activity which people periodically engage in enables it to be shorn of any pretence or arcane mystery. We do not need to dress up our considerations of teaching in jargon or fancy language. Discussions about the nature and quality of teaching can be conducted in ordinary language using the everyday or vernacular ways of talking which we routinely use. There is no need to invoke theory or terminologies shipped in from elsewhere. We do not, for example, need to draw upon a body of psychological or curriculum theory in order to reflect critically upon a teacher's questioning skills; this may be done within the context of the material being taught and what the teacher aims to achieve, and we can engage in this process using everyday language.[15] There is no need to invoke complicated conceptual schemes in order to understand the process of teaching normal children in conventional classrooms. We can and should use familiar language because, essentially, both teaching and learning are commonplace activities. In asserting this I am in no way attempting to belittle or question the teacher, her work, and expertise. The task of undertaking the normal human activity of teaching within the peculiar and demanding circumstances of the school and classroom is a challenging undertaking which requires special abilities, knowledge, and professional training. It does not follow that because teaching is difficult and complicated that we need esoteric explanations in order to account for what is going on. I may illustrate the point as follows. As I write this sentence I am, as ever, amazed that something is going on in my head – indeed it may not even be in my head – which can be translated, via my physiological system, to my hand and this enables me to make marks on a sheet of paper which can rapidly and easily find their way back into the minds of the teeming masses of English-speaking human beings. At one level this is a remarkably complicated process and I could spend years studying biochemistry, neurophysiology, and cognitive science seeking an understanding, or various understandings, of my routine everyday behaviour. At the completion of my studies I would have acquired many interpretations and conjectural accounts of how I am able to write. I may be more enlightened but if my concern is to improve the quality of my performance, that is what I write, all this studious endeavour is simply redundant. So, too, with teaching. The teacher will be concerned about the content of her lessons and the quality of her performance. She hardly requires educationists to provide their own complicated accounts of her sophisticated behaviour. Second, there is a distinctive emphasis upon the teacher's own knowledge of the content of lessons. In order to teach the teacher must be a possessor of, and to some degree expert in, the knowledge which is to be taught. It is the knowledge of the subject matter to be taught which is a distinctive hallmark of the teacher. Third, the recognition that the process of teaching involves not only skill or technique but also the execution of a sensitive performance by a person whose dispositions fit them for the task of teaching in that they care for their subject, take it seriously, and are concerned that their pupils learn it effectively.

The view of teaching as a familiar practical activity claims our attention because it emphasises the putative teacher's knowledge of the material to be taught and her disposition to teach; what it fails to recognise is that school teaching takes place in a peculiar arena, namely the school classroom. Teaching in this distinctive environment requires special training during which appropriate professional expertise is acquired.

THE INHERENT STABILITY OF TEACHING

Teaching in primary schools presents a special challenge because the practical activity of teaching is pursued within classrooms. This may seem so obvious that it should remain unsaid but it must be stressed that the essence of the teacher's job and the justification for her professional authority is not only that she teaches and is responsible for learning but more significantly that she teaches within a distinctive institutional arena (the school) in which she is responsible for the learning of a large group of diverse individual learners (the pupils), and that what the learners are required to learn and the nature of their learning are not necessarily what they would choose to learn (school learning is, in a sense, imposed learning). The form of this familiar activity has remained remarkably consistent over time. We may regard the ways in which the majority of teachers actually teach as being successful and enduring adaptations to the problem of how to teach many children within the confines of classrooms given limited resources of space, time, materials, and energy. We should use the information that most teachers spend much of their time teaching in established ways in the majority of classrooms as the basis for understanding and developing professional expertise.

In the late 1920s my mother trained to become a teacher. Her method notebook contained a model lesson plan, 'How to Make a Jam Roly-Poly'. The basic structure of lesson plans which can be drawn from my mother's model lesson and early twentieth-century methods texts is comparable with contemporary students' plans and many of the methods texts they turn to for advice. The substance of the lesson is 'content' or 'subject-matter'; the teacher describes what she is going to do in terms of her own teaching (using words such as 'purpose', 'aims', or 'goals'); she describes what she expects the pupils to achieve (using terms such as 'children's learning', 'objectives', or 'learning outcomes'); she lists the resources and materials which will be required and how they will be made available and describes how the children will be organised; she describes how the lesson will be introduced, developed and concluded; and finally there is a section in which she comments upon and evaluates her own teaching and the children's learning. There are, of course, elaborations and variations upon this basic model. What is remarkable about primary teaching is not how it has changed over the years but how stable it has remained. Since the 1944 Education Act the rhetoric which has surrounded primary education has consumed forests of paper as partisan groups have debated and squabbled over the merits of traditional and progressive methodologies and other nostrums. While the politicians, pundits, and educationists have argued with each other it has been teaching much as usual in the majority of primary classrooms. To the unpractised eye it may appear that primary teaching has changed substantially during the post-war era but we must not be deceived by changes in the context in which teaching takes place. There can be no doubt that the teaching environment has altered dramatically. Red brick, Victorian two-storey primary schools set in asphalt playgrounds, with infants downstairs and juniors upstairs and separate entrances for boys and girls have been supplemented with open-plan single-storey schools on greenfield sites. Older schools may have had their ceilings lowered and been fitted out with modern facilities. Institutional browns and greens have given way to bright and pastel colours and wall space is planned so as to promote displays of children's work and visual aids. Rows of cast-iron, fixed desks have been replaced by flexible, Formica-topped furniture. Chalk and slate have been superseded by the overhead projector, felt pens, and the micro-computer. Parents and helpers mingle in many classrooms and pop in to see the head teacher rather than wait deferentially at the main gate. There are, of course, changes in form also. Children are less likely to be streamed and are more likely to be organised into small groups within the class and much of the work in humanities and arts subjects has been integrated into topics or themes. All this change should not divert our gaze from teaching and learning as they actually take place in the classroom.[16] The various surveys undertaken from time to time all report evidence which indicates that primary teaching practices, especially in the junior (KS2) years, follow well established procedures.

In the late 1970s Her Majesty's Inspectors (HMI) published a major survey of primary education based upon their visits to 542 schools.[17] They reported that three-quarters of teachers employed a mainly didactic approach and that less than one in twenty relied primarily upon an exploratory approach. The teaching of mathematics was given a high degree of priority with considerable attention to computation, measurement, and calculation. The language curriculum was also given preference with three-quarters of classes making use of reading schemes and with considerable efforts devoted to teaching syntax and spelling. At about the same time, a survey[18] of 1,258 primary classrooms found that most teachers sat pupils separately or in pairs and that they remained in the same seat for most activities. Individual work was more favoured than group work and of the average twenty-five hours devoted to teaching each week in primary schools, fifteen-and-a-quarter hours were allocated to academic subjects, five to aesthetic subjects and four-and-three-quarters to integrated studies. Eighty per cent of teachers used a timetable (and over half of them admitted to smacking children!). The ORACLE survey[19] of fifty-eight classrooms found that nearly 90 per cent of teachers never used co-operative group work in single-subject teaching and that nearly 70 per cent did not use it in their art and craft teaching. Thirty per cent of the curriculum was devoted to maths and 37 per cent to reading, writing and spoken English. Progressive teaching hardly existed in practice and when individualised teaching did occur it was over-whelmingly factual and managerial, it was not concerned with promoting child-centred learning. Similar findings emerge from an NFER survey[20] of 2,519 junior school teachers carried out in 1982. The majority of teachers were firmly in control of their classes, were making use of class teaching, and preferred didactic teaching methods. The predominant feature of junior classrooms was an emphasis on practice and basic skills in English and mathematics with class teaching and ability group teaching predominating. The ten most common activities in junior classrooms in rank order were: work in mathematical computations; silent reading; practice in learning tables or number bonds; vocabulary and dictionary work; descriptive writing; learning lists of spellings; creative writing; spelling tests; formal grammar. In 1984, sixteen infant teachers, carefully selected because of their ability, were subjected to detailed observation.[21] Of the 417 'task demands' they made on pupils in maths and language sessions, 60 per cent were concerned with practice; 25 per cent with introducing new ideas, procedures or skills; and only two tasks (in number not percentage) required the child to invent or discuss an idea for themselves. While there was variation in the detailed content of the maths curriculum, there was a heavy emphasis upon the four rules of number and a large amount of pencil and paper work in routine calculations. There was a lack of attention to the practical relevance of the maths experiences provided. The predominant feature of the infant language curriculum was writing practice in one guise or another with most tasks set for the whole class. Teachers placed great emphasis upon the quantity of work produced and simple punctuation. Requests for spellings constituted the predominant teacher–pupil exchanges in language lessons. A substantial longitudinal survey[22] of some 2,000 pupils in fifty London junior schools confirms the picture. The vast majority of teachers used reading schemes and 95 per cent taught language as a separate subject. In maths most teachers used textbooks. Some form of testing was used in all but three schools and a quarter of them set homework. Three-quarters of the lessons observed were single-subject lessons. Many teachers grouped children according to ability and not a great deal of collaborative work was observed. To come up to date, an extensive evaluation of Leeds primary schools,[23] including detailed observation in ninety of them, revealed that the curriculum is dominated by language and mathematics and that some teachers use aspects of the curriculum such as art, craft-work, and topic work, as a means of creating time for them to concentrate their attention on language and maths. The children's activities were dominated by writing, reading, use of task-specific apparatus and listening. Children spent over half their time reading and writing. All this evidence, it must be stressed, was collected before the introduction of the National Curriculum and the current emphasis upon standards in basic literacy and numeracy.

In North America things are no different. An analysis of nearly 7,000 accounts of classroom practice[24] from 1890 to 1980 concluded that stability had characterised classroom instruction which is teacher centred and dominated. Where change has occurred it has been limited and on the margin and has involved hybrid forms of teacher-centred progressivism which, except for a few teachers, has not incorporated teacher–pupil co-operative planning, determination of content, or allocation of class time. A further survey[25] of 1,000 classrooms concluded that the majority of class time was spent in teachers lecturing to pupils and pupils working on written assignments. Patterns of teaching and learning demonstrate a consistent and persistent preference based upon didactics and practice. Nearly 100 per cent of elementary (i.e. primary) classes are teacher dominated and the most frequent form of interaction is pupils responding to teachers. The modal classroom configurations are: the teacher explaining or lecturing to the class, pupils working independently on written assignments either in a large group or in the whole class, and clearing up or preparation. There is an overwhelming curriculum emphasis upon English, reading, and language (64 per cent of the time) and mathematics (18 per cent of the time).

The cumulative effect of this evidence is compelling. If ever there was a straw man in primary education, it is the idealised image of progressive child-centred teaching. The view of the teacher as 'facilitator' who encourages self-motivated pupils to engage in exploratory learning within a curriculum shaped by their own interests and needs has little substance in reality. For most of the time the substantial majority of primary teachers give most weight to teaching basic numeracy and literacy, employing didactic teaching methods in teacher-centred classrooms. Whole class teaching is common and there is little time allocated for children to explore, solve problems, and engage in co-operative group activities. As Richards has remarked, the interesting questions are, 'How and why did the myth of the "primary school revolution" arise? How was it sustained for such a long period? In whose interests was it perpetuated?'[26]

There are two plausible ways in which to account for the consistency of primary practice and the 'failure' of teachers to bring about changes advocated by educationists. One is to appreciate that the teacher is only a single element in the complex structure of schooling where the overwhelming press of the institutional environment, such as the competing demands of thirty-odd children in a confined environment, lack of resources, limitations of time and money, and having to cope with the piles of paper, advice and recommendations from local educational authority (LEA) advisers, HMI reports, and so on and so forth, all add up to a context in which the teacher must resort to well-established strategies in order to accommodate competing pressures and make life bearable. It is only through a substantial investment of time, money, and staffing that more progressive and flexible changes could be brought about and established in a manner which could offer some guarantee of enduring success.[27] A problem with this interpretation is that even in quite different learning contexts where structural and contextual conditions are such as to indicate that teachers could exert much more control over how they choose to teach there is not, in practice, much variation from the methods usually adopted by junior school teachers. Universities for example, have, for the most part, compliant learners and staff with adequate resources, light teaching loads, and the professional autonomy to determine their own teaching practices. Yet university lecturers are particularly prone to adopt methods of teacher-centred instruction where the curriculum is delivered to large groups of learners using traditional methods.[28] An alternative view is to recognise that the enduring forms of teaching and learning found in classrooms are a creative response by people that allows them to cope with the workplace conditions, conflicting expectations, and structural arrangements of ordinary classrooms.[29] The facts that most teaching in primary classrooms is, in practice, teacher centred and that teachers control the content and delivery of knowledge which is typically addressed to the whole class is not a state of affairs which must be reformed. It should be recognised as an intelligent way in which teachers, down the ages, have responded to the contextual pressures of the classroom and gone about the business of being responsible for the learning of a large number of diverse pupils. We must appreciate that teachers teach as they do for sound and understandable reasons and we should not seek to change the manner in which they teach unless we can adduce convincing evidence that our proposals would lead to significant gains in children's learning. This we are not in a position to do. All this is not, for one moment, to say that notions of quality cannot be attached to teaching or that there will not be significant and substantial variations in teachers' teaching, depending upon the content of the lesson and the learning which the teacher aims to promote. It is, however, to suggest that we must recognise that the essence of teaching is the communication of designated subject matter and that generations of teachers have developed appropriate strategies for undertaking this task within the constraints of space, time, and resources found in crowded classrooms. Any prescriptions for how teaching should be conducted in junior classrooms should be based upon this 'conservative' account of enduring classroom practice.

Deliberations about the nature and quality of teaching and how professional knowledge may be advanced should recognise and be placed in the context of how teachers actually teach. The point can be illustrated by reference to the age-old debate about the merits or otherwise of 'traditional/subject-centred' and 'progressive/child-centred' theories of primary education. There is little point in addressing the question of 'Which method is best?' The discussion must be considered with reference to the practicalities of teaching and learning in classrooms. One of the distinctions often made between traditional and progressive approaches is that the traditional theory holds a view of the child as a 'passive' learner whose mind is a 'bucket to be filled' while the progressive theory views the child as an 'active' learner whose mind is a 'candle to be lit'. A little thought renders such crude distinctions meaningless. Presumably being an active learner does not refer to the idea of the child being physically active and engaging in practical activities so as to promote learning. We all know that children are adept at being physically active in and around the classroom without actually learning anything (beyond learning how to behave so that the teacher thinks they are busy) and presumably being a passive learner cannot carry the connotation of children sitting at their desks, say, listening to the teacher read or engaging in solving a mathematical problem; such physically 'passive' learning should stimulate and engage a very active mind. The effective teacher's task, within the confines of the classroom is to ensure that children's minds are actively engaged in learning and various forms of physical movement and practical activity may or may not be associated with that learning. If, say, the teacher is conducting a science lesson on flotation it may be a good idea to organise some practical experimental activity, not because it accords with some educational theory advocating 'active learning' but because it will be appropriate – given the subject matter of the lesson. Another way of characterising the traditional and progressive approaches is by making the distinction between the traditional teacher as someone who uses a 'delivery' model of learning, while the progressive teacher is seen as a 'facilitator' who creates the conditions in which children may discover for themselves. Such a distinction falls apart in practice. There are some things that the child cannot discover for himself, and even if he could it would be to engage in a very inefficient mode of learning, such as learning how to spell correctly. On the other hand, there are other instances where the teacher must rely, in part, upon the child's capacity to invent or discover, as when stimulating the children to write a poem. In most teaching situations the distinction between a child 'receiving' or 'discovering' knowledge does not genuinely operate. Consider the teacher giving a lesson on the angles of a triangle summing to 180°. The 'traditional' teacher may teach the information in a formal manner as a geometrical theorem using, say, a blackboard presentation and didactic questioning. The 'progressive' teacher may set up an exercise whereby the children discover the answer for themselves. The children cut out paper triangles of different configurations and sizes and then they are required to rip off the corners and join them together along their adjacent sides and asked, through a process of careful questioning, what they have found out; the questioning should lead them to 'discover' that the angles can be arranged so that the unjoined sides make a straight line. It is misleading to see this type of exercise as a form of 'child-centred' or 'progressive' teaching. The teacher has had a very clear idea of what she wished to achieve in the lesson and she has organised a structured activity which has only one correct upshot. This may be seen as an example of skilful teaching and the employment of a neat practical activity which should reinforce what has to be learned. The method arises from the nature of the subject matter and the teacher's desire to teach in a stimulating manner; it does not come from the application of a separate body of educational theory. We always have to ask how good the teacher is at teaching within the confines of her method and the classroom and what she is seeking to achieve in terms of the children's learning. We should not judge our 'traditional' and 'progressive' maths lessons in terms of their theoretical basis but by reference to how successful the teacher was at promoting the sorts of learning which take place in schools. Did the 'traditional' teacher reinforce her blackboard exposition with practical examples? Did the 'progressive' teacher manage to make the difficult transition from the children 'discovering' that the angles joined up to make a straight line to the formal proposition that they summed to 180°? In a word, we must plan teaching, judge teaching, and seek to improve teaching within the context of teaching and learning as they are usually found in school settings and for this we need frames of reference drawn from schools which are related to classroom practice.

THE CLASSROOM CONTEXT FOR TEACHING AND LEARNING

If the primary teacher was able to teach one individual child for much of the time her work would be very much easier; she could focus upon the particular personal qualities of her pupil and the material to be taught. The teacher's undivided attention would ensure that the child engaged with its learning. One-to-one teaching has much to commend it, as is recognised by those who have the wealth to hire private tutors for their children and the Oxbridge tutorial system. Perhaps this is why parents can have such an impact upon their children's learning during their formative years and why parents may be better at getting their children to learn than teachers.[30] School teachers, however, must teach in peculiar institutions called schools. Schools provide an excellent means of ensuring that a limited number of adults may teach all the children that society produces in a tidy and economic manner but they are not necessarily the ideal institutions in which to foster effective learning. Classrooms are environments which have particular characteristics which create problems for the teacher. Primary classrooms contain one adult and thirty or more children. They are rather small places in which to herd so many children for long periods of time – if they were zoo animals we may be tempted to call in the RSPCA; there are many classrooms where space is so tight that it is literally very difficult to move around the room. The resources available for teaching and learning in these confined spaces are strictly limited and must be kept tidy in the few locations available for storage. The most valuable resource in the classroom is the teacher's time and attention and, as far as each of her children is concerned, it is the most limited. These constraints alone indicate that to a marked extent the class teacher's job, unlike that of other professionals and other types of teacher (such as health visitors or university tutors), is concerned with maintaining order, namely: allocating resources, regulating the sequence of events, and directing her own attention. By maintaining order I am not referring to discipline problems and disruption; I mean orchestrating the flow of people, events and materials in a confined space with few resources. Someone has to be in charge.

This is hardly the end of the matter as far as the class teacher is concerned. The thirty-odd children in the class will all have their peculiar quirks of character, disposition and ability and must be treated as individuals. They are in the class for a long time, typically every weekday for the whole school year. The primary teacher may be more familiar to the child than its father or grandparents.[31] Classrooms are not only small, they are very public places. Where else in ordinary life is success or failure so exposed to public scrutiny? The child's performance is open for all to see; everyone knows what's going on and how everyone is doing. Emotion, too, cannot be hidden in the classroom. Children's tears, laughter and illness are on view, as are all sorts of embarrassing situations. Much of what takes place in classrooms is unpredictable and immediate. In a word, the classroom is a lively social community and much of the teacher's professional work is devoted to sustaining physical, social and emotional order within this community. The manner in which a teacher reacts to a child on one particular day will have an effect upon it and other children during subsequent days. The teacher must think carefully before publicly criticising a child's failure because of the effect it may have upon the child's motivation to learn and contribution to future lessons. The teacher may, on some occasions, decide to devise lessons which guarantee that all the children can be successful and have something to go on the wall and show their mums. Within this arena primary teachers are incredibly busy people; detailed observations of their behaviour suggest that on average they shift the focus of their attention and engage in different acts about four times every minute of every school day.[32] For example, Alexander's survey[33] observed teachers making, on average, the following numbers of interactions per hour: work interactions – fifty-eight; monitoring interactions – forty-three; routine interactions – fifty-eight; disciplinary interactions – twenty-two; others – ten. Coping with the idiosyncratic and peculiar demands of classroom life, *per se*, sets school teaching apart as a distinctive professional activity. For the teacher, maintaining order within this arena is demanding enough of itself but it is to do no more than create the circumstances within which she must engage in her essential work which is to foster learning in an environment which does not offer the ideal conditions for it to take place. In a word, the essence of the primary class teacher's professional work is to organise and promote learning in an arena in which she must also sustain order and be sensitive to the nuances of social relationships. There is nothing novel in what I am saying. At the turn of the century Dewey wrote perceptively on the relationship of educational theory to classroom practice and noted that

> The would-be teacher has some time or other to face and solve two problems, each extensive and serious enough by itself to demand absorbing and undivided attention. These two problems are:
>
> 1 Mastery of subject matter from the standpoint of its educational value and use; or, what is the same thing, the mastery of educational principles in their application to that subject matter which is at once the material of instruction and the basis of discipline and control;
> 2 The mastery of the technique of classroom management. This does not mean that the two problems are in any way isolated or independent. On the contrary they are strictly correlative. But the mind of a student cannot give equal attention to both at the same time.[34]

It is possible to claim that each separate part of the primary teacher's expertise is not of itself particularly complex or difficult,[35] that the content of her lessons is not particularly academically advanced or intellectually demanding and that organising and controlling children are ordinary straightforward activities. This may be so, but what is difficult and presents the teacher with her particular challenge and requires special expertise is the ability to integrate all these aspects of her work into one coherent performance so as to teach effectively within a special set of circumstances. It is this notion of practical performance which is central to the teacher's pedagogical expertise; the ability to keep all the balls in the air as she attempts to promote children's learning in the social arena of the classroom with its special circumstances and limited resources. This is one of the defining characteristics of the primary teacher's professional behaviour; namely having the knowledge, skill and expertise to foster learning in the particular organisational context of the primary classroom.

Chapter 2

On learning

Primary school teaching differs from teaching in many walks of life and circumstances because, among other things, the teacher cannot assume that her pupils are on the same mental wavelength as herself. One of the reasons why teachers in higher education and those who teach in the professions and industry may find teaching relatively straightforward and not requiring much special training is that they can take it as read that the members of their audience have mastered the basic skills and competencies required for learning and that they know and understand in ways which are similar to their own. What Jackson refers to as the 'presumption of shared identity'[1] means that teachers of adults may not need to inquire into the nature of their learners' minds as a necessary preliminary before engaging in pedagogical practices. In short, setting aside the question of whether or not they ought to, teachers of adults can assume that their audience is like themselves in terms of the ways in which its members think, know, and comprehend. The teacher can proceed to teach almost with 'eyes closed', to use Jackson's terminology, upon the belief that the significant difference between her and her learners is that they are ignorant about what she is to teach them and then proceed to convey knowledge to her audience in the belief that members will assimilate her lessons as she intends and as she herself understands the material. The primary teacher cannot make such an assumption since young children are still at the stage of acquiring the basic skills, of literacy, numeracy, and oracy and may appear to interpret and understand their world in different ways from adults. It is during the formative years in primary school that children's mental capacities 'develop'. The presumption that there is something special and distinctive about the ways in which primary children learn and that they thereby need treating in special ways is typically regarded as an important consideration which must inform the primary teacher's training and expertise. In this chapter I consider the issue of what the primary teacher needs to know about her pupils' abilities and capacities to learn and how they learn so as to better understand them and thereby aid her teaching. Given the nature of this theme it is hardly surprising that educationists have turned to the social sciences for theories, models, and evidence which it is hoped will enhance our understanding of children's learning. Primary school teachers need to know something of how children learn and the social factors which affect their learning and at first sight educational psychology and sociology would seem to offer appropriate information and advice. It is necessary to attend carefully to psychology's and sociology's claims and ask whether the endeavour is necessary or worthwhile.

THE PSYCHOLOGICAL CONTRIBUTION

Many educationists aver that psychology has the potential for enhancing our understanding of children's learning.[2] Psychology is concerned with how people learn and develop and since official educational documents and teachers themselves make claims about how children develop and also construe education in developmental terms then presumably the social science which addresses human development has something to contribute to educationists' thinking and practice. Teachers obviously have an interest in how children learn and progress through their formative years but it does not necessarily follow that the psychological study of learning and development will inform their teaching practices.

An essential question to ask of psychology is whether psychology itself has yet reached the stage where it has acquired, through a process of theory building and empirical testing, a substantial and verifiable corpus of knowledge which can be passed on to the teaching profession. The opinions of well-established psychologists who can reflect upon their discipline from positions of security and seniority may raise doubts in our minds. One authority opines that psychology has not reached the stage where it can provide scientifically established knowledge about human behaviour which passes beyond common sense.[3] Indeed it has been argued that the task for psychology is to explicate and systematise the common sense psychology embedded in our culture.[4] An extension of the notion that psychology is 'common sense' is the claim that much psychological research is pointless because in effect it attempts to verify logically necessary statements by definition.[5] In other words, the 'findings' adduced by psychologists are logically entailed in the process of stating a psychological proposition in the first place. For example, it is only necessary to raise the question 'What is involved in holding children's attention when teaching them?' in order to explicate the range of techniques and ploys the teacher may bring into play. An alternative view is that psychology is characterised by 'ameaningful' inquiry which assumes that knowledge can be acquired by methodological procedures and that it is then contained within cosy conceptual boxes which distort our view of the human condition.[6] As we bear closer upon higher order human learning psychology's promise seems to become even more fragile. Memory is an important aspect of learning yet a distinguished authority[7] argues that psychological research has nothing to say about the interesting questions which lay people ask about memory and that the generalisations about memory which have been verified empirically are 'familiar to the average middle class third-grader in America from his own experience!'[8]

The tentative nature of psychological knowledge which illustrates that its contribution should be treated with extreme circumspection can be illustrated by quoting from a symposium[9] reporting work at the forefront of investigations into teaching and learning

- As yet there is no comprehensive and universally accepted theory capturing complex human intellectual functions in a single conceptual framework.[10]
- How people acquire and add to complex bodies of knowledge is poorly understood, in spite of recent dramatic advances.[11]
- To what extent are cognitive skills general, to what extent specific? To what extent are younger and older learners and thinkers alike, to what extent different? To what extent, and by what means, can the skills of learning and thinking be taught?[12]
- Learning theory, which should come to our aid, is working its way out of a recession.[13]
- This research has led to questions about implications for curriculum development. But I am not yet sure what they are.[14]
- Our research to date is still well short of providing instructional prescriptions, but we have identified two promising approaches.[15]
- In those ancient years of the mid-1960s when I was a stage theorist (a bogus one really), I tried to deal with the shift from one stage to the next by introducing a notion of conflict in representations with resulting cognitive incompatibility. But to have conflict, the child must in some way be able to represent problems in different ways at any stage. So that made mine a rather half-baked stage theory at that.[16]

Those generations of student teachers who have sat through (and they still do) lectures on 'Bruner' will gain little comfort from learning that the originator himself admits to being both bogus and half-baked in his psychological theorising.

Given the provisional state of psychological knowledge one wonders how so much of it can and should flow over into education. The deluge can only be hinted at. For instance when considering only those psychological perspectives which claim to bear directly upon teaching and learning there is one authority[17] which provides us with three approaches offering 'useful guidelines for the teacher', another group[18] provide eight models describing conceptions of pupil learning in classrooms, although they have the grace to hope that further research will lead to a degree of consensus. The prize must go to a text[19] providing the teacher with some twenty models of teaching based upon different psychologically orientated theories. Such riches may spoil the teacher for choice but also suggest that as far as psychologists are concerned the classroom is a gigantic Rorschach inkblot test which can be interpreted in a variety of ways depending upon the personality, beliefs and values of the psychologist. The blame should not necessarily be attributed to psychologists since it tends to be educationists who appear to need theoretical crutches in order to think about learning and, thereby, psychology has been drawn into the business of applying its findings to classroom learning. Educationists' bewitchment with Piaget offers a nice illustration. Piaget was an epistemologist who said very little about learning in general and even less about school learning[20] and his constructivism can be shown to be either necessarily or trivially true while also failing to account for the public nature of knowledge.[21] The limitations in attempting to relate Piagetian developmental psychology to the process of teaching and learning in school have been exposed by numerous commentators.[22] Bereiter, for example, has observed that Piaget's theory is abstract, complicated and concerned primarily with the development of reasoning and is, 'devoid of practical guidance on any matter. It is, in short, about the last thing that one would expect informal educators to seize as their torch'.[23] What, therefore, is its attraction? According to Berieter, Piaget provides, 'a license for calling virtually anything a child does education'.[24] Moreover, an analysis of the development of the progressive movement in the UK[25] suggests that it was only after child-centred methods were established in some schools that educationists turned to psychologists such as Piaget to provide a theoretical justification for classroom practice.

Since it has been claimed that developmental psychology is characterised by ignorance about the very process of development and that it is in precisely this area where the practitioner would need information in order to optimise children's learning that it is at its most deficient,[26] one wonders why educationists continue to press its claims. Psychologists have, at various times, attempted to remind educationists that psychology is an academic discipline which is distinguished by debate and controversy about what it actually knows, with competing schools of thought offering alternative interpretations and accounts of the mind and its functioning, and that even if psychological knowledge was in some sense 'fact' or 'true' it would not translate readily into classroom practice. For instance, even if we knew the 'correct answer' or 'facts' what does it matter to the teacher and what follows in terms of practice whether 20, 40, or 80 per cent of a child's 'intelligence' can be explained by genetic or environmental factors? It is salutary to remember William James's cautious words of some eighty years ago:

I say moreover that you would make a great, a very great mistake, if you think that psychology, being the science of the mind's laws, is something from which you can deduce definite programmes and schemes and methods of instruction for immediate schoolroom use. Psychology is a science, and teaching is an art; and sciences never generate arts directly out of themselves.[27]

A similar message was echoed by Bruner some half a century later and well before his ideas were adopted by educationists:

I should warn you . . . to beware of the likes of us. We do not have a tested theory of instruction to offer you. I warn you for a good reason. Educators are a curiously doctrinal or ideological kind of people. You are given to slogans and fight and bleed in their behalf. You have looked to psychology for help and have often been misled into accepting mere hypotheses as the proven word.[28]

Perhaps teachers should heed these warnings. The primary teacher must have the strength of mind to question and if appropriate reject that which outsiders who carry academic kudos seek to impose upon her. It is worth bearing in mind that teachers have managed to teach and children to learn despite the rise and fall of the competing psychological theories which claim to address these matters. Professional diffidence should not dispose teachers to fall into the trap of being tempted by psychologists' claims and nostrums. Once teaching becomes 'psychologised', the psychologist controls the terms in which debate about teaching is discussed. Thereby the teacher's professional expertise may be discounted and the teacher portrayed as the unscientific bearer of folk wisdom who resists psychologists' attempts to improve her teaching.[29]

THE SOCIOLOGICAL CONTRIBUTION

It is not only children's 'minds' which may influence their capacity to learn but also the social environment into which they are born and spend their formative years. The family, neighbourhood, and ethnic group, provide social contexts which may influence children's attitudes, beliefs, and values, and have a fundamental effect upon how they regard their world and their attitude to learning.[30] Hence it is also claimed that in order to better understand her children and their disposition and motivation to learn, the teacher must attend to the social factors which may shape children's capacity to learn. Thus we are invited to consider sociology's contribution to educational discourse. There is a sense in which one would hope and expect that the teacher will know something of her pupils' home circumstances and be interested in their life and experiences outside school. If there has been a recent birth or bereavement in the family, if there is a suspicion that the child is being abused, or if the child has a chronic illness, it is important for the teacher to know since such factors may well have a deleterious effect upon the child's behaviour and learning. A child who is under emotional stress is unlikely to give of his best and the teacher may need to allow for this in her teaching. Having said this it is unlikely that the academic discipline of sociology will provide the teacher with necessary additional information. Sociology is, essentially, a cerebral activity through which supposedly disinterested academics seek to develop their theoretical understanding of human social behaviour and buttress their analytical constructs by an appeal to empirical evidence. Knowledge is advanced and truth pursued through a process of intellectual debate. The sociologist is essentially a commentator. The teacher, on the other hand, is essentially an actor; an actor who must reflect upon practice but who must, paramountly, perform in the classroom.[31] It will be the teacher's personal concern for her pupils and her preparedness to show an interest in them and talk to parents and relatives which will influence her acquisition of information about the home circumstances of individual children; this information cannot be derived from the generalised findings and propositions drawn from sociology. Sociology's potential contribution must be treated with caution and we must consider exactly what constitutes its claim for our attention. The burden of the sociological case, in so far as it may interest educationists, is that the particular matrix of circumstances within which the child is nurtured will shape its beliefs and values, the ways in which it acquires thought and language, and what constitutes acceptable behaviour. In short the social environment of the child will endow it with a 'culture' which may or may not be in accord with the general 'culture' of the school. As far as certain social groups are concerned schooling may be regarded as the imposition of an alien culture upon children who do not know how to make sense of it. The degree to which the child learns successfully in school can be accounted for in terms of the child's capacity to adapt from the cultural environment of the home to the cultural environment of the school.[32] The most familiar manifestation of the sociological evidence is the undoubted fact that there is a correlation between social class background and educational achievement. There can be no doubt that the 'higher' the child's social class background, the more successful it is likely to be in school. This suggests that certain qualities or characteristics of middle-class upbringing or culture dispose children from this background to be successful in school; while factors associated with 'working-class' culture such as the facility with which members use language or the value placed upon education militate against successful learning in school. It is difficult to know how the primary teacher may interpret this information and evidence (even if she accepts its validity) and how she may take it into account in her teaching. Particularly when it is remembered that while social class background is associated with successful school learning, it is also the case that there is significant variation in the ability and educational success of children from the same family and that in numerical terms many children from working-class backgrounds are very successful in school.[33] Grammar schools, for example, made a particular contribution to enhancing working-class opportunity. In 1953 two thirds of grammar school pupils came from working-class backgrounds and it can be claimed with some justification (in terms of promoting educational opportunity) that, 'The twentieth-century grammar school has been the great success story of England's large skilled manual working class.'[34] Indeed in the 1964 election campaign the socialist leader, Harold Wilson, campaigned in favour of grammar schools for all.[35] The issue may also be illustrated with reference to social factors such as gender, religion, or race and I will focus upon race. The Council for the Accreditation of Teacher Education (CATE), for example, lays upon teacher trainers a specific requirement that 'students should learn to guard against preconceptions based on race, gender, religion or other attributes of pupils'.[36] This prescription is, of course, part of the laudable attempt to eradicate any racial bias or prejudice from the classroom since teacher partiality may affect pupils' motivation and their consequent learning. Children from racial groups are cast as minorities who are disadvantaged within the educational system. However an examination of the available evidence does not support the sociological claim that variations in educational attainment in school are rooted in racial discrimination.[37] While there is variation between different minority groups there is very little difference between the educational performance of children from minorities and those from white backgrounds.[38] The school a child attends makes far more difference to a child's examination success than the ethnic group it belongs to[39] and the differences in the circumstances in life between racial groups are greater than their educational differences.[40] The evidence[41] provided by the Inner London Education Authority (ILEA) before its demise confirms the general picture. In Inner London there is considerable variation in the educational performance of different ethnic groups. Children from African, Arab, Greek, Indian, Irish, Pakistani, and Southeast Asian backgrounds perform better than expected while those from English, Scottish and Welsh, Bangladeshi, Caribbean and Turkish families fare less well than the average. Some schools are better than others at raising the educational performance of children from one or more ethnic groups but the effectiveness of such schools is not stable over even a three year time period. The ILEA report contains a salutary warning:

> It is also not clear, from this research, what actions a school might take to eradicate factors militating against the best performance of every

student irrespective of gender, ethnicity, social class or disability, nor even what these factors are.[42]

In our society it can be claimed as a mark of achievement that Asian and West Indian children are more likely than white pupils to pursue both full-time and part-time study after leaving school[43] and that in the capital city children from nine minority groups perform better than English, Welsh and Scottish children[44] but it does make one wonder what information educationists should be providing for teachers about the partial treatment of minorities within our schools. The dangers attendant upon teachers seeing children as members of disadvantaged minorities were nicely illustrated by the 'William Tindale Affair'.[45] One of the ways in which the 'progressive' faction among the school staff sought to justify their child-centred approach to primary education was by reference to the undoubted achievement of the school's Jamaican steel band. The teachers made a specific attempt to identify an element in the culture of one of their ethnic minority groups and build upon it so as to enable children to demonstrate one form of success within the school system. But in our society this can be no more than a diversion; in order to promote opportunity teachers must focus upon the central activities of learning. Prowess on the steel drums can be a worthwhile and entertaining adjunct to schooling and the brilliant performer may even manage to earn a living as a musician but the vast majority of steel drum players will need a good job to support their hobby; as, of course, is recognised by the middle classes who will gladly encourage Charlotte and Simon's clarinet and violin lessons and celebrate their achievements in this extra-curricular activity, but they are unlikely to think that a child's musical accomplishment is more important than success in the basic subjects, unless their offspring has a rare talent. What is particularly worrying about the evidence and messages coming from sociology, especially when conveyed in textbooks which prepackage and simplify the complexities and disclaimers of the original material, is not so much that they have little to offer the teacher but that they may have a negative impact. It is the teacher's responsibility to do her best by all children but unfortunately an unintended consequence of sociology is that it may build up the expectation that children from minority and deprived backgrounds may be unsuccessful at school-learning. Sociological theories carry the danger that they provide teachers with myths whereby they can explain or even explain away children's failure to learn.[46] Such powerful myths imply a deterministic thrust which renders the teacher helpless; how can she, in a busy classroom, overcome the home and parental circumstances of a disadvantaged child? Teachers should, of course, acquire information which ensures that they appreciate the particular qualities of individual children but they must also recognise that they are free agents who must do everything possible to promote the learning of each child in their class. Teachers need to know about and respond sympathetically to family circumstances which may have an effect upon the child's behaviour or motivation. It is quite another matter for teachers on initial or in-service courses to receive formal information from lectures and textbooks which lays out a series of explanations for working class or minority group failure within the educational system which range from their linguistic deprivation[47] to their preference for immediate gratification; how did the trade union movement develop if the working classes are linguistically deprived and does plastic money take the waiting out of wanting for the middle or working classes?

It is misguided to slip into debates about teaching and learning information which is little more than a point of view backed up with partial evidence. An essential responsibility of the teacher is to promote the educational and life chances of all her pupils and help them transcend any limitations of their particular autobiographical circumstances. Each child is an individual, not an entity defined by social characteristics (rich/poor, black/white, boy/girl) which in part describe what the child is capable of before embarking upon the educational journey and also offer an easy explanation for any subsequent educational failure. The great Polish educator Korczak,[48] who chose to go to the gas chamber with his Jewish orphans, warned against stereotyping children by social background. All children, he argued, should be treated as mature people with different conceptual scales, different experiences, urges and emotional reactions. They should not be treated as if they are at an immature stage of development; that is a way of keeping them down, he claimed.

THE CHILD'S DISPOSITION TO LEARN

An examination of the standard psychological and sociological contributions fails to provide information about how children learn which may be of value to the practising teacher. An alternative approach is required. As with teaching, my starting point is the proposition that learning may be regarded as a 'natural' activity which human beings have a disposition or propensity to engage in. Indeed, as far as most 'normal' people are concerned who do not have some psychiatric or clinical disorder it is difficult to envisage how they can avoid learning. There are few things which we know conclusively about teaching and learning but we do know with certainty that children learn in school and that they do so as a consequence of being taught in classrooms. (The apparent naivety of this statement will be resolved.) There is huge variation in what children learn in school, the level at which it is learned during primary education, and in individual differences in achievement. The UK, for example, is one of the minority of countries in the world which does not require children to

learn a foreign language during the junior years. There are huge differences between the resources nations allocate to education and variations
in the resources which individual states allocate to schooling, during
periods of war for example, and these do not appear to affect significantly
children's capacity to learn.[49] A glance at a photograph of a Victorian
classroom provides *prima facie* evidence that resources and visual aids are
not a necessary requirement to induce learning. A child's first reader may
be the Koran, the Pentateuch, or Janet and John book one, and we dispute
endlessly the competing merits of 'phonetic' and 'look and say' reading
methods. Despite what they are offered the vast majority of children learn
to read. For most of this century children have memorised number bonds,
chanted tables, and completed endless exercise pages of sums; yet in spite
of what the constructivists say about children's minds, pupils have
learned. In fact specific attempts to base a programme of mathematics
instruction upon Piagetian principles seem to have no substantial advantage over traditional approaches to pupils' learning of basic mathematics.[50] None of this is to advocate that we resort to the Lancaster and
Bell monitorial system or starve primary schools of resources. Neither is
it an attempt to avoid the fact that teaching may have a detrimental effect
upon learning; witness, for instance, the pre-war practice of forcing left-
handed children to write with their right hand or the radically different
treatment of boys and girls throughout most of education's history. What
I seek to do is pose the question: given that it is demonstrably the case that
children learn in classrooms (setting aside for the time being questions
about the quality of and variation in their learning) whatever is provided
for them in the way of curriculum and method,[51] what sort of explanation
can we offer of how children learn? Clearly if a Piaget, Skinner, or
Vygotsky or anyone else actually knew how children learned and if their
theories could be verified experimentally then, presumably, schools
which did not base their teaching methods upon the correct psychological
principles would find it difficult to induce effective learning in their
pupils and they would be exposed as ineffective. It is instructive to
remember that the root meaning of 'theory' refers to viewing, a sight or
spectacle[52] and this perhaps is the way in which we should regard those
contributions which provide theoretical explanations of how children
learn in primary classrooms.

It may be argued that I am posing the wrong question and that in order
to demonstrate how learning theories have an impact upon children's
learning it is necessary to focus upon the approaches to classroom teaching which are based upon theoretical positions. This, too, is a futile quest;
for example, the 'progressive' theory embedded in the Plowden Report
led to the practical recommendation to abandon streaming in primary
schools.[53] The research sponsored by Plowden was totally inconclusive in
its findings and could not demonstrate that either streaming or

de-streaming had an identifiable effect upon pupil learning.[54] The general picture arising from other studies is equally confusing; some studies demonstrate a positive effect associated with streaming, others have associated the positive effects with de-streaming, and a third group is equivocal.[55] An obvious case to take is the research which has investigated the effects of teaching styles based upon 'progressive' and 'traditional' educational ideologies; the progressive approach, of course, being underpinned by constructivist psychologies. In 1976 the data reported in a major survey[56] which had been based upon rigorous and sophisticated statistical analyses demonstrated that traditional teaching styles had a marked effect upon primary children's learning. By 1981, however, even more sophisticated re-analyses of the same teaching style data revealed that the original findings had to be modified and that at best there was a statistical difference in one subject only[57] and that even if there was an effect it was not statistically, let alone educationally significant.[58] That the same data permit alternative explanations is of concern enough but as subsequent investigations demonstrated, back in the world of the primary classroom, teachers, in practice, adopted a variety of styles and strategies in their everyday teaching.[59] In some desperation we may turn to those studies which have investigated the characteristics of effective schools. The conceptual underpinning[60] and methodological and statistical procedures[61] of the research are distinctly fragile but if we take their findings at face value we discover that effective schools (as defined by schools where pupils do better on formal tests of attainment) are characterised by factors such as: school ethos, maximising time engaged on learning, orderly behaviour and classroom management,[62] or purposeful leadership, structured sessions, work centred environment, maximum communication between teachers and pupils and record keeping.[63] Such factors may well be characteristics which, if they are promoted in schools, influence their pupils' learning. But what they are not are factors which relate to styles or methodologies of teaching in so far as these may be informed by psychological theories of teaching and learning. We are thus no further forward with providing a parsimonious explanation for our problem. Whatever we throw at children in the name of teaching, they continue to learn. For those proceeding by way of Occam's razor a useful starting point is the proposition that a major factor explaining children's cognitive growth is simply the fact that they get older. Children may reach different stages at different ages but this is a natural process of maturation; it is not a process of psychological mastery, the child has no choice.[64]

    That children do learn, despite the plethora of experiences they are subjected to in the name of education, may be explained by children's natural propensity to learn. They learn because they are endowed with the capacity to learn and, as with all higher forms of life, this capacity is necessary in order to ensure evolutionary success.[65] This is not a novel view of learning and it has been subscribed to in different ways and to varying degrees by some educationists. At the turn of the century Madame Montessori sought to develop her proposals for a scientific pedagogy upon her principle that 'social man is natural man yoked to society'.[66] Turning to more recent times, Chomsky argues that the principles underlying the structure of language are so specific and so highly articulated that they must be biologically determined and be genetically transmitted from parents to children.[67] It may be noted in passing that Ryle[68] in his critique of the Chomskian notion that there is some innate apparatus or schemata which underpins children's language acquisition, offers an alternative account of how children learn which also supports my argument since it nicely illustrates the 'natural' teaching and learning which takes place between parent and child:

> They [parents, relatives etc.] sing to him, and then with him; they recite to him and then prompt his return recitations to them; they provide, wittingly and unwittingly, what he models his own actions, accents, intonations and nascent phrases on; they challenge him, race him, practise him, test him and correct him, . . . they applaud and laugh at his earliest puns and word-coinages; they feed his nascent hunger for consecutive prose with bed-time stories; and they listen with fond patience to his own first self-invented stories.[69]

The theoretical position which underlies Eisner's educational proposals can be seen as an elaboration of a similar thesis. He argues that the creation of meaning is a biologically determined need of the human organism and that there is a biological basis for learning in that humans have a sensory system which endows them with the ability to learn.[70] There is, moreover, a burgeoning of experimental work which supports this view. The very earliest learning of infants appears to be more general and abstract than adults may expect and they have the mental ability to transfer what they learn to novel situations. Infants can be seen as rational learners whose learning is a logical consequence of what adults provide for them.[71] Accumulating evidence suggests that children's natural learning during the pre-school years is impressive and that youngsters should be recognised as remarkably competent active learners with an ability to learn rationally in natural settings.[72] Indeed it has been recommended that the proposition that children are extremely capable natural learners constitutes the essence of what it is necessary for the teacher to know about the child.[73] This notion may be pursued into the institutional context of the school. Stephens, for example, argues that the essential features of education which bring about children's learning do not reside in the educational programmes provided for them but within underlying forces which accompany any educational programme.[74] These are powerful spontaneous tendencies, such as the human disposition to communicate, which engage the mechanisms of learning whether or not it is our intention to teach. The mechanisms responsible for academic growth 'reside in humble, spontaneous tendencies which are always in operation when an adult consorts with maturing children'.[75] The sheer fact that a child, with a propensity to learn attends an institution which has as its goal the fostering of learning of one sort of another provides an explanation of why children learn and why children learn whatever the teaching method, however the materials are presented, and whatever educational innovations they are subjected to. It cannot be too strongly stressed that this is to say nothing about the quality of learning or to be seen as absolving the teacher from her responsibility to promote learning. It is simply to provide the context for my response to the question: what does the teacher need to know about the child as a learner? The essence of the reply is that children have a natural disposition to learn as is impressively demonstrated by the learning which they manifest before and outside formal schooling, and during schooling, whatever the methods employed by the teacher or other adults. In terms of pedagogical practice this is how the teacher needs to regard children's learning. Knowing this places a considerable burden of responsibility upon the teacher and requires that she think seriously about what children should learn and how it can best be presented to them, rather than become overconcerned about conjectural accounts of what may or may not be the child's mental capacities and dispositions to learn.

Thus far I have sought to demonstrate that children may be thought of as having a natural propensity to learn and that we need not seek complicated accounts of how they learn and that we do not require sophisticated theoretical models which have been devised in other contexts to explain how children learn. But it is hardly adequate to offer an account of children's learning which fails to go beyond the claim that children are 'natural' and usually very able learners. (If, for no other reason, because such a view of the child as learner carries with it the temptation to remove the onus from the teacher to be responsible for the child's learning.) If we know anything about schooling it is that children do learn as a consequence of attending school, but we also know that some children learn better than others, and that some schools and teachers are better at fostering learning than others. The apparent simplicity of these truisms may be contrasted with the views of those educationists who invoke sophisticated and complicated explanations of school learning which, while they may beguile and impress, fail to offer any coherent theoretical explanations which readily translate into propositions which enable the teacher to organise her teaching so as to legislate for desired learning to take place. Theory and research informed by the social sciences cannot provide the teacher with information which will enable her to bring about learning. Yet, and this is the crucial issue, the teacher has the unequivocal professional responsibility to act in ways which are most likely to promote children's learning. To say that the child will learn to some extent whatever the teacher does because the child has a natural propensity to learn is to eschew professional responsibility. Hence the notion of learning as a natural activity can be no more than the basis of a more extensive account of what we need to know about the relationship between teaching and learning.

Chapter 3

The teacher's responsibility for learning

In this chapter I address the relationship between teaching and learning and consider the extent to which and the manner in which teachers may be held responsible for children's learning and also offer a preliminary account of how children's learning may be regarded as a consequence of the teaching they receive.

In a seminal paper the educational philosopher Paul Hirst sought to distil the essence of teaching.[1] His aim was to identify specific teaching activities which can be distinguished from what he calls the general enterprise of teaching, which includes activities such as playground duty and ordering stock which are part of the teacher's job but not actual teaching. He defines teaching as an intentional activity which has as its purpose the bringing about of learning, formally expressed as follows:

> A teaching activity is the activity of a person, A (the teacher), the intention of which is to bring about an activity (learning) by a person, B (the pupil), the intention of which is to bring about some end state (e.g. knowing, appreciating) whose object is X (e.g. a belief, attitude, skill).[2]

He goes on to add:

> From this it follows that to understand what is involved in teaching, one must start at the other end of a logical chain of relations, with an understanding of the end achievements to which everything is being directed.[3]

Hirst appreciates, of course, that his definition of teaching focuses upon the unobservable intention of the teacher and it thus becomes necessary to attach observable features to the act of teaching in order to be satisfied that it is taking place. The first is that the teaching activity must express or embody that which is to be learned and those parts of the teacher's activity which do not exhibit this quality are not teaching because

> Specific teaching activities must be indicative of what is to be learned and it is for this reason that the opening of windows and the shar-

pening of pencils could never be themselves the teaching of historical facts or 'Pythagoras's Theorem'.[4]

The second is that teaching acts must be expressed in such a way that it is possible for pupils to learn what is intended.

> One might teach an undergraduate class in philosophy Wittgenstein's criticism of the idea of a private language, by reading to the students from the *Philosophical Investigations*. But to carry out such an activity with a class of six-year-olds would, I suggest, not constitute teaching at all.[5]

This attempt to analyse what teaching is has much to commend it in one respect but it also suffers from a severe limitation. Its strength is that it places an onus upon the teacher to be responsible for the child's learning and to act in those ways which will bring about learning. Teachers must have a clear idea of what they require children to learn and then teach so as to ensure that children will learn. What is valuable in Hirst's attempt to engage in a dispassionate analysis of 'what teaching is' is, paradoxically, professionally prescriptive. The limitation of his account is in the analysis itself. Hirst allies learning too closely to teaching and posits a logical chain of relations between teaching and learning. One has only to spend five minutes in a classroom to appreciate that the pupils may not necessarily be consenting participants in the enterprise which Hirst is analysing. Children may be willing or not so willing learners. Whether or not children learn will depend, in part, upon their motivation, ability and preparedness to do so. Even if one goes as far as saying that teachers are responsible for the activities associated with learning which children are required to undertake and even if the children engage in these activities it does not follow that children will learn.[6] It should be recognised that there comes a point at which children must be implicated in their own learning and also be regarded as responsible for it although it is difficult to know to how young an age this argument can be extended.[7] We must appreciate that, in part, learning has to be seen as the independent achievement of the pupil.[8] It is not possible, for example, for a teacher to make a child swim. She can take the child to the pool and encourage the child to engage in a variety of confidence building exercises and she can employ floats and other aids. But whatever efforts the teacher makes the child will never learn to swim unless it wants to and makes the independent contribution itself. Moreover, it is difficult to determine when specific teaching acts actually result in learning. The teacher may decide to teach her class the three-times table. Over the weeks there may be, say, class chanting, quick-fire questioning, and paper and pencil tests. The upshot will be that most children will eventually learn their multiplication table as a consequence of these diverse activities. It is usually difficult to pinpoint exactly when and how the child learned.

It is, therefore, necessary to relax any tight bond between teaching and learning.[9] Philip Jackson, for example, has proposed that the apposite metaphor is one that casts teaching as the 'blowing of bubbles' because it highlights the fragile and transient relationship between teaching and learning.[10] He suggests that elementary (primary) school teaching is more to do with maintaining children's involvement with activities in the classroom in the hope that these will bring about beneficial learning. In a sense, he argues, learning is a by-product of children's activity; it is not directly caused by it. Jackson makes an important point and it resonates with classroom experience. The relationship between the teacher's teaching and children's learning sometimes seems ephemeral. One day everything will have been planned in detail and the teacher will have thought carefully about the children's work but for some reason the lessons fall flat and the children fail to be engaged or produce anything worthwhile; and the only plausible explanations are along the lines of 'perhaps it's the weather' or 'because it's Friday'. Perversely, on another day without too much effort on the teacher's part all seems to flow along with the children involved and producing interesting work. Jackson's interpretation is illuminating and 'makes sense' in terms of classroom experience but we can accept it only so far, because teachers' professional expertise does and should extend beyond providing children with activities in the hope that they will learn.

It is necessary to reconcile Hirst's and Jackson's ways of considering the association between teaching and learning. This may be achieved by proposing that while teaching should be seen as an intentional activity whereby teachers should teach so as to promote children's learning, it must be recognised that however 'good' the teaching and firm the intention, the teacher may 'fail' because, due to factors beyond her control, the children for one reason or another do not learn as she intended.[11] We must recognise that even when some children fail to understand or learn the teacher may have engaged in 'good' teaching. Conversely, children may learn successfully as a consequence of 'bad' teaching; because of fear of physical punishment being an obvious example. The reasons why 'good' teaching can be unsuccessful include difficulties inherent within the lesson content itself, pupils' disinclination to make their contribution, or their deliberate attempts to thwart the teacher's intentions. Hence the quality and nature of the teacher's teaching should be judged not only by reference to children's learning but also by what we know about the various ways in which teachers may teach and what these tell us about keeping children productively engaged with learning activities. We should appreciate that there are alternative approaches, methods and ways of casting subject matter and ask how a particular teacher's performance compares with alternatives which may be acceptable alternative forms of good practice. In doing so we are not so much judging the teacher's performance in the light of children's learning but rather by reference to alternative ways of teaching in a nominated set of circumstances. There are no hard and fast rules but there are different ways of trying to teach whatever it is that children are being required to learn. Consider, for example, the case of the teacher teaching subtraction (examined in more detail later). There are a number of techniques and ploys which the teacher can call upon in attempting to teach this basic skill such as alternative practical activities, ways of explaining, and routines to follow. We can make an informed judgement about what we think is more preferable in a particular context but what we cannot do is make a prediction to the effect that if the teacher teaches in one particular way she will ensure that children learn. We must evaluate the teacher's performance according to her ability to call upon different ways of representing subtraction computations and provide alternative explanations so as to do everything possible to overcome children's difficulties. We would be concerned if a teacher doggedly persisted with a method which was demonstrably failing to help children learn but we may applaud another teacher who was deploying all her powers of exposition and trying different approaches even though the child still failed to learn.

The essential purpose of teaching is to foster learning but there is a limit to the extent to which the teacher may be held responsible for learning. How, then, are we to construe the relationship between teaching and learning. I propose that the appropriate manner in which to understand the association between the teacher's teaching and her pupils' learning is by thinking in terms of learning as a contingent process. The dictionary definitions of contingency embrace notions such as: non-essential, conditional, a thing that may or may not happen, conditioned by something else, and not logically necessary.[12] I wish to be more precise and employ the idea of contingency as it is used by Stephen Gould[13] in his discussion on evolutionary theory. He demonstrates that an (historical) explanation does not rest upon direct deduction from laws of nature but arises as an unpredictable sequence of antecedent states. Thus while we cannot, beforehand, foresee the outcome of events we can, after the event, offer an explanation or account in the light of what had occurred beforehand. This seems to offer an appropriate and useful way of considering the relationship between teaching and learning in the classroom. Learning can be thought of as having a contingent association with teaching because while the teacher cannot, beforehand, legislate (on the basis of any theory or set of rules) to ensure that learning will take place she can, after the event and if learning does occur, offer a reasonable account of why the child learned in terms of the antecedent activities which preceded that learning. Because learning is contingent upon teaching there will be times when teaching 'works' and children learn and there will be others when it does not. This does not mean that the teacher abandons hope or that she has failed. It means that the teacher will need to engage in a variety of intentional activities and strategies in the hope that she can engender learning. When her pupils learn she is likely to be able to offer an explanation of why they did so; when they fail to do so she will need to try a different approach. She will win some and lose some.

This way of viewing teaching and learning has the merit of matching primary school experience and the sorts of accounts which teachers offer for their pupils' learning. The notion that learning takes place alongside the teacher's teaching rather than being brought about as a direct consequence of the teacher's intended instructional procedures at a particular point in time is nicely illustrated by an extract from a report which is based upon the close and sympathetic observation of the teaching and learning of mathematics in the infant classroom:

After the first lesson on place value, Kerry was shown the phrase, '1 ten and 5 units' and asked to show it with Unifix cubes. Kerry put out the following and said:

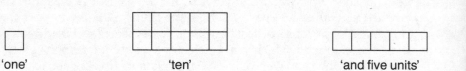

'one'   'ten'   'and five units'

When she was asked 'How many are there?' she counted the cubes and announced 'sixteen'. When asked how many the phrase, 'one ten and eight units' was she said 'nine'. Gary's answer to these questions were similar to Kerry's. When asked for the value of 'one ten and five units' and 'one ten and eight units' he said 'six' and 'nine' respectively. Four days and three lessons later the children were shown a cluster of fourteen dots. By counting, they each ascertained that there were fourteen. They also knew that meant there was one ten in there but they did not know how many units that left over. After only one more lesson in which the teacher discussed place value using the numbers twenty to twenty-nine, both children showed a clear understanding of place value. They could split any numbers under one hundred into their component tens and units (the teacher had not covered beyond twenty-nine) and describe their reason for doing so. Gary described 'forty' as 'four sets of ten' and Kerry said that 'thirty-three' was 'three lots of ten – ten, twenty, thirty – and three left over'. All the questions that had defeated them in earlier interviews now seemed trivially easy and they got them right quickly.

These children's successful performances, over a week, on tasks they certainly did not understand, seemed·closely associated with their

apparently sudden grasp of a notoriously difficult concept. By reward-
ing their efforts and performances the teachers had kept the children
engaged on a series of tasks which, in the end, paid dividends.[14]

Primary teachers will be familiar with similar events which are often
referred to as breakthroughs in learning; the teacher will have tried all
sorts of strategies to promote learning and then suddenly in a moment the
child somehow makes the leap or connection. Cortazzi[15] investigated the
various metaphors which teachers use to describe such sudden advances
in learning, these include: 'click' (e.g. 'it seemed to click'), 'there was a sort
of click in their minds'; 'jigsaw/mosaic' (e.g. 'it all fell into place'); 'seeing
light' (e.g. 'daylight has dawned at last', 'their eyes light up'); 'movement'
(e.g. 'she's just come', 'I could see him beginning to go', 'this girl has
suddenly taken off', 'they zoomed away').[16] Interestingly Cortazzi reports
that teachers, in their conversations with him, never made reference to
children's breakthroughs in learning in terms of psychological theories of
learning.[17] In another study a primary teacher who engaged in classroom
based, teacher focused inquiry into children's reading[18] used the notion of
'the jumps' to describe children's acquisition of the abilities which
enabled them to make the connection between what was taught and what
they needed to know in order to become readers. 'The jumps' provide a
way of illustrating that it is the child who has to make the step of seeing
the possibilities of reading which extend beyond the reading scheme and
being heard to read by the teacher; while 'jumps' could not be predicted
and made to happen they could be attributed to a key antecedent event.

The nature of the relationship between teaching and learning in the
classroom is such that while the teacher cannot legislate for or predict that
learning will take place as a consequence of her teaching, the teacher must
act upon the assumption that learning will occur. This is because learning is
a contingent event and it is likely that there will be some teaching ploy,
procedure, analogue, trick, method or whatever which should enable the
child to learn. Teaching entails the skilful deployment of alternative ways of
seeking to promote learning in the purposeful and hopeful expectation that
one of them will be successful eventually. It also involves sustaining children's motivation, attention, and engagement with learning activities even
when they are finding the tasks tedious or demanding because, while from
the children's point of view the tasks may seem difficult or uninteresting, the
teacher who has the longer term aspiration must keep them involved with
their work in the expectation that they will learn in due course.

LEARNING AS A PRACTICAL ACTIVITY

Learning, I have suggested, has a contingent relationship with teaching,
but it must also be appreciated that school teaching and school learning

are practical activities which take place in a particular set of circumstances which bear upon the nature of children's learning.

To summarise elements of my argument thus far:

- Teachers have a professional responsibility to promote their pupils'
  learning.
- Children may be regarded as having a natural propensity to learn and
  what they learn in school may be accounted for in terms of the manner
  in which learning is contingent upon teaching.

It is quite unsatisfactory to leave the matter at this juncture. Although
teachers may engage in different tactics and approaches to promote
children's learning, and although learning may be seen as contingent in
that one approach 'works' but another does not, and although we may
only be able to offer an account of why it worked after the event it does
not follow that the ways in which the teacher decides to teach are hap-
hazard and unplanned. The teacher should be able to give a reasoned
account beforehand as to why she decides to teach as she does. We expect
her account to have an awareness of the child as a learner which extends
beyond the claim that the child is a 'natural' learner who will eventually
learn as a consequence of one strategy or another. Moreover, explanations
of children's learning which, by implication, add credence to the idea of
contingent learning but which do not extend beyond explanations of the
form 'it just happened' or 'he took off' are hardly satisfactory as a basis for
professional practice or as accounts which can be built upon when seeking to enhance the knowledge base for teaching. We require, for example,
a more coherent account of why a child may have learned within one set
of circumstances rather than another. In particular, it is necessary to
elaborate on the notion of learning as a natural activity. To illustrate with
a horticultural analogy, the plants in our garden may grow naturally but
we do not leave things to nature or chance. Plants will thrive with neglect
but the keen gardener acts with purpose in the expectation that his plants
will flourish. He cannot predict success and his best efforts can be
defeated by the weather but he can at least assist nature and encourage it
in the right direction. So, too, with teaching.

In order to extend the notion of learning as a natural activity so as to
embrace the idea of learning as a practical activity it is necessary to regard
the child as a learner who seeks to understand the world around him. The
child should be considered as an active agent in his own learning. The
child does not just receive the teacher's teaching and spontaneously
respond to it without thought. The child will attempt (but not always
correctly) to make some sort of sense out of what is required by the
teacher. The child must interpret the teacher's accounts, instructions,
demonstrations, or requirements and discern what he thinks the teacher
expects, so as to produce the work or results which the teacher will accept

as evidence of learning. I use the term 'practical learning' to convey the notion that when we regard children as learners in the classroom we should consider them as what has been termed 'just plain folks'[19] who seek to make sense of their immediate surroundings. They attempt to 'suss out' what is required of them as learners within the particular classroom environment in which learning takes place. Our appreciation of learning must recognise the context in which it occurs. Classroom learning may be regarded as an authentic activity located in the classroom whereby children act in the ways which are expected of them in that particular set of circumstances.[20] The issues, problems and tasks presented to them by the teacher as she goes about her teaching must be resolved somehow by the children and fed back to her as a demonstration of their learning.

When the teacher teaches she places children in the circumstances in which they must interpret the learning they are expected to engage in but it does not follow that all children, acting as 'just plain folk' will make sense of it in the same way. Factors such as their academic aptitude, their ability to read the teacher's instructions, their motor skills and competencies, and their determination and interest will affect the way in which individual children seek to make sense of a teacher's teaching and shape how they will respond. Some of them may, in fact, decide that the way to proceed is not to 'learn' but to cope with the situation by drifting off for a chat with a friend or to 'hide' from the teacher's gaze (by, say, reacting to questions they do not understand by putting up their hands when nearly every other child does with a good chance of not being called on but not doing so when only a few hands go up). Individual differences among children and quirks of personality go some way to accounting for why learning may be seen as contingent upon teaching because the teaching of the one teacher will be received, interpreted and responded to in different ways by different children.

The task, then, is to articulate frames of reference in terms of which we can think about the nature of learning as it is experienced and made sense of by children in classrooms. This should both inform the manner in which we think about and plan teaching and also provide contexts within which to develop professional knowledge. The first issue to consider is the extent to which and the manner in which the teacher can and should relate what she teaches to the prior knowledge and capacities of the children she teaches.

Chapter 4

Relating teaching to children's aptitudes

In order to promote learning teachers need to consider two essential professional tasks. These may seem self-evident or common sense but they must be examined in some detail and their implications for teaching considered. One is to provide information and materials together with learning activities which are closely related to pupils' abilities and what they already know and which may advance their learning in terms of knowledge, understanding, and skill. The other is to provide and optimise the time and opportunities for children to learn so that for as much of the day as is reasonable each child is productively engaged in learning activities during the time that they are in school. These two issues will be discussed in this and the next chapter before considering in Chapter 6 the central complicating factor which must be addressed in practical teaching, namely how the content of lessons shapes the teacher's reflection upon and execution of these professional tasks.

The issue of relating teaching to children's aptitudes is usually referred to as *matching*. This entails, among other things, providing *differentiated learning activities* for the individual children in mixed-ability classes. In what follows I identify the available evidence and then go on to discuss the issues which arise and consider their implications for learning.

MATCHING TEACHING TO LEARNING

To recall part of the argument from Chapter 1, Hirst, in his analysis of teaching, argues that it is not sufficient for the teacher to claim to be teaching; in order to be satisfied that the teacher is teaching we must be able to observe two essential features of her teaching. The first is that teaching activities must be indicative of what is being learned; that is they must express or embody whatever it is that has to be learned. The teacher cannot claim that she is teaching 'the addition of fractions' unless she is providing information, examples, and practice which are related to fractions. The manner in which the teacher ensures that her teaching is indicative of what is to be learned can be discerned in different ways.

What is indicative of what is to be learned in the teacher's formal presentation of information may be quite different from what is indicative when children are engaged in problem solving exercises. The second is that teaching acts must be indicatively expressed; that is the teacher's teaching must be expressed in such a way that it is possible for children to comprehend and learn what is intended. Hirst cites the example of reading from Wittgenstein's Philosophical Investigations to a class of 6-year-olds to illustrate the point that if there is too great a gap between the knowledge, skills and state of mind of the learner and what the teacher is teaching then the teacher cannot claim to be teaching. These two characteristics of teaching should not be seen so much as part of a formal analysis which seeks to define teaching but as criteria attached to descriptions of good teaching.[1] There are no hard and fast rules or procedures whereby we can decide that a teacher's teaching is indicative and indicatively expressed; it is a matter of making informed judgements within practical contexts. The point can be made in a clear-cut and straightforward manner by citing the example of a teacher reading an advanced philosophical text to infants but this is unrealistic. Consider, rather, the case of my grandmother. During the 1930s this formidable lady taught in an elementary school in a depressed Durham mining village where she was responsible for the 'remedial' class consisting of sixty-odd 'backward' children. She used to teach Shakespeare's plays because she considered that deprived children living in an impoverished environment should not be denied what is best in our culture, whatever their academic abilities. Was she or was she not engaged in teaching and, more intractably, was she a 'good' teacher? An informed reply would have to rest upon judgement arrived at from observing the teacher at work within the particular mix of circumstances in her classroom. Did my grandmother have a distinctive knack or skill which enabled her to communicate and teach Macbeth in a way which engaged slow learners, or was she a strict disciplinarian whom the pupils attended to while her attempts to impose the culture she valued floated above their heads?

THE EVIDENCE

In the first instance it is necessary to examine the available information describing matching practices in the classroom. In 1978 HMI conducted a survey of teaching practices in representative English primary schools[2] and what they discovered about teachers' matching of work to children's abilities[3] placed matching firmly upon the primary education agenda. The survey reported on the education provided for 7-, 9-, and 11-year-olds in 542 primary schools. When they visited classrooms HMI asked teachers to identify within their classes groups of more able, average, and less able children. The teachers were not expected to make comparisons with other classes or other schools but to make a judgement about their pupils. HMI then examined the standard of work being undertaken by the children in these ability groups and they then compared it with what they thought the children were capable of. The relationship between the work children were actually doing and what HMI thought that they were capable of doing was referred to as *match*. A reasonably satisfactory match was noted and recorded when the tasks which were presented to children were related to their existing skills and knowledge, and where there was evidence of the acquisition of further skill, information and understanding. When work was presented at the right level children were confident and not afraid and they displayed a sense of purpose and appeared to enjoy the challenge of the increasing but realistic demands placed upon them. When work was not reasonably matched in nearly all cases it was not sufficiently demanding. It was rare for children of any age or ability to be required to undertake work which was too difficult for them. At all levels work was least well-matched for able groups. With respect to specific areas of the curriculum HMI reported that

- The teaching of reading was most frequently judged to be reasonably matched.
- Mathematics was reasonably matched for most average and less able children but for more able children a reasonable match was achieved in only half the cases.
- Work in writing and spoken language was matched for about three-quarters of below average and average children but only in about half the cases for above average pupils.
- There was a poor match in science in about two-thirds of the cases observed.
- Work in music and arts and crafts was matched in about half of all cases but in history and geography there was a considerable under-estimation of children's abilities.
- The more reasonable matching in language and maths reflected the high priority given to teaching these subjects and the availability of graded schemes of work.
- In general teachers were relatively successful at matching work in basic skills for slower children but more able children were less likely to be provided with work which was challenging.

Following the publication of the HMI Report the Department of Education and Science (DES) funded a research project which investigated the problem of matching in infant classrooms.[4] This study was devised so as to explore the fine-grain of matching and as such a considerable amount of information was collected in sixteen classrooms. The teachers involved in the research were specifically selected because they had been judged to be good teachers. In their classes six children, 6–7 years old, were targeted for observation (a high, average, and low achieving boy and girl). The typical research procedure was for an investigator to question the teacher, prior to the beginning of the school day, in order to establish the work and tasks she was to give the six target children during the day and to ask her about the rationale for setting the work she was providing and to discover what she expected in terms of the quantity and quality of each child's work, and any problems she anticipated. Following the interview the researcher would closely observe two target children and make a continuous record of their activities and work. When children had completed tasks set by the teacher they were interviewed by the researcher in order to discover directly from pupils their understanding of what had been required of them and their emotional and motivational reactions to the learning tasks. On the basis of their observations the researchers devised diagnostic questions to assess whether the tasks set by teachers matched children's levels of ability and understanding. Finally the work completed by the child and the record of the researcher's observations were discussed with the teacher. The teacher was invited to comment on the quality of the child's work and the appropriateness of the task she had set the child. Over 400 tasks set for children were analysed in this way. Two salient issues emerged from the analysis of the evidence; these concerned the nature of the tasks themselves which the teachers set the children and the extent to which the tasks were matched to pupils' abilities.

In order to discover what sorts of tasks teachers set and the learning processes they required from children a category system was devised which described different types of learning task, namely:

- Incremental tasks which involve the process of accretion in the acquisition of new facts, skills, rules or procedures.
- Restructuring tasks which have the pupil working predominantly with familiar materials, but discover, invent or discuss new ways of looking at problems.
- Enrichment tasks which require the application of familiar skills to new problems.
- Practice tasks which demand the repetitive and rapid application of familiar knowledge and skills to familiar settings and problems.
- Revision tasks which demand attention to materials or skills which have been set aside for some time in order to minimise memory loss or provide a foundation for learning new or related material.

The close observation of individual teachers and children revealed that practice tasks predominated and involved 60 per cent of all tasks. This contrasts starkly with the incidence of incremental tasks which comprised 25 per cent of observed tasks. There was a low incidence of enrichment tasks at 7 per cent, and 6 per cent of the tasks were revision tasks. Of over four hundred tasks analysed only two (in number) were concerned with restructuring; that is to do with discovery or invention. The types of tasks set for children were not related to their attainment levels. Teachers gave similar proportions of practice and incremental tasks to children of different abilities. Thus, for example, the quantity of practice tasks involving the consolidation of learning required of slow learners was no different from that required from high achievers.

Having discovered what sorts of learning tasks children actually engage in the researchers sought to assess the degree of matching between the tasks and children's ability. They did so by asking to what degree a particular task contributed to the learning processes of a particular child and they used as evidence: the product of the child's work; the record of the child's strategy when undertaking the task; and the record of the post-task interview. The assessments revealed that, overall, 43 per cent of tasks were matched for number and 40 per cent for language work. Forty-one per cent of the tasks set for high attainers underestimated their ability and 44 per cent of tasks overestimated low attainers' ability. There were considerable variations to this pattern within different classrooms.

At first sight it would appear, from this evidence, that teachers are not particularly effective at matching their teaching to their pupils' abilities. More recent investigations provide additional confirmatory information and indicate official concern. The HMI survey of newly trained teachers undertaken in 1987[5] reported that the needs of primary and middle school pupils of average ability were well provided for in eight out of ten lessons and those of more able or less able children in seven out of ten lessons. Too often more able children were expected to work at a faster rate, rather than be provided with more demanding work, and on occasions less able pupils were allowed to spend much time on undemanding tasks. A substantial evaluation of one LEA's primary schools[6] noted that teachers tried to strike a reasonable balance between the challenges they set and the skills of their pupils but it was not easy to balance challenges and skills even when working with individual children.

In sum, the available evidence indicates that for many children for a substantial part of their time in primary schools the tasks set and learning required of them do not match their abilities. This information is easily conveyed as a 'problem'[7] and provides the grounds for admonishing teachers. For instance the 1985 White Paper, *Better Schools*,[8] reported that the government believed that the curriculum offered each child should reflect a number of fundamental principles, which include

> There should be careful differentiation: what is taught and how it is taught need to be matched to pupils' abilities and aptitudes. It is of the greatest importance to stimulate and challenge all pupils, including the most and least able: within teaching groups as well as schools the range of ability is often wide.[9]

A degree of circumspection is in order before rushing to judgement. The evidence must be weighed carefully before criticising teachers' ability to match and before assessing its implications for practical pedagogy. This is particularly so at the present time because the introduction of the National Curriculum places particular burdens upon teachers in terms of their ability to match learning tasks to children's abilities. Each National Curriculum subject is organised according to levels of attainment and identifies attainment targets which, it is claimed, are 'on a single continuous scale'[10] and which define by Statute the knowledge, skills and understanding which pupils of different abilities and maturities are expected to have by the end of each key stage. A curriculum which envisages children proceeding in an orderly manner from one level of attainment to the next presents the teacher with the problem of matching in unequivocal terms. How in a busy classroom is she to provide differentiated learning activities in all core and foundation subjects for pupils who have reached different levels of attainment? Before proceeding some searching questions must be asked about the matching problem.

ASSESSING THE EVIDENCE

The evidence indicates that for a significant proportion of the time teachers fail to match tasks to children's abilities. Without further reflection this 'fact' becomes accepted as an implied criticism of teachers. But it is a fallacy to engage in research, acquire evidence, and then attach a value to it. We need to ask at the outset (a) what constitutes success and (b) what are the bench-marks by which we assess the teacher's performance? We may argue, for example, that the primary classroom is a complex environment within which the teacher must perform many functions besides attending to the instruction of children with different abilities and aptitudes.[11] It has, for instance, been argued that the child care, wider educational, and training demands which are placed upon primary teachers are such that schools would be more effective in fostering numeracy and literacy if their instructional role was clearly demarcated from their other functions. If, say, small groups of children were removed from the hurly-burly of normal classrooms and spent an hour or two each day in separate rooms with teachers who instructed them in basic skills they would learn more effectively since the teacher would be able to devote all her time and effort to instruction.[12] Given the circumstances in which teachers must work we may plausibly argue that if teachers can match for, say, half the time that constitutes success, it would seem unrealistic to establish the bench-mark at, say, 80 per cent. It is instructive to bear in mind that the studies which have identified high rates of failure to match have employed a methodology which requires an independent, experienced educationist to be present in the classroom who focuses his attention upon target children during designated lessons. Under such circumstances it is easy for the observer to spot mismatching and no doubt any teacher who was asked to address the learning of a handful of children would have few problems with matching. All this is conjecture but it is to establish the point that it is misleading and of little value to obtain research evidence which slips easily into an implied criticism of teachers. One needs to look carefully at the circumstances in which teachers teach and ask what may be expected from them in terms of matching.

While we have no agreed standards by which to determine what constitutes success it is still necessary to explore precisely what are the particular circumstances in primary classrooms which may affect adversely teachers' capacity to match, especially with reference to the work provided for below average and above average pupils. If we have some understanding of the reasons why teachers fail to match then it at least becomes possible to suggest procedures for maximising the opportunities for matching to take place. We may not be able to set an independent bench-mark for measuring success but presumably as an aspiration we would prefer teaches to match learning tasks to pupils' abilities as often as is possible. Evidence from a number of sources point to the nature of the problem. The ORACLE project[13] entailed detailed observations of primary teaching in fifty-eight classrooms over a 3-year period. While the study did not focus directly upon matching one of the key themes emerging from the research is pertinent. The ORACLE report noted that over the past twenty years there have been changes in primary schools which are best explained by the rise of the 'post Plowden' progressive movement. The result of these changes is that schools have adopted flexible forms of classroom organisation and there has been an emphasis upon the individualisation of work and attention. These managerial changes have not been linked to the development of changes in the forms of learning associated with progressive education such as child-centred exploratory learning with an emphasis upon finding out for oneself. Teachers have focused upon the problem of keeping individual children involved with tasks. By doing this they have neglected pedagogical considerations concerned with the quality of their teaching and the quality of pupils' learning. Teachers have concentrated on keeping children busy rather than attended to the quality of instruction which includes, among other things, matching work to ability. This theme is echoed in other, more recent, studies. The ILEA survey[14] of over two thousand pupils in some fifty London junior schools which tracked pupils through their years of junior education identified the problems inherent in attempting to organise too many learning experiences in any one classroom. Where this was the dominant organisation mode teachers were too often unable to cope with the myriad demands made upon them and consequently could rarely ensure that learning in each separate area was progressing satisfactorily. In addition, because pupils were engaged in such different tasks the teacher's attention tended to be upon management rather than teaching, so opportunities for . . . intellectually challenging teaching arose too rarely. The results . . . are poorer teaching and learning.[15]

This research suggested that pupils are more industrious when teachers are able to provide pupils with feedback about their work and communicate with the whole class, and that teachers are able to spend more time interacting with the children when the work being covered is in one curriculum area. Children's progress is more likely to be promoted when the teacher takes responsibility for providing a structure which gives order and facilitates a balance of work during the day and where there are clearly defined periods when children work broadly within one or two curriculum areas.

Finally, the evaluation of primary education in Leeds[16] makes similar comments. Classroom observations, as noted previously, revealed that teachers tried to strike a balance between the challenges they were setting and the skills of their pupils. Their ability to motivate children was dependent upon the precision of this balance because tasks which were too difficult tended to generate frustration and anxiety and those which were too easy lead to boredom and loss of direction. It was not always easy to maintain the balance, especially for teachers working with mixed ability groups where the normal practice was for there to be several different tasks in different curriculum areas. In these classrooms maintaining an adequate balance was an, 'aspiration rather than an achievement'. Teachers often adopted strategies which camouflaged the intractability of the problem such as asking large numbers of questions or imposing small amounts of extremely easy work. The reduction in task demands maximised the numbers of children who could proceed without assistance and offered the illusion of motivation through enjoyment.

The general theme which emerges from these surveys is clear. The more complicated the organisation of the classroom and the greater the variety of curriculum activities going on at the same time, the more difficult it is for the teacher to match learning to pupils' abilities. The teacher's energy and attention are devoted to sustaining order in a complex environment rather than focused upon pedagogical matters relating directly to children's learning. (This theme is explored in detail in the next chapter.) The justification for organising the classroom and curriculum according to 'progressive' principles is, presumably, because this has a worthwhile effect upon the nature and quality of pupils' learning experiences which are more 'child centred' and activity based. But, as the evidence from these and the other studies outlined in Chapter 1 demonstrates, 'child-centred' organisation does not necessarily lead to child-centred learning. Children continue to learn in teacher-centred ways and engage in the sorts of learning tasks usually found in traditional classrooms. The difference is that the work is probably done less efficiently. The implication for classroom practice is that the teacher will be better able to focus upon pedagogical matters such as matching if she organises the classroom and curriculum in a structured manner which specifies a limited number of tasks and activities children should engage in at one time.

CLOSENESS OF MATCH

There is no agreed or satisfactory answer to the question of how frequently we should expect the effective teacher to be able to match and to complicate matters we must introduce another issue for consideration. How do we decide whether or not a satisfactory match has been achieved? Again we lack established criteria or guidelines. This is awkward because, presumably, if we consider an ability to match to be an important part of the effective teacher's expertise then it follows that we should have a clear idea about what constitutes an acceptable degree of matching. Leaving aside the investigations reported in *The Quality of Pupil Learning Experiences*,[17] attempts to define the closeness of the degree of match are couched in broad terms and rest upon subjective judgements.[18] There is no difficulty in accepting that teachers should match in a very general sense but the issue of matching focuses upon the specific learning tasks which children undertake and hence assumes that a reasonably precise degree of matching can be maintained on a regular basis. The achievement of close matching may be a worthy educational ideal but it is very difficult to attain in practice. Any attempt to match closely must be based upon the presumption that the teacher can have a detailed and extensive appreciation of the knowledge that is contained in each child's mind and also know that this knowledge is organised in accordance with some systematic hierarchic principles. Furthermore it assumes that facts and skills exist independently and can be built upon, like adding stones to a cairn, rather than appreciating that knowledge, skill and understanding are better regarded as existing within complex networks and that individual children will interpret and incorporate new knowledge into what they already know in different ways. As one educational philosopher has pointed out, we lack in principle a simple and clear means of uncovering what is 'new' for a pupil. Davis argues[19] that it is naive to consider the child's mind as a receptacle containing facts to which new facts can be added. Among his many illustrations he cites the example of the geographical 'fact' that Edinburgh is west of Bristol. There is no sense in which this new fact can be simply added to the store of knowledge already in the child's mind because it must be interrelated with what the child already knows. One child in an East Anglian primary school may have only a hazy idea of where Scotland is and lack any sense of direction. While another child living in Edinburgh knows that the rival Glasgow is to the west and that England is to the south. What this fact means to the two children and how they understand it may depend upon what they already know. Davis goes on to argue that fine-grain matching is simply not possible and that all the teacher can be expected to do is to match in the most general sense. Hence, he suggests that the notion of matching should not provide a means of criticising teachers since at best they can match in only the broadest of terms. This analysis has considerable force. Nevertheless, it does not provide a defence against some of the teaching practices identified by matching studies such as providing children with manifestly easy work which does little beyond keeping them busily employed. While it may be difficult to match we should at least be prepared to challenge children and extend what they know rather than devote too much time to the undemanding practice of what is already within their compass. Rather than advocate that teachers should match closely, a better guide may be to suggest[20] that they should avoid deliberate mismatching. Much of the information reported in the research indicates that in many cases, such as when children carry out routine low level tasks which merely keep them employed, mismatching could be avoided comparatively easily.

The notion of close matching is also open to a logical objection. The teacher's task is to advance and develop what the child already knows hence any new learning entails a forward jump which in a sense is a leap into the dark, the outcome of which cannot be predicted. The shift to a new state cannot be exactly matched to the child's current knowledge. Any teaching involves making an effort in the hope that it will be success-ful but most attempts to move learning forward carry the risk of failure. In a sense advancing learning entails risking a deliberate mismatch. Con-sider the case of Mary learning to ride her bicycle. At the outset her father will walk beside her supporting the cycle and, as she grows in confidence, he slackens his hold and eventually lets go. Mary might manage to balance or she might crash. But the father has no option; if Mary is to learn to ride there comes a point where he must let go and pass from the stage where she cannot ride to being able to do so and thereby risk a 'mis-match'. Consider also the plight of most of us in our attempts to learn, say, mathematics. We reach a stage where we simply no longer understand. However close the matching and however clear the exposition we cannot comprehend and the subject becomes a closed book. Considerations such as this may explain why matching studies report that teachers do not provide sufficient tasks which extend able children. Attempts to advance learning involve a challenge and carry the risk of failure. They demand that the teacher devotes considerable attention to a group of children and engages in a variety of activities so as to promote new learning. Difficult work which has moved beyond obvious matching may generate opportunities for frustration and failure and may affect children's enthusiasm and commitment to learning. The teacher may need to weigh the claims for (a) risking new learning that carries the possibility of failure and disaffection and (b) providing work that she knows that children will be able to manage and thereby sustain their enthusiasm and commitment.

Thus far my exposition has rested upon the presumption that matching is important if children are to learn successfully. In a sense this would seem to be part of our common sense understanding of what is involved in teaching. In any walk of life people who engage in teaching, be they driving instructors or professors, proceed from the easy to the more difficult and from the simple to the more complex and progress by building upon introductory or elementary materials.[21] The educational case for matching is, however, not only based upon common sense and in its stronger and more persuasive form draws upon psychological theory. We must therefore examine the theoretical case for matching. Over two hundred years ago the German philosopher and psychologist J.F. Herbart sought to establish a scientific pedagogy with psychology as its basis.[22] He developed a set of principles for enabling children to acquire knowledge. Herbartianism became one of the standard and enduring approaches to methods work in teacher training institutions. One of Herbart's fundamental principles is that ideas are associated together in groups in the human mind. During the process of learning the child makes contact with the outer world by sense perception and any new perceptions are influenced by what is present in the mind and must be built into what is already there. From this is developed the Herbartian psychological principle of 'associationism' which, in terms of his recommended pedagogical practice, leads to the association stage in the lesson when the teacher presents content so that it may be associated with what is already in the child's mind. Modern psychology continues to reflect Herbartian notions. In the 1960s Ausubel[23] developed a model of meaningful learning whereby he proposed that worthwhile learning results when new information is related to the cognitive structures already in the learner's mind. (To pre-empt later discussion it must be emphasised that Ausubel focuses upon the particular cognitive structure of the individual learner.) The pedagogical principle which follows from his theory is summarised in a quotation familiar to generations of student teachers, 'The most important single factor influencing learning is what the learner already knows. Ascertain this and teach him accordingly.' More recently, schemata theory continues the tradition.[24] A schema is conceptualised as an organisational structure within the learner's mind which summarises knowledge about a number of cases which are linked to one another on the basis of similarity or difference. The manner in which what the learner already knows is structured within mental schemata influences how he perceives, understands and remembers new information. The schemata which come into play on particular occasions lead different children to focus upon and interpret learning in different ways. As children acquire new knowledge through instruction and experience the way in which they remember, interpret, and understand is shaped by the prior knowledge structures within their minds. A particular theme addressed by schemata theory which is of relevance to classroom practice is that children's experiences of growing up, behaving and acting in contexts outside the school lead to the development of schemata which may not necessarily be conducive to the assimilation and understanding of the new knowledge taught in schools.

In sum, these psychological perspectives offer us a view of the child as an independent learner who comes to any teaching–learning encounter with its mind already containing a considerable amount of knowledge. The knowledge in the child's mind is not stored in an arbitrary manner but is organised according to some principles. New knowledge which the teacher requires the child to learn will be perceived, mediated, understood and assimilated within the context of what the child already knows and the ways in which it is structured and organised. This model has clear implications for matching in that it offers a theoretical basis for justifying matching and for claiming that teachers must match closely for learning to be effective. This is an appealing proposition but except in the most general sense offers little in terms of proposals or prescriptions for pedagogical practice. It is, moreover, unworkable and unnecessary. When we focus upon practice it is unnecessary, beyond providing general guidance, because it is demonstrably the case that much successful and effective teaching is necessarily carried out without the teacher having any detailed information concerning what may be in each child's mind or even being aware of individual learners. Television and radio school programmes do not, because of their very nature, match learning to what individual learners already know and neither do many computer programmes designed to foster learning. Beyond a broad 'sense of audience' none of the textbooks, learning programmes or aids which are devised by people who are not in the classroom and have no appreciation of individual children can be based upon an informed understanding of the knowledge already in the individual child's mind and the ways in which it is organised. Yet such materials are constantly used in the classroom to good effect. The psychological theory is unworkable because it places an unrealistic, if not impossible, burden upon the teacher. It is wishful thinking to imagine that the teacher could have access to the minds of the thirty odd children in her charge and thereby discern both what they already know (across, say, all subjects within the National Curriculum) and how their knowledge is organised. Moreover, even if in an ideal world where the teacher has all this information, it is never clear in terms of suggestions for classroom practice how exactly new knowledge is perceived by the learner, interpreted, and incorporated within the existing corpus or schemata.

Consider the story of Alfred and the cakes. I can still remember that one of the first occasions when I began to suspect that teachers were fallible was when, as an infant, the teacher told us the story of Alfred's inept cooking. The teacher illustrated the story by holding up the stereo-typic picture of a bearded man pondering deeper matters while the cakes on the open hearth burned. I knew perfectly well what cakes were; my mother used to give us them for tea when we got home from school. It was silly to imagine putting cakes by a fire, the cream would melt and in any case if you were offered a cake you eat it. The infant teacher cannot 'get inside' each child's mind so as to assess how he will understand and interpret new learning. Why should she, *a priori*, consider 'cakes' to be a problem rather than say 'burning'? The National Curriculum for history includes a level one statement of attainment, 'place in sequence events in a story about the past' and gives as an example, 'Re-tell the story of the Gunpowder Plot'. If the successful teaching of the story to infants entails matching the lesson content with what the children already know, then presumably the teacher needs to check up beforehand on her infants' understanding of notions such as 'gunpowder', 'plot', and 'Houses of Parliament', perhaps to discover later that they have been bemused by 'Guy's forks'.

There is an additional substantial practical problem which is not addressed by psychological theory but which is drawn to our attention when we consider its practical application. It is that during the years of primary schooling it is not always possible or desirable to organise knowledge so that it proceeds from the 'easy' to the 'difficult' or more complex and thereby make matching possible. An obvious example is reading. A vast proportion of infant teachers' time and resources is devoted to teaching reading during the early years. It is at least possible that reading could be taught more effectively and rapidly and with a greater degree of success if formal instruction was delayed for a year or two, as in most European primary schools. School time could then be devoted to more productive learning activities which were closely related to infants' aptitudes. Perhaps they could learn to speak another language rather than read their own. In mathematics there are instances where we persist in teaching material when we know beforehand that many children will experience considerable difficulty and which we also know is probably difficult to relate to what they already understand. The formal procedures or analogues for subtraction and the invert and multiply rule for dividing fractions are notorious examples. Perhaps if we put these activities at a later stage in the curriculum children would learn more quickly and effectively. There is, of course, a valid and sound educational reason for not always delaying the the introduction of skills and knowledge which we know will be difficult to teach at an early stage. It is that we expect children to be able to have mastered certain skills and routines at an early stage so that the curriculum can build upon them. What we require children to know early on in the learning process is not necessarily that which it is easiest to acquire. Children must learn to read when they begin schooling because education within literate societies is based upon the presumption that children can read. Subtraction is taught in the infant classroom because it is an important skill needed for a wide range of mathematical activities later on. The practical pedagogical task facing the teacher, especially during the early years, is not always matching her teaching to children's abilities but rather persisting with attempts to teach knowledge and skills which often appear to be beyond the child and which he continually struggles with. The teacher's job is not so much matching learning tasks to the child's ability but rather matching the child to the task and to deploying various motivational strategies in the hope that the child will remain engaged with tasks and thereby learn eventually. Indeed it can be argued[25] that if we take the theoretical and research evidence concerning matching seriously then the educational prescription is that we give children considerable responsibility for their own learning in terms of what they need to know and the pace at which they acquire it.

WHAT CAN AND CANNOT BE SEEN

Finally we must examine closely both what teachers are actually doing and also the nature of the evidence they use when making judgements about matching and mismatching. The burden of the case for matching is that in order to teach effectively the teacher must have a reasonable idea of the state of the learner's mind in terms of what the child already knows and how this knowledge is organised and then provide learning tasks in the light of this information. But, as has been argued, we cannot have access to the child's mind. I suggest that when the teacher is teaching she does not usually attempt to gain some sort of independent information about the child's mental structures and abilities before introducing new knowledge; it is, rather, that she assesses how well the child manages with school work in terms of his actual behaviour and performance on tasks during the time when curriculum content is being introduced.

When schema theory is drawn upon to make suggestions for educational practice it is proposed, for example, that the crucial teaching skill is to do with ascertaining children's various schemata.[26] This involves diagnosis and finding out what children already know and understand of the subject or topic in hand in order to establish a profitable starting point. It requires careful observation, testing, conversation with the child, and teaching, so as to add to schemata, and involves the skills of explanation, description, demonstration and modelling. These are established teaching skills although not necessarily deployed equally effectively by all teachers and we need to ask precisely what teachers are about when they use them. These skills cannot be employed so as to give us direct access to the contents and structures within the child's mind and it would not, I suggest, occur to teachers, if asked what they are doing when they question or test, to say that they are attempting to elicit the schemata within the learner's mind. When teachers deploy these skills it is always with reference to some aspect of the content of the lesson and the performance of the pupils in relation to that content. The teacher's interaction with the child focuses upon what the child has produced on paper or what he has said or made and she observes, questions and tests with reference to this product in an attempt to discover whether or not the child knows and understands. The intention is not to penetrate the child's mind but to teach the child content. The teacher interprets what the child 'thinks', 'knows', or 'understands' by reference to a substantive performance related to the subject matter being taught. While the teacher may, *a priori*, be able to match learning in a very general sense to children's abilities it is only after the child has produced some learning outcome that she can gain any detailed information about exactly how well the child has understood. This information relates to performance with specific tasks rather than to mental states or aptitudes. When children fail to understand, have a block, or fail to 'see' then the teacher is placed in the situation where she must think carefully about how she is going to teach the child in order to get over the present hurdle. Her only realistic option is to proceed in terms of how she can represent the lesson content in ways which help the child grasp its meaning. There is no need for an intermediate process involving gaining access to the learner's mind before teaching. The sorts of tasks which teachers set and the way in which they may interpret any evidence obtained will vary in different subject areas and according to the nature of the learning required. When, for example, a child is progressing through a structured maths scheme the teacher may judge the child's performance by reference to the rate of progress and proportion of correct answers. Matching in this circumstance includes checking that the child has, say, a workbook pitched at about the right level and then ensuring that the child remains engaged with the required exercises and offering help and advice when sticking points are encountered. On the other hand, the teacher may play a piece of music as a stimulus for imaginative writing. The same task will elicit a variety of responses and the only way in which the teacher could be said to be matching is in terms of keeping the children involved with their writing through, say, encouragement, praise and advice and helping to develop individual children's skills and abilities while they are engaged with the activity. Once the work has been completed the nearest we can get to considerations of matching is by reference to the teacher's comments which assess the quantity and quality of manifestations of learning in the light of her general impression of individual children's abilities and aptitudes such as, 'This is a very good piece of work for Jim, he has only produced four lines but this is an advance, ' or, 'I know Jane can do much better if she tries'. In this sense any judgement made about the quality of match rests upon a comparison between what the individual child actually produces and what the teacher would have expected in the light of her general knowledge of the child.

This suggests, as far as practical pedagogy is concerned, that in so far as matching may be a characteristic of effective teaching, the teacher's task in many contexts is to match the child to the subject content of lessons, rather than vice versa and then ensure that the child remains productively employed with learning activities. It further suggests that knowledge about the child's performance should direct us not so much to conjectures about the child's mind but to a more substantial consideration of the material being taught and how it is taught. If the child encounters difficulties, then teaching involves attempts to recast the material, offer alternative illustrations or metaphors, and so on in an attempt to assist the child. Practical pedagogy entails thinking carefully about the content matter of lessons, the nature of the associated learning tasks, and the use of various teaching skills which may encourage children to remain pro-ductively engaged with their work in the expectation that they will learn successfully whatever the teacher intends that they should learn.

SUMMARY

Classroom observations in primary schools that have focused upon matching have provided evidence, which cannot be dismissed, which indicates that for significant proportions of time work is inappropriately matched in that children of different levels of ability are given learning tasks which are not closely related to their aptitudes and attainments. An examination of the evidence indicates that we have no agreed standards by which to determine the quality of the closeness of match and the optimum frequency of match. Even if we did have a bench-mark, judge-ments would need to bear in mind those circumstances in which teachers teach which are not always conducive for promoting optimum teaching strategies. Nevertheless, as an ideal it is presumably preferable for teachers, in a general sense, to match learning to pupils' abilities as often as is possible and especially ensure that children do not spend too much time engaged in low-level repetitive or practice tasks which keep them busy but which do not advance their learning.

Close matching based upon the teacher's appreciation of what individual children already know and the mental structures organising what they know is an unattainable ideal. Only in broad terms is it possible for the teacher to make use of what she thinks she knows about her children's abilities and aptitudes when planning her teaching. The practical pedagogical imperative facing the teacher is rather one of matching children to the tasks she sets in the expectation that through involvement with activities they will learn. This includes deploying her organisational and motivational skills so as to encourage children to remain engaged with learning tasks and focusing her attention upon the content of lessons and how it is presented so as to engage her pupils in learning and facilitate their understanding. The old adage has it that in order to teach history to Johnny the teacher must know something about history and something about Johnny. What is being suggested is that the teacher should focus very much more upon what she knows about history because it is through the medium of teaching history that she comes to know about Johnny.

Chapter 5

Organising teaching to promote learning

In this chapter I consider teaching and learning within the wider context of the classroom environment and explore how the teacher may manage her classroom and organise her teaching so as to optimise children's opportunities to learn and engage with the learning tasks which are provided for them.

MAXIMISING THE TIME AND OPPORTUNITY FOR LEARNING

The teacher should be responsible for ensuring that as much time as is reasonable is allocated for learning. It may seem trite to suggest that the more time that children spend in school and the more time that they are engaged in learning in the classroom, the more they are likely to learn, but an important theme emerging from classroom studies is that there are significant variations in the length of the school day and the proportions of time during which children are involved with learning tasks in class-rooms. Time and the opportunity to learn are key factors affecting the quality and quantity of children's learning. The hours in the school day, the proportion of the day devoted to the curriculum, the amount of time allocated to different areas of the curriculum, and the amount of time in lessons during which pupils are employed in learning are factors which teachers should attend to if they wish to optimise their pupils' learning.[1]

The requirement to maximise the time available for learning must, of course, be considered not as a slogan to be implemented but as a guideline for pedagogical practice. Teachers need to consider for instance how much learning their pupils can take. Lengthening the school day and lesson time only to be confronted by weary children subjected to incessant teaching is unlikely to lead to worthwhile learning. Time is only the 'container' for the curriculum; what is particularly important is the quality of teaching and learning which goes on during lessons.[2] While bearing these disclaimers in mind, it should, nevertheless, be recognised that there are often significant differences between, for example, the time schools take over assembly, registration, and other preliminary activities in the morning, the length of playtimes, the amount of dislocation caused at lunch-time (often created by organisational factors beyond teachers' control), and the time taken by teachers to get their pupils involved with lessons. The proposal to optimise the time available for learning should not be taken as an invitation to cut five minutes off playtimes or for the head to march around the school, stop watch in hand, measuring the time allocated to learning. It is to suggest that primary teachers need to reflect upon how the school day and lessons are usually structured and sequenced and ask whether the best possible use is being made of the time available for learning.

The expectation that the teacher should optimise teaching and learning opportunities in the classroom must be tempered with consideration of a factor which educational outsiders and pundits fail to appreciate and which even conscientious teachers may not acknowledge. It is to recognise the importance of energy as a factor in teaching and planning for teaching.[3] Teaching is demanding work. The primary class teacher is usually responsible for her class for all of the school day and free periods are a luxury. She is on public view and must perform for all the time that the children are in school and usually beforehand and afterwards as well. This is another of the distinctive characteristics of primary teaching which must be born in mind when considering the teacher's professional expertise. Secondary teachers will expect their fair share of free periods for preparation and no teacher in higher education could contemplate the primary teacher's contact time. It is important for the teacher to pace herself and ration her energy and enthusiasm; a burnt-out teacher is of no use to herself or her children. It is unreasonable to expect the primary teacher to spend the whole day engaged in intentional teaching activities designed so as to advance learning. Even if the teacher could bear sustained teaching from nine in the morning to four in the afternoon it is unlikely that her pupils could take so much purposeful learning. It is professionally appropriate for the teacher to consider her own needs and convenience when organising the classroom so that the arrangements enable her to manage her own stock of energy and attention and ensure that they are husbanded so as to provide for maximum effect within the class. It is not fanciful to suggest that if young children engage in, say, two or three hours structured, purposeful learning each day during which the teacher is making a direct effort to teach them, then they will make better progress than is often the case in primary classrooms where the teacher tries to do too much with too many children and thereby dissipates her efforts.[4]

TO GROUP OR NOT TO GROUP

The policy of grouping children in the primary classroom has probably reached the status where for many primary teachers it is accepted as characteristic of good primary practice.[5] It is seen as the way to organise children, usually so that they can be allocated to ability groups. Often the groups will move from one activity to another during the day and group composition may change from time to time depending upon the nature of the learning and area of the curriculum.[6] The thrust of the previous chapter carries an implication that in mixed ability classrooms it may be appropriate to group children according to aptitude if teaching is to be matched to their ability. Before deciding to group it is important to consider carefully whether this is necessarily good practice and weigh the benefits and costs. For instance it does not follow that in order for the teacher to provide differentiated learning that pupils have to be physically grouped within the classroom. The groups can, as it were, exist in the teacher's mind and learning activities can be provided for children of different abilities who are randomly distributed throughout the class.

When children are grouped in class it is usually so that the teacher can form homogeneous groups for learning but it is important to remember that to group children according to one characteristic, say, their reading ability, does not get over the fact that they may still be very different on other characteristics which may be related to learning such as mathematical ability, motivation, or the social adaptability necessary to work effectively in groups.[7] Moreover, grouping children according to ability may, as a consequence, mean that the groups are alike in terms of social class background, ethnicity, or gender and thereby possibly expose the teacher to the charge that discrimination or partiality has influenced group formation (this problem can be worse if children are grouped according to friendship choices). The issue should also be considered with reference to streaming. One of the important reasons for abandoning the practice of streaming children in separate classes according to academic level and for creating mixed ability classes in their place is to overcome the social problems and stigma attached to labelling children according to whether they are in the A, B or C stream. But grouping children within classrooms according to ability, and this is the most common method of grouping,[8] does not disguise the fact that the children are still being organised according to their ability.[9] Indeed the kudos of able children may be enhanced within the unstreamed class because less able children can turn to them as a resource for advice and help when the teacher's attention is elsewhere.[10] If the teacher's aim is to disguise differences in ability it is probably preferable to disperse children randomly throughout the class.[11] The teacher cannot organise children into groups and then expect the groups to work productively and harmoniously. The evidence suggests that it is necessary to prepare and train children if they are to work effectively in groups;[12] pupils must be taught to co-operate and provided with appropriate skills if they are to work together. The irony is that classroom studies report that children work best in groups when they receive clear-cut assignments which are closely monitored by the teacher.[13] The notion of children working co-operatively together on creative or discovery orientated tasks is not supported by the available evidence; in fact creative work is probably more likely to be found during whole class instruction.[14] The evidence[15] also indicates that homogeneous ability grouping may be detrimental to the learning of children in low ability groups; it is able children who are more likely to be able to cope with and prosper in group settings where pupils are less likely to be under the eye of the teacher.

In sum, there are sound reasons for grouping children in primary class-rooms but there are equally convincing reasons for not doing so and for engaging in class teaching. Grouping places a particular burden upon the teacher in terms of the management and organisation of the class and the problem of sustaining order may become paramount, resulting in the teacher having less time to attend to teaching and learning. The teacher should not assume that grouping is a prerequisite for good primary practice; whole class teaching has an equal claim to the teacher's attention.

The practical pedagogic problem facing the class teacher is that she is likely to want to adopt different forms of classroom arrangement from time to time and switch from one to another. A recent report on primary education[16] proposes that it is necessary to strike a balance between the organisational strategies of whole class teaching, group work, and indivi-dual teaching. In order to strike a balance the teacher must ask, 'What is a good balance and how is the classroom to be organised so as to enable the smooth transition from one organisational form to another?' Advice available to teachers tends to fall silent when these awkward practical questions are posed.[17] One possible solution is to arrange the desks in a square or horseshoe figuration as the basic form of organisation and switch from this to individual, group and whole class teaching as desired.[18] The square or horseshoe pattern allows the teacher to see every child and every child to see the teacher during class lessons. Desks are arranged around the sides of the classroom with children facing into the middle of the room. This method has the following advantages:

- Children can see each other and are more inclined to listen to each other's contributions than when seated in rows with their backs to colleagues, or in groups where eye contact and audibility are difficult.
- A large space is available in the middle of the room for stories, large pieces of artwork and so on.
- Children are able, when required, to work in pairs or threes, that is group sizes which are productive and unlikely to exclude people. (Often group size is determined by the number of children who can sit around table arrangements, rather than educational considerations.)
- The teacher can see, at a glance, what every child is doing and reach those with problems quickly.
- Desks can quickly be formed into tables of four when required.

This approach allows flexibility and enables a variety of teaching methods to be employed. Class teaching should be successful because children are facing the teacher and are not able to conceal themselves behind others, as they can be when sitting in rows which all face the front of the classroom. Group work can be employed easily, with group sizes determined by the task rather than by the number of children who fit around a table. In addition, some children can work in groups while others work individually.

There are, in sum, possible managerial solutions which make it possible to switch from one form of classroom organisation to another and accommodate the advantages of both whole class teaching and group work.

TEACHING AS PRACTICAL PEDAGOGY

At the conclusion of the first chapter it was argued that the essence of the teacher's work is to communicate subject matter to pupils and, at the same time, sustain order within the particular social context of the classroom where one adult is responsible for the education of thirty-odd children in a constrained space with limited resources. It is the teacher's ability to teach successfully within the demanding circumstances of the classroom which is central to the primary teacher's professional expertise and distinguishes her from teachers in other walks of life. In practice it is not, of course, possible to make a clear distinction between the imperatives for teaching subject matter and sustaining order, since they are inexorably linked with each other. The professional challenge facing the teacher in her endeavours to foster children's learning in her class may be seen as resolving and manipulating the tensions between the need to teach subject matter (however defined) and the need to sustain order (in the broad sense of organising the classroom, monitoring the flow of events, and allocating resources). We can view class teaching as a series of bargains or accommodations which must be made between promoting learning and sustaining order. The skilful resolution of these tensions may be referred to as 'practical pedagogy'. The teacher's practical pedagogy should be based upon informed choices so that she is aware of the costs and benefits entailed in pursuing one course of action rather than another. In what follows I elaborate upon this theme[19] and outline the issues which teachers need to bear in mind when making their pedagogical choices.

Social arrangements

There is a relationship between the nature of the social arrangements in a classroom and the amount of time which the teacher devotes to maintaining order and the amount she devotes to fostering learning. As a guiding principle it is likely to be the case that the more complicated the social arrangements, degree of pupil choice, number of ongoing activities, degree of mobility, etc., the more time which the teacher may need to allocate to maintaining order. It is not so much a teacher's style or philosophy which determines the proportions of time devoted to maintaining order and promoting learning but, rather, the nature and variety of activities going on in the class. This is not, of course, a hard and fast rule. There are some teachers who are superb managers who can organise and orchestrate complicated classroom arrangements so that they can, at the same time, direct most of their attention to classroom learning. And there will be those occasions when the teacher decides that complicated arrangements are justified on edu- cational grounds and the fact that she has to devote most of her time to maintaining order is a price worth paying.

Content and continuity

The content and continuity of a lesson, or block of time, may, on the one hand, be controlled by the teacher and involve her in directing the work, ordering the sequence and structure of activities, and controlling the allocation of materials. On the other hand, content and continuity may, in effect, be controlled by the children who are, say, engaged in role play, creative exercises, or group discussions. These alternatives create different problems for the teacher in terms of maintaining order and ensuring pupil involvement with learning. The greater the degree to which the teacher takes responsibility for controlling content and continuity the greater the amount of time which she may be able to allocate to promoting learning and ensuring that children attend to their work. The greater the degree to which children are responsible for content and continuity, the easier it is for them to work within their own abilities or take steps to avoid being involved in learning. As ever, practice is more complicated. The quality of the work instigated by the teacher or devised by the children is all important; bored children pretending to attend to a tedious or unintelligible lesson delivered by the teacher are just as unproductively employed as children aimlessly wasting their time in idle chatter during group discussions.

The nature of academic work

The academic work which the teacher provides for her pupils carries implications for maintaining order. If the work is familiar, routine and predictable then most children are more likely to know what to do, will manage to get on with it and be less likely to place demands upon the teacher in ways which require her to direct her attention to maintaining order and away from helping those children who need assistance with their learning. Routine work involving practice tasks and requiring straightforward responses is more likely to lead to a smooth running and efficiently ordered classroom. When work is novel, ambiguous, challenging or just plain difficult, there are more likely to be problems of order for the teacher to attend to because the children are more likely to question her and ask for guidance and negotiate with her about what to do, or attempt to tease out from her the correct way of proceeding. They are more likely not to pay attention or attempt to do something else. Hence at those times when the teacher should be devoting her attention to promoting learning she may find herself having to allocate more effort to maintaining order. This is a particularly challenging problem for the teacher since it is on precisely those occasions when she may wish to advance the children's learning by presenting new or difficult material or to take risks with her teaching so as to encourage imaginative or creative responses that she is most likely to be confronted with the problem of order. In addition, it is always possible for the teacher to use the content of lessons as a means of imposing order. A familiar strategy for coping with a class which is getting restless is for the teacher to threaten them with tedious routine drills while sitting at their own desks.

It is necessary to elaborate upon this general picture. The manner in which the content of lessons is related to problems of order will vary for different subject or topic areas and the teacher may wish to resolve the balance between fostering learning and maintaining order in alternative ways depending upon the content of the lesson and the sorts of learning she aims to promote. For example, the teacher may cope with getting across a tricky mathematical notion which children must learn if they are to progress beyond a difficult part of the syllabus by breaking it down into easy stages and reinforcing learning with practice drills whereas if, in the adjacent lesson, she wishes to encourage the children to let their imagination roam while doing clay work she may be prepared to accept the inevitable problems she will have in terms of maintaining order so as to foster a different kind of learning.

Finally there can be lesson content which takes a simple organisational form but which entails challenging pupil learning (undertaking difficult arithmetic computations for instance) and there can also be lesson content which requires relatively complicated organisational and social arrangements but which is straightforward in terms of the work required (as with some science experiments for example). These factors also raise issues for the teacher. She may decide, for example, that the effort and time involved in the children setting up an experiment themselves is simply not worthwhile in terms of what they are likely to learn and that she can make more productive use of lesson time by giving a single demonstration herself.

Completing work

When people are engaged in work there is a need to show that it has been completed, preferably successfully. This is certainly the case in the classroom where finishing work can also be seen as an aspect of achieving order. When the teacher plays the dominant role in controlling the class and deciding what is to be done, acceptable and satisfactory work is more likely to be produced than when the work is selected and determined by the children. A possible dilemma for the teacher is between, on the one hand, ensuring that work is completed at a level and in a manner which ensures that, say, it may be displayed or put in the folder and, on the other hand, say, valuing work which is a creative contribution from the child but which is full of mistakes and untidy. Again life is more complicated in practice, as for instance, when the teacher devises work which leads to a pleasing product which may be displayed on the wall and proudly shown to mum but which may not advance the child's learning and understanding.

Summary

It must be stressed that when describing ways in which the teacher's work can be seen as maintaining a balance between order and learning that order should not be taken as referring to discipline. (Although teachers who are successful at maintaining order are less likely to have discipline problems or need to act as disciplinarians.) Sustaining order refers to coping with the problems generated by locating teaching in the peculiar environment of the classroom. This framework offers a useful context for thinking about the tasks of teaching in primary classrooms. It also offers a frame of reference for moving the teacher's expertise to centre stage since it is the class teacher who must resolve the tensions, dilemmas, or bargains which I have described. She must make informed judgements, often very rapidly. Her decisions will be shaped by a number of factors, these include: her own values about the proper way to treat children; what she knows of individual children; her intuition about the current state of the class (she may react to a similar set of circumstances differently from day to day depending upon, say, whether the children are fractious or calm); and her own reserves of energy (the teacher may organise her teaching during the late afternoon in a particular way because everyone, including herself, are feeling weary). There are no firm rules to guide the teacher and what is distinctive about the teacher's professional expertise is how she brings to bear her experience, judgement, nous, intuition and skill in the particular mix of circumstances found in her classroom. This practical pedagogical expertise lies at the heart of teaching.

DEMONSTRATING TO CHILDREN THE IMPORTANCE OF WORK

In order to enhance their children's learning teachers need to emphasise the importance of work and achievement within their classrooms and develop an atmosphere which is conducive for learning. This is not to advocate for a moment a return to the authoritarian school teacher forcing reluctant children to work; what is conducive to learning is a business-like and purposeful classroom climate in which the teacher plays a positive part in making clear her purposes and expectations for her pupils. It is a matter of professional judgement and balance rather than an all or nothing pre-scription but it is one that teachers need to reflect upon regularly.

One of the better ways in which to demonstrate the importance of work and foster children's learning is to employ direct instructional techniques. Many educational investigations and reports have been devoted to emphasising that direct instruction has a positive effect upon children's learning but they are limited in that they embody rather restrictive notions of what constitutes learning and many teachers may consider that they are too detailed and prescriptive in suggesting how teachers should teach.[20] One list of recommendations proposes, for instance, that when teaching structured subjects the teacher should:[21]

- Begin a lesson with a short review of previous, pre-requisite learning.
- Begin a lesson with a short statement of goals.
- Present new material in small steps, with practice at each step.
- Give clear and detailed instructions and explanations.
- Prove a high level of active practice for all children.
- Ask a large number of questions, check for understanding, and obtain responses from all children.
- Guide pupils during initial practice.
- Prove systematic feedback and corrections.
- Provide explicit instruction and practice for seatwork exercises and, where necessary, monitor progress during seatwork.

This and other similar guidelines for systematic teaching[22] contain sound pedagogic advice but they carry the danger of forcing teaching into a straitjacket and open up the possibility of stereotypic lessons run accord-ing to a formula. I prefer to use the phrase 'active instruction' to describe the teacher centred classroom in which the teacher takes clear respon-sibility for teaching but does not reduce her performance to the carrying out of prescribed skills or routines. Active instruction refers to classroom contexts in which the teacher is responsible for providing the input or content of lessons; the teacher introduces information and concepts through descriptions, accounts, explanations and presentations; the teacher closely supervises the work of pupils, where appropriate; pupils are given ample time to engage in tasks related to what they are learning; and provided with feedback indicating how well they have done, together with additional practice and revision if indicated. All this, it must be acknowledged, is at variance with the notion (admittedly not often found in practice) that children should be provided with an ample choice of learning activities in an environment rich in resources and opportunities. As Bereiter[23] has pointed out if you provide children with interesting and worthwhile activities then children will tend to involve themselves with these worthwhile activities which may be experientially rich. But this does not make them either education or training. In a work orientated classroom the teacher – obviously – provides her children with tasks of one sort or another. If we are to regard learning as work it becomes necessary to consider what learning tasks may mean for the children.

LEARNING AS WORK

Thus far I have cast the problem from the point of view of the teacher. The matter is more complicated than this because the teacher must also consider how her pedagogical choices and the work she sets have an influence upon children's learning. Hence we must explore the probable impact of the teacher's practical pedagogy upon children's perceptions and their dispositions to learn. It is by attending to the teacher that the child discerns what to learn and how to learn. The notion of schooling as work is also useful, when attempting to gain some idea of how teachers' actions impinge upon children and their learning. Children do not volunteer to attend school or determine the content of schooling. Indeed the very rationale for schooling is that learning is imposed upon children. This does not mean for one moment that schoolwork is necessarily harsh or miserable; many people look forward to their work and classroom work can be exciting, stimulating, and enjoyable. It is, nevertheless, work. The pupil who will not sit and listen to the teacher's entertaining story is a nuisance. The pupil who will not join in a team game is misbehaving. Children who behave well may be allowed into the playground early and bad behaviour may result in the culprits being required to spend more time at their desks. We can only use reward and punishment in these ways if we think of schooling as work. In the perceptive words of the infant whose animated conversation has been interrupted by the teacher, 'Oh, bugger! It's talking time again'.

It is illuminating to go into classrooms, sit with children and ask them what they are doing and then talk to the teacher and ask her about her aspirations for the lesson. The flavour of many such encounters can be illustrated with a couple of examples. I was sitting with a 7-year-old in a class where the children were string printing. After a preliminary chat I asked her what she was doing. She showed me, rather than described, her work (dipping the string into a jar of paint, placing it on the sheet of sugar paper, folding the paper, and drawing the string through, and thereby leaving a random pattern). I asked why she was doing this and the reply was, 'Because Miss told us to'. I persisted but however I attempted to rephrase my question, the answer was always in terms of, 'This is what the teacher has told us to do, so I am doing it'. Other children at the table contributed and indicated that if you did not do what Miss said you had better watch out. I attempted to talk about the emerging patterns and asked whether she noticed what happened when different colours crossed and so on, but with little impact. The girl was more concerned about avoiding dripping paint and keeping the work tidy. When she had completed a print she was pleased with she asked the teacher if it could go on the wall. I then read the student teacher's lesson plans and discovered that the work being undertaken was justified in terms of art education and that the objectives were to develop certain aspects of the children's aesthetic appreciation and artistic skills. All of which flowed above the children's heads as they diligently did what they interpreted their teacher as wanting, namely pulling coloured string through folded paper without making drips so as to produce neat designs which could be displayed on the wall.

On another occasion I sat with a group of upper juniors during a maths lesson. They were copying out the two-dimensional nets of three-dimensional solids. When completed and coloured in, the nets were to be cut out and glued together. Again the question, 'Why are you doing this?' As ever the children were somewhat taken aback since the answer was so obvious, 'This is what the teacher told us to do', they said, in effect. Observing the children it was clear that considerable effort was going into completing the work neatly. There was much rubbing out and redrawing of lines, sharpening of crayons, and careful colouring in. Discussion among the children was in terms of matters such as who had the easiest shape to do, did they have to get it done by playtime, and the whereabouts of the glue. Various efforts were made to get me to help with the tricky bits, especially the cutting out. When this did not work expeditions were organised to the teacher's desk to elicit her help and when a child managed to get the teacher to do some glueing it was displayed around the group with a self-satisfied, 'Miss did this'. A reading of the student's lesson note indicated that the teacher's purpose was to develop the children's mathematical understanding by encouraging them to find out certain information about the relationships between two- and three-dimensional shapes. For the children, however, the lesson was all about how to complete the task of making the three-dimensional shapes; any learning which took place was to do with developing craft skills and manipulating other people to help them complete the work.

These two examples illustrate my theme, which is that from the point of view of the pupil, being in the classroom involves doing work. When it comes to the crux point where the teacher attempts to teach the child she necessarily, in some shape or form, presents the child with tasks which can be thought of as work. The pupil's problem is to accomplish tasks to the satisfaction of the teacher. What the teacher intends is not necessarily received and understood by the child in the same way. In another lesson I sat and listened to the teacher expound on eels; unfortunately his speech was characterised by excessive sibilance. When he had finished his talk he set the class a learning task by asking, 'What else can eels do?' The hand of a well-behaved and keen boy shot up with a, 'Sir, sir, they balance balls on their noses'. This was received as cheek and he was promptly put down. I wonder how many other children sat through the lesson thinking it was about seals rather than eels.

It is helpful to regard the teacher as the person who determines how schooling is to be accomplished by deciding how content is to be represented to children, in the broadest sense, and who also engages in pedagogical tasks in order to achieve this. (These two processes of deciding upon the subject content of lessons and the deployment of appropriate pedagogical moves are crucial to my argument. For present purposes, so as to focus upon children's work, I defer discussion on the organisation of subject matter until the next chapter and skip to the point at which the actual curriculum which the teacher employs so as to engender learning can be thought of as the various tasks which teachers give to children and which are received by them as work to be undertaken and completed.) Work can be seen as the way in which children make sense of being in classrooms. It is more useful to think of what children do in classrooms as 'working', rather than as 'learning'. Learning is a somewhat elusive and unobservable notion[24] and is not the direct consequence of teaching. Learning is something which accompanies classroom events and which may follow from how children interpret and process the information contained within the tasks which teachers allocate. In a word, the actual curriculum which exists in classrooms and which constitutes the work which children undertake may be seen as a series of tasks which the teacher gives the pupils and which they are expected to accomplish. It is through completing tasks that they eventually learn. Tasks embrace a wide range of activities including: sitting in a circle and listening to the teacher playing the piano, individual seat work following a maths scheme, being a mouse in a movement lesson, composing a poem, and so on. However long the list, tasks, for the purpose of exposition, may have a number of attributes attached to them.[25] These are:

- A product – that is an end result such as: a completed work card, the rough version of an essay, reporting the results of a group discussion to the class, a piece of craftwork, or answering a question.

- Production process – that is engaging in the activities which generate the product such as: following instructions and using apparatus as indicated on the work card, writing notes for the essay and making a word list, engaging in group discussions, measuring, cutting and gluing, or listening.
- Use of resources – that is having access to and getting hold of the resources needed to produce the product such as: collecting maths apparatus from where it is stored, having access to a dictionary or pencil sharpener, finding a quiet space for a group discussion, acquiring card, paint and glue.
- Significance – that is the value or weight which is attached to both undertaking and completing the task such as: the marks awarded for completing a task and how they 'count', the public display of completed work, the degree of attention given to pupils' reports of group work.

It is also necessary to note additional themes associated with tasks, namely:

- That the way in which tasks are socially organised will have a bearing upon the four characteristics described above. For instance, tasks undertaken when children work individually at their seats must be distinguished from tasks undertaken and completed by children working as a group.
- That tasks may be analysed from the point of view of the teacher or from the point of view of the pupil. For instance, the teacher may express the product of children's work as a set of objectives related to the content; it does not follow that the pupils will see their work in this light. It is always possible that it is the teacher's lack of clarity in specifying tasks or the child's misinterpretation of task requirements which account for learning failure, rather than lack of ability or understanding.
- That there are different types of procedures for completing work such as using memory, applying routines, or voicing opinion. These embody different accounts of what constitutes successful completion and different notions of what constitutes learning.
- Tasks are not discrete episodes; they are set within the context of the social life and flow of events within the classroom. Thus when completing a specific task the pupils will have a history of previous experiences to guide them when interpreting how it should be accomplished.
- Finally, it is important to appreciate that tasks carry an affective dimension which will influence children's responses. Some children just do not warm to music, games, maths or whatever because they have some prejudice against the subject or because they feel that they lack the requisite skill.

By thinking about what children do in classrooms in this way it becomes possible to appreciate what work and learning may mean to children and to relate their activities to the teacher's work in ways which may assist the teacher's efforts to promote learning when determining pedagogical choices. A range of issues are exposed by regarding children's work in this manner.

Learning

From the point of view of the pupil, learning consists of work which must be attended to, produced, or completed. As such children are not so much likely to be concerned with the meaning of the content of their lessons as with the meaning of their tasks. For children, learning the intrinsic meaning of content is likely to give way to questions about what they have to do in order to produce acceptable results and what value the teacher attaches to what they have done. Children can become remarkably competent at coping with their classroom tasks and pleasing teacher.[26] Learning for children can involve them in devising means of completing work to the satisfaction of the teacher. Children may not necessarily follow the teacher's required procedures in order to complete a task, even though for the teacher the process, itself, may constitute an important part of the children's learning. As indicated previously, tasks which the teacher has set which are intentionally novel or challenging and lead to unpredictable outcomes are more likely to create problems for the children. They will, for instance, attempt to negotiate with the teacher, ask her for cues, or make preliminary guesses in order to discover what she really wants. They may ask how long they have got to finish or wonder whether their neighbour is doing the work correctly. The classroom bush telegraph will be active as children attempt to elicit from others, 'what she really wants'. In a word, for the child learning may be a matter of production rather than of understanding or meaning.

Reward

Children are no different from adults in that they may do work for its intrinsic satisfaction but they also expect to be rewarded. Children will become engrossed in tasks because they find them interesting and satisfying but much of what is learned in classrooms is routine and it is here that the perceived value of a task comes into play. Children will take steps to work out the real weight which a teacher attaches to a task and what she really rewards. Since children have previous experiences to go on they become adept at predicting what the teacher actually requires. She may say that she wants them to use their imaginations and produce an exciting story but the children may well know that on the basis of her track record she rewards tidiness and length; hence they will see their real task in these terms. If the teacher considers that the process of learning is important then she may need to provide ways in which this, as well as the finished product, can be rewarded. One has only to observe a few primary science lessons to realise that often the children are more concerned to discover what they should be finding out rather than learning to engage in and value the process of scientific discovery itself.

Because classrooms are open arenas much of the teacher's praise and blame is delivered publicly, thus children will take steps to ensure that they are not shown up or admonished by the teacher. They may avoid putting their hands up, they may complete as little work as is possible (because they know that if they do any more they will get it wrong), or they may ask the teacher for reassurance after having done so much. Thus, for instance, when the teacher introduces new material which is difficult or challenging it may be preferable to suspend any system of rewards or blame because rather than encourage children to learn it may actively impede their first hesitant steps to grapple with novel material; they are unlikely to try if their attempts are 'punished'.

Procedures and resources

In order that tasks can be completed children may need resources to support what they do. It does not necessarily follow that procedures and resources facilitate task accomplishment. They can easily become a hindrance and cause the children problems. In an example I described earlier the process of drawing and making two-dimensional nets of solid shapes was so complicated that it became an end in itself, rather than a means of promoting mathematical learning. When one watches infants struggling with joining together long rows of unifix cubes which often fly apart when pushed too hard one does wonder how they are supposed to aid children's understanding of simple addition or subtraction, although the exercise may do wonders for developing their manual dexterity. I once observed in a classroom where the teacher did not believe in excessive rubbing out and the children were supposed to cross out instead. There was only one rubber which could be taken from the teacher's desk with permission. From where I was sitting it was clear that there was roaring activity in surreptitious rubber trade and use which consumed much time and effort as, for example, children waited for a rubber to reach them. All this activity was hidden from the teacher and hindered the efficient completion of tasks. In order to promote the effective completion of tasks and maintain order it is important for the teacher to ensure that appropriate procedures and resources are available so as to allow children to work purposefully. It is useful to bear in mind that procedures which are intended to promote learning may be so unwieldy or complicated that carrying them out becomes an end in itself, rather than the means of achieving the learning the teacher has in mind.

The child as practical learner

The frame of reference I have described offers a context in which to regard learning from the point of view of the child as a learner in the classroom. It does not follow, of course, that children will necessarily learn at all or respond to learning tasks in the manner indicated by the frame of reference. This is because learning has a contingent association with teaching and children may respond to learning tasks in different ways depending upon their individual quirks of personality, motivation and ability. The range of possible variation will, of course, be constrained by the nature of the subject matter being taught. While there will be a measure of predictability in the children's learning it still requires each individual child, as a practical learner, to make sense of the tasks the teacher has set, depending upon the particular subject matter being taught. Writing an account of the corny 'Day in the Life of a Penny' permits greater latitude in terms of the meaning imposed by the learner and the quality of his response than computing '47 – 3', which may be interpreted in different ways by different children but which permits only one acceptable response, and solution.

Children must be regarded, to some degree, as independent practical learners who attach their own meaning to the tasks set by the teacher in the classroom and who are agents in their own learning. It follows that there will be individual variation in learning and that the teacher cannot legislate for learning to take place. The teacher through her pedagogical practices can plan for learning but because children are practical learners who seek to make sense of learning tasks and thereby become implicated in their own learning she cannot make learning occur. Nevertheless the teacher, by appreciating how her plans may be interpreted by children and how as a consequence they go about their learning, is well-placed to take informed pedagogical decisions.

SUMMARY

The frame of reference outlined provides a structure, is rooted in the constraints and practicalities of classroom life, for regarding teaching and learning in primary schools. It is a framework which suggests how the teacher's teaching may be linked to children's learning in an albeit contingent relationship. It emphasises the need for the teacher, when planning teaching, to consider what learning may mean for the child and suggests how the class teacher must balance the claims of promoting learning with those of maintaining classroom order.

The frame of reference, teacher's pedagogical decisions, and children's learning tasks are, themselves, empty; they are form without content. It is the material that is taught as subject matter in the classroom and that is embedded in tasks which gives content and substance to the form and also affects the nature of the form itself. In the previous chapter the content of lessons was considered, in passing, in terms of matching tasks to pupils' abilities. This chapter has developed this theme by (a) locating the setting of tasks within the wider context of the classroom and examining the pedagogical choices which the teacher must make so as to accommodate the requirements to both communicate subject matter and also maintain order and (b) considering what tasks may mean to children and how they perceive and accomplish them so as to demonstrate to the teacher that they have learned. There is, therefore, an additional crucial theme to consider in order to flesh out the analysis thus far and it is the subject matter itself which provides the substance of lessons. Central, then, to the teacher's work is her knowledge and understanding of subject matter and the manner in which she makes curriculum content available to children so as to foster their learning.

Chapter 6

Organising subject matter for learning

To state the obvious, teachers teach subject matter. Whatever the teacher's style, methods and approaches, the teacher is of no consequence if she does not intend to communicate subject matter to her pupils. (The phrase 'subject matter' is used as a shorthand at this stage to include material which is taught within the context of conventional subject boundaries such as 'maths' or 'history', and material collected together according to different principles, as with 'topic work' or 'centres of interest'.) Subject matter not only includes formal information and facts, it also embraces an understanding of related underlying concepts, the acquisition of skills, and the development of relevant attitudes. All discussions about teachers' teaching styles and their methods, as well as conjectures about the nature of children's learning and how teachers may promote that learning, count for nothing unless the subject matter which is communicated during the teaching–learning process is brought to the forefront of our consideration of teaching and learning in the classroom. It is doubtful whether individual teachers have a distinct style or one approach to their teaching all the time.[1] As one would expect, teachers teach differently in different circumstances and the manner in which they teach depends, in part, upon the material they are teaching.[2] Subject matter itself has a significant effect upon the way in which teachers teach. This may be because characteristics inherent within the subject itself dispose the same teacher to deploy alternative pedagogic practices in different subject areas.

The subject content of lessons has an important part to play in guiding pedagogic considerations,[3] and it must be recognised that the variety of teaching acts which teachers engage in when communicating subject matter cannot be separated from the subject itself and the teacher's personal knowledge of the subject.[4] For example, the teacher's ability to question appropriately is not a teaching skill which may be demonstrated independently from the material being taught. The manner in which a teacher questions in order to probe or advance children's understanding may be quite different in, say, a maths or a music lesson and will depend, in part, upon the teacher's own knowledge and skill in the subject. Moving beyond classroom practice, it may be claimed, with some justification, that the basis for teachers' authority and what establishes their claim for professional recognition is their knowledge of subject matter and a belief that the passing on of that knowledge to subsequent generations is a worthwhile and socially valuable activity.[5] Indeed, there are those who claim that the essence of what a prospective teacher needs to know is the knowledge of the subject to be taught and that any other teacher training can be provided 'on the job' in the classroom.[6] The failure of the research community to identify the central importance of subject matter in the teaching–learning process has been referred to as the 'missing paradigm' in educational research[7] and in recent years there have been determined efforts by a group of educationists to remedy this gap in our knowledge.

The teacher's knowledge of subject matter presents a particular problem for primary education, especially during the junior school (KS2) years. In secondary education the situation is comparatively straightforward. Secondary school teachers are expected to have a degree or advanced qualification in the subject they teach and they are usually members of subject departments and spend most of their time teaching their speciality. The circumstances are quite different in the typical primary school; while there may be some specialist teaching in subjects which require distinctive expertise such as music, the usual pattern is for the class teacher to be responsible for most of the curriculum. In a small or medium size primary school there are simply not enough teachers to permit specialist subject teaching, even if this was thought desirable. The junior teacher requires a formidable amount of subject matter knowledge over a broad field. Unfortunately, the extent and depth of primary school teachers' subject matter knowledge does not receive the recognition it deserves in our contemporary society which values advanced specialist expertise within narrow subject fields. The demands which the National Curriculum place on junior teachers' knowledge of subject matter are considerable and indicate that we should think in terms of a regeneration of Renaissance man and woman if teachers are to be educated at a level which will enable them to teach successfully across the range of the National Curriculum core and foundation subjects. HMI, for instance, have reported that there is a greater proportion of poor and unsatisfactory work in the upper reaches of the primary school and that the curriculum is not demanding enough for older pupils. They envisage the introduction of the National Curriculum as remedying the situation[8] but this can only be achieved if junior school teachers receive the additional education required to enhance their subject matter knowledge and skills across the core and foundation subjects. Each junior teacher will be expected to acquire a vast range of information which she understands in a manner which enables her to teach across all ability ranges for all subjects in order to cope effectively with children's learning in the upper reaches of the junior school. The magnitude of the problem facing junior teachers may be appreciated when it is realised that the average level of attainment for secondary pupils at the completion of Key Stage three is expected to be five or six. In other words, the single teacher responsible for the final year of junior teaching (KS2) will need to provide educational experiences for her class which will enable them to reach the average level of attainment of 14-year-olds who in secondary schools will be taught by specialist teachers who are members of subject departments. As far as the teacher is concerned, acquiring a substantial amount of knowledge across a range of diverse subjects is only the start of the problem; her purpose is to teach subject matter effectively to the mix of individual children in her class. She must provide differentiated learning for all National Curriculum subjects in a programme which must clearly distinguish different levels of attainment. The issue facing the teacher as a professional educator is not so much what she needs to know about a subject herself but rather how she needs to know about a subject in order to communicate it effectively, within the constraints of ordinary classrooms, to children who are at different levels of attainment. The teacher has to be able to translate her own personal knowledge of subject matter into a form which is appropriate for teaching in the classroom and which, it is envisaged, will promote pupils' learning.[9]

If there is one distinct merit in the changes wrought by the 1988 Education Reform Act and the introduction of the National Curriculum it is that subject matter knowledge is placed firmly at the forefront of the educational agenda. The emphasis upon subject matter has been presaged by reports on primary education[10] and related official discussion documents.[11] There are now regulations to ensure that initial teacher training courses place considerable stress on prospective teachers' subject matter knowledge.[12] Accompanying, indeed heralding, this emphasis upon subject matter has been a programme of conceptual analysis and empirical enquiry[13] which has the potential for making a valuable contribution to our deliberations about what teachers need to know about subject matter and its application in the classroom. This has led to the development of a corpus of formal knowledge and research studies which, while it has not generated unequivocal 'findings' which can offer prescriptions for practice, does provide a basis upon which it is possible to set out and consider the issues related to this central aspect of teachers' professional knowledge.

I shall consider how subject matter may be organised within the curriculum and then go on to explore the issue of what teachers need to know about subject matter in order to be able to teach it effectively to children.

THE ORGANISATION OF KNOWLEDGE

The human mind cannot comprehend the notion of knowledge as being part of a coherent whole; there is so much of it and it takes so many different forms that it is necessary to impose order upon knowledge by arranging it according to agreed principles. As far as primary education is concerned the question is how to organise the corpus of knowledge provided for children within a coherent curriculum which is both appropriate for teaching purposes and which will also engage children's interests and foster learning. Discussion about the nature of the curriculum has achieved the status of a subject in its own right among educationists. I address what I see as the central issue of whether the curriculum should be organised within conventional subject categories or according to principles which it is presumed lend more coherence to a body of knowledge and enable the child to discern the interrelationship of knowledge and linkages between different areas and which find their curriculum expression in topics, projects, or centres of interest. With the establishment of the National Curriculum which is articulated in terms of conventional subjects it may be argued that any further discussion is unnecessary. But it should be remembered that the advice and guidance given with the National Curriculum does (at present) leave it open for teachers to organise the curriculum and to employ approaches that seek to integrate material within topics or projects. So long as the attainment targets for each subject are addressed it is up to primary teachers to decide how they will structure their teaching and for them to select the methods, approaches and teaching aids they wish to use.

I suggest that there should be a disposition to organise teaching within conventional subject boundaries and that however admirable the aspirations of those who argue for organising all or part of the curriculum on a topic basis (hereafter I use 'topic' as a shorthand to include other forms of integration such as projects or centres of interest), they are responsible for some of the major limitations associated with primary education which made the introduction of a National Curriculum necessary.

An eloquent case for the integration of subject matter and one which has probably had most influence upon primary educational thought (if not practice) is found in the Plowden Report[14] where it was argued that, 'Any practice which predetermines the pattern and imposes it upon all is to be condemned'.[15] The report even goes on to propose[16] that one of the reasons for changing the age of transfer to secondary school is so as to delay the provision of specialist subject teaching. In the course of its exposition Plowden offers some halcyon visions of what follows from breaking down conventional subject boundaries, for example with reference to centres of interest:

> When a class of seven year olds notice the birds that come to the bird table outside the classroom window, they may decide, after discussion with their teacher, to make their own aviary. They will set to with a will, and paint the birds in flight, make models of them in clay or papier

mâché, write stories and poems about them and look up reference books to find out more about their habits. Children are not assimilating inert ideas but are wholly involved in thinking, feeling and doing. The slow and the bright share a common experience and each takes from it what he can at his own level. There is no attempt to put reading and writing into separate compartments; both serve a wider purpose, and artificial barriers do not fragment the learning experience.[17]

One must interrogate this beguiling picture. Why on one particular occasion did the birds excite the children's interest? What if in six months' time the children notice the birds again, another project? Is it a sound principle to organise the curriculum according to what the children have noticed and has stimulated their interest; is this not in fact a more arbitrary way of organising the curriculum than within subject boundaries? Birds, of course, are safe; what if the children had noticed a fatal accident or a streaker running by – are these appropriate integrating themes? Why is it assumed that 'inert ideas' are a characteristic of knowledge organised within subjects? Why must it be assumed that involving children in thinking, feeling, and doing are characteristic of the methods Plowden advocates? Is it not possible to entertain the notion that thinking, feeling, and doing are equally possible within the context of formal subjects? When we focus upon the children's activities we note that they are engaged in painting, modelling, writing stories and poems, and reading. Are these not core skills and activities which should be fostered however the curriculum is organised? The charm of Plowden is that it stresses the theme of organising the curriculum so as to awaken children's interests, to relate what they learn to their own experiences, and to provide them with a variety of learning experiences which have a focus and purpose. But it does not follow that these are characteristics of good teaching which are necessarily determined by organising the curriculum within topics; they can flow equally well from organising the curriculum within subjects. If history, maths, or music are the repository of inert ideas and the source of dull, repetitious learning activities that is the teacher's fault not the subject's. These points must be made because organising the curriculum in terms of topics carries the real danger of neglecting coherence, progression and continuity and of not providing the broadly based curriculum which children ought to be entitled to rather than one shaped by their interests.

It is instructive to return to Dewey, who is one of the icons, referred to by advocates of progressive methods,[18] and to look at how children were actually taught in his Laboratory School.[19] Dewey was concerned to demonstrate that learning must be understood from the point of view of the child and that knowledge should not be seen merely as a body of facts but as part of the child's living experience. It was essential for the teacher to relate all learning to the child's experience and actively involve him in learning. It is this focus upon the child, and his experience and activities which leads Plowden to advocate topic work but Dewey was much more circumspect. Dewey's practical curriculum had two sides: the child's side with its focus upon the child's activities and experience and the teacher's side with its focus upon logically ordered bodies of subject matter. As Dewey's ideas were developed in his school he decided that instruction by specialist teachers should begin in the first years of schooling. From the teacher's standpoint it was subjects which formed the basis for their planning and the development of the curriculum, namely: arithmetic, botany, chemistry, physics, zoology, geography, history, geology and numerology, physiology, and geometry. The teacher's task was to teach so as to ensure that the subject related to the real experience of the child and to actively involve the child in learning tasks. It was necessary to have some co-ordinating themes so as to ensure that subject specialists did not go their own way and to lend coherence to the child's total experience, but in order to do this he required teachers with specialised knowledge of subjects so as to develop children's understanding. At the end of his experimental school's first year Dewey wrote:

> The undue separation which often follows teaching by specialists is not inherent in the method, but is the result of lack of supervision, co-operation and control by a unified plan.[20]

Dewey recognised that in order to provide his children with worthwhile learning experiences and a unified view of knowledge their education should be planned, from the teachers' side, by subject experts. It is the failure to appreciate this central requirement which has led to criticisms of some aspects of the education found in 'post-Plowden' primary schools. One of the reasons for the introduction of a National Curriculum which is specified in subject terms, and which provides for children to be entitled to what is thought to be the basic knowledge which all children should acquire, has been the concerns expressed about the content of important areas of the primary curriculum. Deficiencies have been identified, particularly when subject matter has been taught through topic work.[21]

When one examines the information about teaching topic work which is made available for teachers it is hardly surprising that problems to do with lack of structure and continuity arise and that the range of subject matter actually taught emerges in a somewhat *ad hoc* or eclectic manner. Consider, for example, Figure 1[22] which is a recommended flow chart for a term project on 'The Sea'. By the sleight of hand of drawing arrows outwards from the sea to other words it is assumed that connections are established between elements of knowledge. The first wave of arrows shoots out from 'the sea' to 'animal and plant life', 'legends', 'famous names', 'natural resources', 'art', 'famous maritime states', 'transport',

'Royal Navy', 'sea ports' and 'Merchant Navy'; the arrows then travel further to the periphery of the diagram where such diverse topics as 'maritime biology', 'literature and the sea', 'Rome', and 'famous sea battles' are pinned down for consideration. The fact that many of the words hereby targeted are themselves possible centres for topic work, that the various words and arrows can be re-ordered and shifted around at will without impinging upon the (non)sense of the diagram is not recognised. The fact that marine biology, for instance, could either be the subject of a degree or General Certificate of Secondary Education (GCSE) is not entertained and one fails to see how any semblance of sequence, structure or order can be imposed upon diverse bodies of knowledge by the simple device of drawing arrows from one word to another. The glaring problem that at no point is there any attempt to lay down what children might actually do and the nature of their learning experiences when, say, focusing upon 'Phoenicia' must be an additional matter for concern. The second example, Figure 2[23] taken from a Schools Council publication, reinforces the point. 'Transport' becomes the centre for a range of diverse activities which by various connections span 'bathing the baby', 'cogwheels', 'coin recognition' and 'houses'. The connections are made by drawing lines between words and again one can only speculate as to how such a scheme lends itself to the child acquiring a coherent view of knowledge, understanding and skill which is structured and developed over the primary years. Presumably one of the central justifications for topic work is that it should permit the organisation of subject matter according to some principle which demonstrates cohesion and which can be articulated by the teacher and which will also mean something to the child and which, moreover, may also be seen as an improvement upon what is often claimed to be the arbitrariness of presenting subject matter to children within the constraints of conventional subject boundaries. Topic work does not appear to confer any advantage in terms of offering children an integrated or coherent view of knowledge and the observational studies mentioned in the first chapter do not provide any evidence demonstrating that integrating the curriculum enhances the range and quality of children's learning activities. On the other hand, conventional subject boundaries do provide a reasonably established rationale for the organisation of a corpus of knowledge and provide a framework within which to structure and sequence learning and plan for progression.

As far as practical pedagogy is concerned I suggest that, as a guide, conventional subject categories should form the basis for determining learning tasks and activities and that efforts to integrate knowledge and demonstrate links between different areas of knowledge should arise from necessary and manifest associations between different subjects. (Such a proposal conveniently maps on to the requirements of the

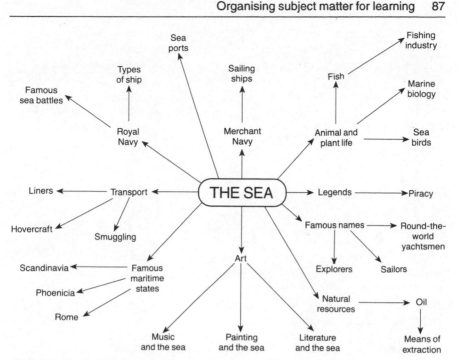

Figure 1 Flow chart for a project on the theme of 'The Sea'

National Curriculum but it must be stressed that the proposal arises independently from considering how best to structure the primary curriculum.) In this respect HMI have noted that the introduction of the National Curriculum is having a marked effect upon the planning of topic work.[24] They remark that in the past much topic work was superficial with too many subjects included under one theme, making it difficult to manage let alone teach in sufficient depth. Consequently subjects such as history or geography were often poorly taught. Now many schools are planning and preparing topics more thoroughly and selecting more unified elements from one subject such as history, geography or science rather than opting for a 'pick and mix' approach across a number of subjects. The Non-Statutory Guidance suggests, for instance, how geography may be taught through broadly based topics such as 'Homes' or subject led topics such as 'Weather in Different Parts of the World' and indicates how clear links can be made with other areas of the National Curriculum. While there is scope for teaching through topics within the National Curriculum and advice is offered as to how this may be achieved, it must be viewed with caution for two reasons. The first arises from a consideration of the treatment of topic work by the Non-Statutory Guidance for each subject and the suggestions for teaching cross curricular themes such as environmental education. From their particular

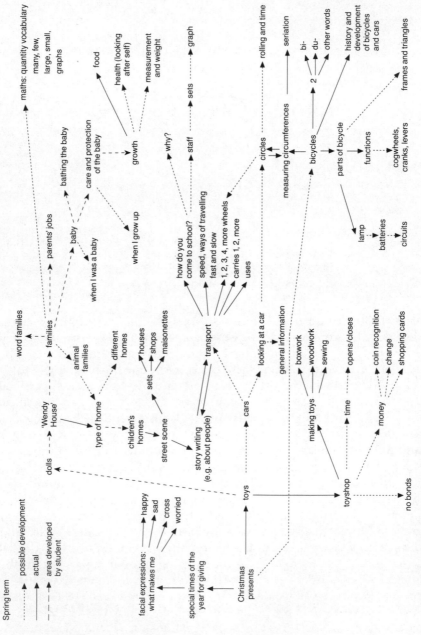

Figure 2 Flow chart for a school's topic work

subject stance the various suggestions for guidance indicate how it is possible to teach through topics and illustrate how aspects of the nominated subject can provide the central theme for topics and make linkages with attainment targets in other subjects. There is not, however, evidence that there has been an attempt to take an overview of the primary curriculum and, bearing in mind the programmes of study for each subject, to identify coordinating themes or principles. The result is that the different sets of advice offer an ad hoc menu of suggestions for topics with divers linkages to different attainment targets in different subjects, sometimes at different levels of attainment. There are signs, however, that deficiencies in the early advice are now recognised and that more realistic proposals will be made available.[25] The other fundamental problem to be faced when planning to teach through topics is that the National Curriculum presents us with the scenario of individual children progressing through the curriculum for each subject and probably being at different levels of attainment within each subject. If we are to take the precepts of the National Curriculum seriously we must envisage each child as having his individual profile of attainments across the core and foundation subjects. If we pursue this impractical logic the implication for teaching is that when designing a topic the teacher must establish linkages between different subjects for different levels of attainment and then provide each child with its own topic work plan. Hence it may be suggested that while the National Curriculum makes a gesture towards topic work, the practitioner may find it preferable to give priority to organise her teaching through subjects. This has the additional advantages of enabling her to provide learning tasks which in practice will make it easier to allow for progression and continuity and to be in a better position to identify and remedy misunderstandings within each subject.

The overriding consideration is that all teaching and learning and proposals for improving their quality must be considered within the context of the material which provides the substance of lessons. The teacher's knowledge of the subject matter she is teaching and her skill in applying her knowledge in the classroom are of central importance for practical pedagogy. As far as children's learning is concerned what is central is not whether lesson content is presented as subjects or topics; it is how the material is made available for children as tasks so as to foster their learning. It therefore becomes necessary to address the issue of what the teacher needs to know about subject matter and its application in the classroom so as to enhance the quality of the learning she provides for her pupils.

KNOWLEDGE OF SUBJECT MATTER AND ITS APPLICATION

A seminal contribution which has directed attention to the study of subject matter has been Shulman's proposal[26] based upon the central question he posed which is how does the successful college student transform his or her expertise in a subject into a form which pupils can comprehend. He asks

> When this novice teacher confronts flawed or muddled textbook chapters or befuddled students, how does he or she employ content expertise to generate new explanations, representations or clarifications? What are the sources of analogies, metaphors, examples, demonstrations and rephrasings? How does the novice teacher (or even the seasoned veteran) draw upon expertise in the subject matter in the process of teaching? What pedagogical prices are paid when the teacher's subject matter competence is itself compromised by deficiencies of prior education or ability?[27]

In order to advance our thinking on these matters he focuses upon what he terms teacher's content knowledge and he makes a distinction between

- Subject matter content knowledge which refers to the amount of subject matter knowledge acquired by the teacher and the way it may be organised in her mind. This should include not only knowledge of facts or concepts within a subject or 'domain of knowledge' but also the underlying structure of its subject matter such as the ways in which truth or validity are established within that subject and why, for instance, some topics will be central to the discipline.
- Pedagogical content knowledge which is the particular form of content knowledge that embodies aspects of content most germane to the teachability of the subject. This includes the most useful forms of representing the central ideas within a subject, the most fruitful analogies, illustrations, examples, explanations, and demonstrations. That is, ways of representing the subject which make it most comprehensible to others – these must provide alternatives since there is unlikely to be one best approach in all cases. Pedagogical content knowledge should also include an understanding of what makes the learning of specific topics easy or difficult and the common conceptions or misconceptions which pupils may have and the strategies for dealing with them.
- Curriculum knowledge which refers to knowledge about the range of curriculum materials and programmes which represent the subject and which are used in teaching it. This includes a knowledge of schemes of work, textbooks, computer software, audio-visual materials, and demonstrations which are available for teaching a subject at a particular stage. The teacher must also have the ability and expertise to evaluate and assess the various ways in which the content is embodied in curriculum materials.

This scheme has subsequently been elaborated and developed in a number of ways and has formed the basis for a range of developmental and empirical studies which have investigated teachers' knowledge of subject matter and their ability to apply it in practice.[28] The work of Schulman and others offers a useful frame of reference for examining the question of what teachers need to know about subject matter knowledge and its application but the corpus which makes up this contribution consists mainly of formal studies and investigations and thereby may suffer from the limitation of not having been tested in practice or of failing to address substantial practical problems presented to the teacher. The great value of this work is that it is genuinely educational in appreciating that the communication of subject matter is central to the teacher's task and in recognising that her effectiveness must be both developed and judged with reference to her ability to translate what she knows about a subject into a form in which it can be best communicated to pupils within the classroom. As with all proposals for classroom practice it is necessary to appraise Shulman's contribution with reference to practical pedagogy.

HOW IS THE TEACHER'S KNOWLEDGE TO BE ACQUIRED?

The teacher will, of course, have passed through the educational system and will therefore have acquired much of the basic knowledge which comprises the substance of the primary curriculum; she will also have received much additional information during her professional training. It is doubtful, however, whether the primary teacher's own personal and professional education will equip her to cope with the demands occasioned by teaching the full range of National Curriculum subjects. One of the reasons for introducing the National Curriculum is to remedy the huge variation in curriculum provision in primary and secondary schools and what are seen as unacceptable gaps in many children's education. Thus, for example, many primary teachers themselves may not have pursued science in school to any great depth and their own personal knowledge may be deficient or they may lack the confidence to teach the subject.[29] While at school teachers were still pupils and therefore learned knowledge for various purposes, such as to pass examinations. It is doubtful whether, during their own schooling, they acquired the sorts of secure knowledge across the full range of the curriculum which would enable them to be confident in the basic principles and concepts which underlie and inform all the subjects included within the National Curriculum. They will not, for instance, during their personal education have been introduced to different approaches to teaching a subject or have appreciated that there are alternative ways in which knowledge can be organised and structured within each subject. Moreover, their own personal skills, aptitudes and attitudes towards subjects such as art, music, or physical education may be such as to limit their ability to teach these foundation subjects. It is doubtful whether even recently trained teachers, whose education has borne in mind the demands of the National Curriculum, will have substantial and necessary expertise across all its subjects. Those children who eventually become teachers will not, while at school, have learned subject matter in ways in which they need to know the material when they become teachers and during their time in the higher education system as students they are likely to have studied subjects as they are usually studied within universities and polytechnics, which is not necessarily the way in which they need to know about subject matter in order to teach it in primary schools.[30]

In sum, during her own educational career the primary teacher will have acquired something of a patchwork of subject knowledge which will have been learned with varying degrees of enthusiasm for varying purposes. It is unlikely that she will be the possessor of the full range of knowledge over the National Curriculum's core and foundation subjects at, say, the seventh level of attainment. It is even more unlikely that she can remedy all the gaps in her own personal knowledge during periods of professional in-service training. Hence the practical problem facing the teacher is that she may, from time to time, be placed in situations where she has to teach information which is unfamiliar to her and which she may have some difficulty with herself. Coping with this challenge is one of the distinct problems facing the junior teacher; namely, how to teach subject matter successfully in a field where she recognises that her own knowledge may be limited in terms of what she knows about the subject's basic information, its underlying principles, and the alternative ways in which it may be organised and presented.

THE APPLICATION OF SUBJECT MATTER KNOWLEDGE

Casting the teacher as a teacher of subject matter and asking the question, 'What does the teacher need to know about the material she is to teach?' carries a danger. It may convey the assumption that the subject matter knowledge which the teacher possesses can somehow be easily 'detached' from the teacher's mind and 'transferred' to the mind of the child and that children will assimilate and understand the subject matter communicated by the teacher in the way in which it exists in the teacher's mind. Teaching, however, is very much more than finding the means of imposing adult understandings of subject matter upon children. Such a simplistic delivery model of teaching has little to commend it; the teacher's task is to teach subject matter to children in ways in which she hopes they will be able to understand it and in a manner which will facilitate their learning. The teacher's skill entails adapting content and providing learning experiences so that it will be accessible to the mind of the child.[31] Shulman's elaboration of his central question, 'How does the teacher transform his or her expertise in a subject into a form which pupils can comprehend?' provides a useful frame of reference for examining what a teacher needs to know about a subject in order to apply it in a classroom, but it is hardly sufficient for the teacher's knowledge to consist only of the content knowledge of the subject; it must also be supplemented with pedagogical content knowledge. This suggests a substantial, additional dimension which should be included in the consideration of the teacher's professional repertoire The relationship between the teacher's knowledge of a subject and her pedagogic content knowledge and curriculum knowledge raises issues about what a teacher needs to know in order to be a successful teacher of subject matter, and these must be addressed with reference to classroom based practice.

For example, it is possible to develop Shulman's scheme and elaborate its elements in some detail with reference to the teaching of specific subject matter. Figure 3[32] illustrates an exercise which lays out in detail the pedagogic content knowledge required to teach equivalence of fractions to fifth graders (say, final year juniors). This may be an admirable attempt but it is also indicative of an unrealistic agenda in that it describes the substantial amount of pedagogic content knowledge which can be linked to one narrow aspect of one subject at one age level; the elaboration of similar exercises for the whole primary curriculum hardly bears contemplation. While Shulman's scheme offers a useful framework for directing our attention and raising issues it must be tempered with a recognition that its aspirations are difficult to realise in practice. First, because it would require a massive investment in research and development programmes to establish and map out the pedagogical content knowledge required across, say, the junior (KS2) curriculum, and when completed the products of such an endeavour would place huge additional burdens on teacher training programmes at both the initial and inservice stages. Second, it has to be recognised that there is no easy or clear distinction between the notion of knowledge of the subject and the notion of pedagogic content knowledge *per se*. To complicate matters it must be appreciated that teachers' personal knowledge of a subject and their capacity to apply it in the classroom can be shaped or affected through their experiences of actually having taught the subject. For instance, as teachers gain experience they may begin to think differently about subject matter, and classroom practice may shape their pedagogic content knowledge. Teachers with only a rudimentary knowledge of a subject may find that their own understanding and knowledge are increased as they gain experience in teaching the subject. The manner in which teachers teach a subject will not only be shaped by what they know of the subject it will also be affected by their own values and beliefs as teachers. There is no 'neutral' and separate body of information which

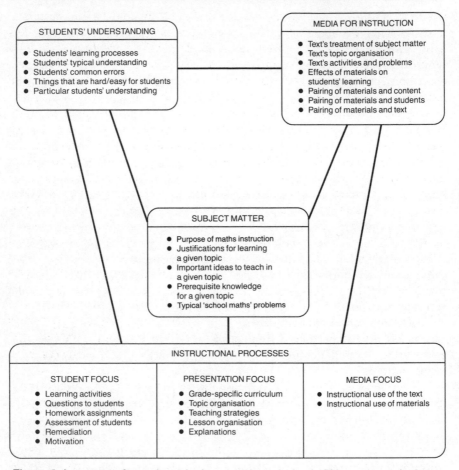

Figure 3 A structure for pedagogical content knowledge in fifth grade equivalence of fractions

can be acquired which tells a teacher how she must apply her subject. To a certain degree her own disposition will shape how she thinks that the subject ought to be taught, how she should relate to children, and how she should communicate information to them.[33]

When considering teaching subject matter it is important to ask what the teacher needs to know about the subject so as to be able to put it into a form which allows her to apply that knowledge in the classroom. But this way of regarding teaching must be located within the practical context of the classroom since it is impractical and unrealistic to establish *a priori* a scheme for, say, the whole primary National Curriculum. Such a programme is too ambitious and, in any case, would not generate the information which could legislate for how teaching should take place since teaching is, to a marked degree, shaped by the discernment and judgement which is exercised by the teacher in the classroom. For instance, one of the important claims made for the importance of pedagogical content knowledge is that it focuses upon the problem of representation; namely the various ways in which a teacher can represent a subject's concepts, ideas and procedures so that they can be best communicated to children.[34] This is because, whether or not they are consciously aware of it, teachers are constantly engaged in a process of constructing and using instructional representations of subject matter knowledge when, for example, they are asking questions, presenting examples, using analogies, or setting children's activities. One would hope that good teachers have an armoury of analogies, illustrations, examples, explanations and demonstrations for representing and formulating a subject so as to make it comprehensible to others but it is not always apparent in practice what is subject matter and what is representation. The nature of the problem with representations may be illustrated with reference to one study[35] of elementary mathematics teaching which found that prospective teachers were able to carry out routine computations such as $1\frac{3}{4} \div \frac{1}{2}$. They knew the invert and multiply rule and could compute the correct answer. But when asked how they could represent the process by some graphical or illustrative means the vast majority of the sample had difficulties. Thus, if they had been presented with a pupil who could not understand the arithmetic problem they would not have been able to provide the child with alternative explanations of the computational processes by, for example, reference to a diagram or a picture which could be used to aid the child's comprehension. Within the context of the classroom, however, the issue is more complicated. If prospective teachers had been asked to provide a representation of the example $2 \div \frac{1}{2}$, no doubt they would all have managed without difficulty but if they had been asked to represent $27\frac{9}{11} \div 7\frac{14}{25}$ it would probably defeat anybody. In this particular case, the practical pedagogical problem facing the teacher is for her to bear in mind that the invert and multiply rule is an algorithm which, if appropriately applied, yields the correct answer. The algorithm is relevant and must be used when the arithmetic becomes complex. Perhaps the reason why students cannot provide graphic representations of $1\frac{3}{4} \div \frac{1}{2}$ is that this problem has already reached the stage where it is too difficult to represent it as, say, a drawing. Hence the real pedagogical task facing the teacher could be whether or not to set the child back to simpler computations which can be represented graphically or to provide extra practice applying the algorithm in the hope that the child eventually realises the correct procedure.[36] The general point to be made is that there is not always a neat distinction to be made between a 'subject' and applied knowledge of the subject, since what at first sight may be seen as an example of pedagogic content knowledge should more properly be thought of as an example of subject matter itself.[37] In other words, that it is the very stuff of pursuing the subject rather than the means of communicating it to others.

Finally, Shulman refers to the range of curriculum materials which embody the content of a subject and which the teacher uses during her teaching. There can be no question that teachers should be aware of the full range of schemes of work, textbooks, audio-visual aids and computer software which they can use in their teaching and that they should know enough about a subject to enable them to make informed judgements about the quality and potential of the curriculum materials available. For example, HMI have reported instances of schools adopting a particular commercial scheme in mathematics to help them implement the National Curriculum at precisely the same time that other schools were abandoning the same scheme, presumably because they considered that it was deficient in terms of delivering the National Curriculum.[38] We need to know very much more about why and how teachers make such curriculum decisions so as to be able to acquire information upon which they can be securely based. It is, however, not often the case that the primary teacher is in a position whereby she can make an informed professional appraisal of the range of teaching materials which are available and which she can then acquire and subsequently employ in her forthcoming teaching, or that she has the financial resources to purchase her preferred teaching aids and books. A practical problem facing most junior teachers for part of the time is 'making do' with the limited materials which are already available to them. When the teacher takes over a class she inherits the curriculum materials which are in place and she may from time to time receive some money to replenish and renew her stocks and even purchase new materials. The teacher's task in classroom is to make the best use of what she has to hand, decide how she can acquire those resources available in, say, the local Teachers' Centre, encourage parents to provide, and beg and borrow. Pedagogical curriculum knowledge should focus not so much upon the *a priori* decisions which teachers in an ideal world would make about the quality of materials and their acquisition prior to beginning their teaching but rather upon how they deploy their skill and ingenuity to make use of what is already available.

In addition, the thrust of this discussion raises searching questions about the teaching of the primary curriculum through topics. The question of what a teacher needs to know about conventional subjects in order to teach successfully presents some challenging issues. But these are straightforward when compared with asking the same question about topic work. In order to prepare and teach a topic such as 'my body' or 'our neighbourhood' or plan a centre of interest based upon 'birds' so as to integrate material from different subject areas, what does the teacher need to know about the body of knowledge embraced by the theme and its application?

SUMMARY

The renewed interest in subject matter and its application has performed a valuable service in that it requires us to focus particularly upon the content of instruction. The teacher's ability to plan the curriculum and lessons within it, employ a variety of styles and methods and approaches when teaching, promote and foster children's knowledge, understanding and enthusiasm by asking the right questions and setting appropriate tasks, to diagnose learning difficulties, and provide appropriate assessments, all depend crucially on the teacher's own knowledge, skill and understanding and confidence within a subject area.[39] We must, however, while appreciating the issues ask how they may be resolved within the constraints of the classroom. We may acknowledge the truism that teachers must have their own personal knowledge of a subject in order to teach it, but we have no firm information about how much of the subject they need to acquire and the nature of what they need to know. The empirical link between what and how a teacher needs to know a subject and the child's own learning of that subject has yet to be established.[40] It is an open question, for instance, as to whether the emphasis should be upon enhancing the teacher's personal knowledge of the subject *per se* or whether there should be a concentration upon a separate body of knowledge to do with its application. In any case, we know that the exigencies of professional life are such that the policy option of devoting substantial additional time to enhancing teachers' knowledge of subject matter is not on the agenda. We also know that there is no easy and direct way in which the teacher can apply her knowledge of subject matter in the classroom. Teaching is very much more than an intellectual activity in which the teacher passes on the knowledge in her mind to the minds of her pupils.[41] The classroom is a complex social setting in which, among other things, the individual children bring to their learning experiences different aptitudes and interests. As a consequence of their personal experience of teaching a subject, teachers' own knowledge of a subject and how best to apply it may develop as they practise relating the subject to children. It is more appropriate, therefore, to recognise that the teacher is already an established practitioner who has been and will continue to be charged with the business of teaching subject matter within the classroom. Hence we need to accept the teacher as a practising pedagogue whose communication of subject matter within the classroom is shaped, in part, by the particular circumstances found in her classroom. A rounded appreciation of how teachers actually teach subject matter must recognise, for example, that the same curriculum will be mediated and taught differently by different teachers and that the distinctive personal attributes and characteristics of the teacher may affect the quality of children's learning and even what they do learn. Because, through their teaching, teachers not only communicate knowledge and understanding they also convey interest and enthusiasm or indifference and boredom for the subjects they teach.[42]

Chapter 7

Pedagogy in practice: the case of subtraction

The argument, thus far, has been couched in general terms. For the purposes of exposition elements within the pedagogic process have been identified and considered separately. In this chapter I illustrate how various themes which have been addressed may be combined in order to examine one particular aspect of children's learning. The aim is to demonstrate how the ways in which I have been regarding pedagogical practice may be brought together so as to scrutinise the teaching and learning process within the context of some of the frames of reference I have been developing. I also aim to show that we may engage in the rigorous and reflective analysis of the teacher's practice and children's learning with reference to that practice and learning itself and without reference to theory and research drawn from other disciplines. I illustrate my case with recourse to formal subtraction.

I take it as read that a task for the teacher is to ensure that her pupils acquire the ability to calculate the answers to subtraction sums correctly and I do not pursue those additional aspects of her task which are concerned with fostering a deeper conceptual understanding.[1] I take this pragmatic approach since in fact the majority of primary teachers set out to teach subtraction as a computational skill and do so using practice routines. [2] The National Curriculum programmes of study, of course, make specific suggestions for teaching subtraction.[3]

At the crux point where the teacher seeks to actively promote her pupils' understanding, deal with their errors and misconceptions, or diagnose the reasons for children's failure the available psychological research is of little consequence. The essential resource which the teacher has to draw upon is her experience which includes her own understanding of subtraction together with intangible qualities such as 'nous', 'intuition', 'common sense', or 'discernment'. It is not the teacher's formal knowledge drawn from research evidence which may enable her to promote children's learning of subtraction, it is rather her knowledge of the subject matter being taught together with her ability to deploy her personal qualities and tacit skills[4] within the time and resource constraints of busy classrooms. Indeed, if the available research establishes anything, it is that the manner in which primary classrooms are organised and resourced makes it very difficult for the teacher to act in any other way.[5]

THE RESEARCH EVIDENCE

The argument is explored and illustrated in detail with reference to the research which has investigated the systematic errors which pupils make when doing subtractions. The ability to compute correctly the answer to 'take aways' is a basic arithmetical skill which it is assumed children must be able to perform at an early age. Teaching young children this skill presents a challenge since it is a procedure which will appear virtually meaningless to many children as they have no appreciation of its underlying semantics and must learn procedures which are unrelated to their everyday experience outside the classroom.[6] It is claimed that knowledge of 'buggy algorithms' will be useful to teachers and inform their efforts to teach abstract procedures and, in addition, 'bugs' may offer an explanation for why children reach an impasse in their learning.[7] The notion of 'buggy algorithms' refers to the systematic errors which children may make when doing computational sums.[8] 'Bugs' are precise descriptions of errors and lead to predictions of what the errors will be, as in the following example.

'Bug'

$$
\begin{array}{r}
207 \\
-169 \\
\hline
162 \\
\hline
\end{array}
$$

Child subtracts the smaller from the larger number in each case

$$
\begin{array}{r}
207 \\
-169 \\
\hline
100 \\
\hline
\end{array}
$$

Child puts a zero when there is a need to borrow

$$
\begin{array}{r}
207 \\
-169 \\
\hline
42 \\
\hline
\end{array}
$$

Child subtracts smaller number from larger instead of borrowing from zero

It is claimed that children who make such mistakes have failed to follow or understand the routines (algorithms) which teachers have taught them and in order to make sense of and complete subtraction tasks they invent their own 'buggy algorithms'. An aim of the research investigating this problem is to discover the ways in which children acquire 'buggy algorithms' since this would prove valuable information for teachers which could help them to eliminate sources of misunderstanding and then take appropriate remedial action.

An initial problem is that the examples illustrated cannot be taken out of the social context of the classroom if one wishes to acquire a comprehensive understanding of the processes which generated the wrong answers. There are a variety of reasons why a child might not have produced the correct answer to the subtraction sum[9] and the child's response could be interpreted in alternate ways such as:

- The child may not have understood place value and have no conception of borrowing, in which case the remedial action may be to return to the meaning of multi-digit numbers or simple addition with carrying.
- The child may always have been used to subtraction sums set out differently for example, written horizontally, and find the vertical format puzzling.
- The child may have copied down the problem incorrectly, in which case the appropriate action would be to check for a careless error.
- The child may simply have made a hurried careless mistake, in which case the teacher would place the onus on the child to make the correction.
- The child may have been idle, fooling around, not interested or emotionally upset. In such cases the teacher's task may be to comfort or motivate the child in some appropriate way.

Direct observation of children's mathematical learning in the classroom[10] indicates that young children use a variety of strategies besides attempting calculations in order to complete mathematical tasks. These include 'recalling earlier work', 'looking back at an earlier solution', '"reading" the teacher' and 'memorising what the teacher said in her description of the task'. Errors in any of these strategies could also lead to a variety of wrong answers to the problem.

Finally, and most importantly, we must consider the distinct possibility that the children have been badly taught and that embedded in the 'buggy explanations' of children's mistakes are prescriptions for further poor practice. Two of the 'bugs' mentioned in the illustrated example assume that the appropriate way to proceed when doing subtraction is, when necessary, to borrow from the next column. Hence we have a problem with the algorithm itself since it does not relate directly to the mathematics involved in doing subtraction. Subtraction algorithms which involve 'borrowing' or 'paying back' do not have as close a relationship to the mathematics of subtraction as do algorithms based upon equivalence or equal addition procedures. Thus a more powerful and arithmetically correct procedure may be to teach subtraction involving 'carrying' using an equivalence method, say

$$\begin{array}{ll} 42 & \text{change 42 to } 30 + 12 \quad - \quad {}^3\!\!\!\not{4}2^{12} \\ -26 & \text{change 26 to } 20 + 6 \quad - \quad 26 \\ \hline \end{array}$$

$$16$$

Hence it is necessary to probe the very algorithms which researchers are employing to explain subtraction errors. Indeed, the current popular procedure for teaching subtraction is the decomposition or equivalence method[11] as illustrated above and an important argument for it is that this method reflects what is actually happening in the operation in a way which young children may be able to understand and model. Moreover, accepted good practice warns against the use of the misleading and mathematically incorrect term 'borrow'. Terms such as 'change' or 'rearrange' are recommended. Yet the term 'borrow' is consistently used in the descriptions of 'buggy algorithms'. Before psychologists seek to offer explanations of why children make subtraction errors it is incumbent upon them to enquire of teachers how they go about teaching subtraction.[12]

It must be stressed that when children's subtraction errors are located in the social arena in which they were generated they can be accounted for in a variety of ways and it can only be the practising teacher with her personal knowledge of the children in her classroom and of her own teaching methods who will be in a position to acquire the evidence which permits the appropriate interpretations. The teacher's available knowledge will not only constitute any formal records she may keep, it will be massively supplemented by her personal, somewhat intuitive knowledge of her pupils and depend in part upon the commitment, industry and flair which she brings to bear in her teaching so as to understand her children and acquire information about them. Her personal knowledge will, for instance, enable her to judge whether a particular child's error is, say, due to a slip in concentration which can be ignored or, say, a more substantial comprehension error which is worrying and requires remedial action on her part.

A close reading of the original research itself casts further doubt upon whether what has been 'discovered' about children's use of 'buggy algorithms' could be of value to teachers. A prodigious quantity of resource and research time has been devoted to investigating children's 'buggy' subtraction errors. Empirical studies have involved some 925 pupils and four or five thousand hours of expert diagnosis of children's subtraction errors.[13] In terms of effort and expertise the scale of the research is more than an army of primary teachers could amass in a lifetime. To duplicate this endeavour for other procedural skills in other areas of, say, only the junior mathematics curriculum would be a daunting task. What has the available research discovered about children's mistakes when doing subtraction? First, that at best 'buggy algorithms' explain only about one-third of the errors children make in subtraction. Hence a comprehensive knowledge of the 'bugs' children may employ when doing subtraction would enable teachers to cope with only a minority of their mistakes. Another notion, that of 'repair theory' is invoked to explain about another third of children's subtraction errors. Repairs are defined as the local problem-solving strategies which pupils devise, such as skipping a bit of a sum, which generate an answer which is not only incorrect but is also not the type of incorrect answer which is generated by the systematic application of a 'buggy algorithm'. Repairs can be proposed as explanations for about another third of children's subtraction errors. Since, by definition, repairs are local problem solving strategies it is only the class teacher who is in a position to find out what they are. The huge research effort can offer no diagnosis for the final third of all subtraction errors.

There is a sense in which this research is of vital interest to teachers. In one narrow but important area of the curriculum in one subject a substantial research effort can offer information which may be of value in helping teachers diagnose children's learning failure in one-third of all cases, suggest that failure is caused by pupils' local strategies in one third of cases, and is unable to offer information concerning the remaining third. What, then, can one reasonably expect of the teacher in the classroom and by what criteria should we judge the teacher's success in diagnosing children's learning difficulties? Moreover, since in 28 per cent of the instances where a 'buggy' error was diagnosed the 'bug' was a failure to borrow and subtract the smaller digit from the larger one[14] (an error which any teacher is familiar with) any practical pay-off is further reduced.

It would seem, to retain some optimism, that in the one-third of cases where children make systematic errors research has something to offer teachers in that 'bugs' provide an explanation which may be used to diagnose learning difficulties. This, unfortunately, is unlikely to be the case; various teams working with the aid of considerable computing power have been able to identify over one hundred subtraction bugs.[15] This is hardly information which may be of value to the teacher with thirty or more children in her care; even if she could assimilate it, how could she deploy it in real-time teaching contexts? Another theme emerging from the studies will at least strike a chord with teachers, even though it presents further difficulties concerning its practical application. It was found that some pupils tested a few days apart answered all problems correctly on the first occasion but made slips on the second and that children could manufacture 'bugs' for the duration of one test and then discard them once they had helped the child get through that particular exercise. This phenomenon is known as 'bug migration'.[16] Thus we are reminded that children can be little 'bugbears' rather than 'bug users'. Indeed it is probably the case that the usual problems facing teachers are to do with children's unsystematic errors and erratic performance from day to day and not to do with systematic errors encountered at specific stages in their learning.

A substantial psychological research programme focusing upon one particular facet of learning fails to provide information for teachers which could enhance their routine classroom practice. The research is flawed in so far as it may have practical application in the classroom. This is because the conceptual framework underpinning the research is based upon a model of learning and terminology drawn from computer programming.[17] Algorithms are important and powerful heuristics which are part of the equipment of practising mathematicians.[18] It is a mistake, however, to accept that conceptual tools which are of value to cognitive psychologists and mathematicians can also be employed as devices for explaining children's learning failure in the primary mathematics class. This may be demonstrated by attempting to consider the problem of doing subtraction computations from the point of view of the teacher interested in the child's learning in the classroom and what we know of how children probably tackle subtraction tasks. It must be accepted that such enquiries are necessarily speculative since all of us, like the psychologist and educational researcher, are denied direct access to the child's mind. There can be no question that children do acquire procedures and strategies from teachers in order to cope with subtraction problems but if the upshot is that they can merely apply these procedures in parrot-like fashion we are unlikely to agree that the child has 'learned' or been 'educated'.[19] Learning involves more than the automatic carrying out of a procedure, it also involves such things as being able to apply the routine in novel situations or scrutinise one's own work and rectify mistakes. If the child could do no more than, metaphorically speaking, apply the algorithm in the manner of a calculating machine the teacher should be just as concerned with that child as with the child who makes erratic mistakes. Presumably it is only the teacher who is in a position to make the judgement about whether the child has learned a procedure in a manner which permits its application with understanding.

There can be little doubt that children can invent their own algorithms and that these may be different from those taught in formal schooling,[20] in so far as they can devise rule governed routines which permit the correct computation of practical transactions. One may wonder, however, whether children conscientiously invent algorithms which are incorrect and which, incidentally but conveniently for the researcher, can be expressed in written form. Is it reasonable to assume that a child who makes use of a systematic procedure to get through a set of subtraction sums which yield rule governed wrong answers has devised and applied what we may term a 'buggy algorithm' and that this notion offers a way for diagnosing and remedying learning failure? Reconsider the original illustration:

$$207$$
$$-169$$

and the examples of 'buggy algorithms' invoked to explain systematic errors such as 'child takes smaller number from larger'. For many children there will be a stage in their mathematical development when this calculation presents a challenge. It will be more difficult than examples they have encountered previously. It is interesting to note that the illustrations of 'buggy algorithms' all provide solutions which are easier to carry out than the correct one for coming up with the right answer. In such circumstances it is difficult to accept the notion that the child has consciously invented a routine (which can be expressed verbally), albeit an incorrect procedure, and that knowledge of the 'buggy algorithm' will aid the teacher in diagnosing learning difficulties and helping the child. Indeed, it is doubtful whether, with reference to the specific case of subtraction, children are actually able to apply an algorithmic model to match the rule.[21] What the teacher needs to know is why, at the outset, the child did not or could not follow the 'harder' correct procedure and decided upon a different 'easier' strategy. Invoking knowledge about 'buggy algorithms' introduces extra redundant information which is unlikely to be of value to the teacher. The reasons why the child got the incorrect answer are probably that the child lacked motivation or, more likely, did not understand place value and carrying (setting aside factors such as carelessness or copying from a child also making mistakes). It is commonplace notions which provides the teacher with the information which she needs to help the child overcome its difficulties. The only person who can have access to plausible and usable explanations of the child's learning difficulties is the teacher. In practice it will be clear to the reasonably perceptive teacher that the child's subtraction errors have been generated because the child followed a systematic but incorrect procedure such as inappropriately subtracting a smaller from a larger number. This is part and parcel of her practical, professional expertise. There can be little point in recasting her commonsensical expertise within a mathematical or psychological framework[22] and elaborating it beyond the realms of practical application.

PRACTICAL CONSIDERATIONS

The starting point for any discussion about the problem of teaching subtraction within the confines of classrooms must be a recognition that the commercially produced mathematical schemes of work which are used regularly in most primary classrooms, the National Curriculum for mathematics and, indeed, parental expectations all require primary teachers to teach what may be crudely termed 'doing subtractions'. More-over, there is compelling evidence that mathematical computation is given a high priority in the primary classroom.[23] Doing 'take aways' must be taken as a given for the primary teacher. How, therefore, is it appro-priate to consider the teacher's task when she has to cope with children's errors?

At the outset it should be recognised that any explanation of a child's failure to produce the correct answer must, if it is to facilitate the teacher's instruction, be expressed in terms of the ordinary language which a teacher uses when talking with a young child. The teacher when teaching the child can do one thing not two. She cannot both at the same time seek to explain to the child and also engage in some additional mental activity which draws upon different language and concepts which may inform her practical activity.[24] Thus we must be cautious if we seek to go beyond commonplace accounts of why children make computational errors. Advice to teachers based upon informed professional experience is more likely to be of value than that which derives from research or speculative notions about how the child's mind works. It is, for instance, a moot point as to whether the prescriptions for teaching subtraction using 'carrying', 'equivalence' or 'equal addition' are methods derived from mathematics or 'common sense'; they are certainly not derived from research investi-gating teaching and learning. What the teacher relies upon when teaching subtraction is not formal knowledge based upon psychological or mathe-matical research but rather those personal qualities which enable her to become a perceptive and sensitive observer of children's learning. It is through watching children, talking with them, and examining their work that the teacher is likely to diagnose their learning problems. This is an ability which, in part, can be developed through practical experience although, of course, beginning teachers can be tutored so as to help them develop these practical skills.

Within the arena of the classroom it is necessary to recognise the crucial importance of time as an essential resource in the teaching process. The best efforts of highly regarded teachers can so easily be deflected by the demands of thirty or more children.[25] An important aspect of teaching is how the teacher uses her scarce time so as to make it available in the most productive manner in order to attend to the needs of most of the children for most of the time. For example, the sort of difficult problem facing the teacher is should she go through each child's work individually – which results in maximum attention being given to one child but none to the rest of the class – or should she run through common errors with the whole class – which results in every child getting some attention but an indivi-dual child's particular difficulties probably being neglected. The teacher's availability to engage closely in productive teaching of subtraction and to attend to children's errors depends particularly upon her ability to organise her classroom, sustain order and juggle the competing demands upon her time. Such skill arises from practice and experience rather than knowledge of theory and research. In order to teach subtraction successfully in busy classrooms with many children competing for her attention the teacher is inevitably thrown back upon her own resources of perception, energy and intuition.

Once the teacher has made the time available to deal with a child's subtraction difficulties she will need to assess the problem facing the individual child and take appropriate action; at this point it will be direct personal knowledge of the child, subject matter knowledge, and experience which informs her teaching rather than research. Experience may indicate that it is quite common for children to subtract the smaller from the larger digit when doing subtraction. The teacher will need to judge in a particular case, whether this was a momentary slip which can be safely ignored or an indication that the child has a shaky understanding and that she must engage the child in conversation so as to gauge the nature of the difficulty and then take remedial action. Several options are then open to the teacher. She may attempt to teach the child a correct algorithm such as the equivalence method which has a clear relationship to the mathematics involved, or she may decide that the child needs practice using structural apparatus. Whatever the teacher decides will be a matter of judgement; she cannot legislate for learning to take place and her decision will depend upon professional nous and experience. Just as the members of the *Gardener's Question Time* panel may offer different advice on how to grow bigger and better begonias, teachers may offer different suggestions for dealing with a learning problem. There are pluses and minuses associated with any tactic. In the above example teaching the algorithm may be objected to on the grounds that it is mechanistic and does not contribute to the child's understanding but the teacher may hope that the child will eventually realise why it works. Requiring the child to engage in practical work using apparatus, on the other hand, may assist the child's understanding but since it is highly likely that the child will have engaged in such practical exercises at an earlier stage the teacher can be fairly confident that such activity has not 'worked' thus far and being set back to an earlier stage may be resented by the child and affect its motivation.

In a word, at the 'chalk face' although the teacher cannot make children learn subtraction – or anything else – she must take steps to foster children's contingent learning. As such she will be required to make professional decisions in conditions which are not conducive to sound decision making, such as lack of time, lack of information, and competing demands for her attention. Research has little to offer the teacher in these circumstances. When the teacher teaches she acts as a human being making decisions about the behaviour of young children so as to promote their learning, in doing so she brings into play a subtle amalgam of nous, intuition, and professional experience together with her understanding of the material being taught. The teacher's task involves maintaining children's involvement in classroom activities and making informed and educated judgements about how to help a child in a particular circumstance. The transmission of knowledge from teacher to child should not be likened to the path of an arrow.[26] Much of the teacher's work has a fragile and ephemeral quality; sometimes the teacher's ploys are successful and on other occasions they fail. What works with one child does not always work with another. This is because learning has a contingent relationship with teaching.

Chapter 8

Teachers' pedagogic expertise

I have articulated the case for construing primary teaching in terms of practical pedagogy. It is important to bear in mind that every teacher, from the student on her first practice to the experienced deputy head, is already a practising pedagogue and as such has her repertoire of pedagogical skills and expertise. In this and the final chapter I address the issues of how teachers' pedagogical expertise can be incorporated within a body of knowledge which contributes to primary teachers' professional credibility and authority. At a time when a plethora of experts, politicians and parents seek to shape educational policy, and press their particular interests it becomes necessary to ask what is the distinctive professional competence of the class teacher and what special reasons are therefore attending to her expertise. It is the teacher who has direct personal responsibility for promoting learning within that peculiar learning environment which is the classroom. If any policy for change is to have a significant impact upon the quality of children's learning in the classroom it is prudent, if not mandatory, to listen to the professionals whose expertise and experience is directly concerned with practical pedagogy and involve them directly in deliberations concerning teaching and learning in the primary school.

TEACHERS' PRACTICAL PEDAGOGY

There have been various attempts to determine the essence of teachers' practical expertise and proposals made for how it may be identified and codified. The notion of 'situated knowledge'[1] has been used to describe teachers' contextually developed knowledge which is acquired and deployed in ways which tend to make use of characteristic features of the environment as solutions to problems. Situated knowledge is a form of expertise in which efficient trial and error procedures are used as solutions for solving specific problems. A similar notion is that of 'practical knowledge'[2] which refers to the procedural information that is useful in one's everyday work. It depends upon the practitioner and the context in which she works; what may be practical knowledge for one teacher may not be so for another. An alternative is the idea of 'personal knowledge'[3] which refers to the personal judgements whereby a theoretical body of knowledge is brought to bear upon experience; it relies upon tacit knowledge and entails integrating information and skill in practical activities. More specifically the term 'craft knowledge'[4] is employed to describe the particular strategies adopted by teachers attempting to instruct their pupils. Craft knowledge encompasses the wealth of teaching information that skilled practitioners have about their own practice. It includes location specific knowledge of teaching and also fragmentary, superstitious, and often inaccurate opinions. Some descriptions of practical expertise are avowedly prescriptive, for example the notion of 'pedagogical intelligence'[5] is used to identify the characteristics of inspired teachers who have the ability to facilitate significant learning, with maximal efficiency, under the conditions which prevail. Pedagogical intelligence is individualistic and each teacher must draw upon personal attributes and competencies in fashioning an efficacious method of coping with learning problems. Shulman[6] has extended his scheme to include 'wisdom in practice' which refers to the maxims that guide (or provide reflective rationalisation for) the practices of able teachers. This, he argues, is the least articulated part of the knowledge base for teaching but a potentially valuable and extensive source of professional knowledge.

These terms seek to capture the essence of classroom based, professional expertise but they suffer from one or more limitations. First, they all carry the connotation that each teacher has personal expertise which embodies her own solutions to teaching in the particular mix of circumstances in which she is required to teach. There can be no doubt that the concrete circumstances of different classrooms are, to a degree, idiosyncratic[7] and that the teacher is an individual who teaches her pupils in her own manner. It does not follow from this that each teacher always finds individual solutions to the problems of teaching in classrooms and that these should constitute her own personal professional knowledge. Such a view is both mistaken and dangerous. It is mistaken because, in practice, there are unlikely to be more than a limited number of ways in which the teacher may resolve a particular problem to do with teaching and learning. The ways in which a teacher may respond to a particular child's reading difficulty, say, are not infinitely variable depending upon the personal qualities of the teacher and child and the particular classroom environment in which they are located. There are unlikely to be more than a few reasonable alternatives in any one case. It is dangerous because it invites us to accept a view of professional expertise which retreats into solipsism and which rests upon the individual teacher's experience. It is a view which negates attempts to develop a formal corpus of systematic professional knowledge which may inform practice and which also suggests that teaching expertise should be 'acquired by experience'. Second, these definitions are too broad in that they do not prescribe or set limits upon the nature and range of teachers' professional knowledge. Presumably teachers' professional knowledge may extend from, say, taking playground duty to organising morning assembly. These are important aspects of the teacher's work but for my purposes it is necessary to focus upon that part of teachers' expertise which is concerned with fostering children's learning of subject matter. Third, it is necessarily the case that all attempts to identify and capture teachers' practical expertise will be prescriptive; this cannot be avoided and there comes a point when value judgements must be made. These accounts, however, are too prescriptive from the outset in that reference is usually made to 'skilled', 'inspired' or 'effective' teachers. All teachers however 'good' or 'bad' they may be have professional expertise and in the first instance it is preferable to recognise that it is necessary to identify variations in and alternative examples of professional practice before attaching notions of 'success' or 'effectiveness' to them. Certainly outsiders who investigate professional expertise should at least attempt to set aside their own assumptions about what constitutes good practice. Indeed we may learn as much about improving teaching by seeking to identify 'poor' practice and taking steps to eradicate it as by defining 'good' practice and attempting to promote it.[8]

It is not appropriate to regard each teacher as a unique individual who develops her own distinctly personal professional knowledge which is the product of her subjective experience. To adopt this position is to suggest that all teaching practices and expertise are shaped by a distinctive set of circumstances for each individual teacher and to accept that teachers' strategies and solutions are idiosyncratic and probably whimsical. Such a view also embraces the assumption that it is not possible for the teaching profession to contribute towards developing a systematic body of professional knowledge which may underpin and inform teaching. If we wish to propose ways in which teachers' expertise may become established as part of the knowledge base for teaching it is necessary to acknowledge that while there are individual differences in the ways in which teachers engage in teaching there are only a limited range of acceptable alternatives and that these may be articulated and exposed to scrutiny. The knowledge base for teaching should focus upon the heart of the teacher's work, which is to do with fostering children's learning of subject matter in the classroom. It should do so in a manner which permits practical experience to be identified, codified and subjected to professional scrutiny and eventually incorporated within the professional knowledge base for teaching. In this respect Shulman's scheme (see Chapter 6) provides a useful starting-point for examining and developing teachers' pedagogic expertise.

The value of Shulman's model is that it focuses upon classroom practice and encapsulates the notion of teaching as a pedagogic activity whereby the teacher is required to think carefully about how best to communicate subject matter to pupils so that they may comprehend it. Moreover, it embodies a notion of pedagogy which is derived from considerations of the subject matter to be taught, rather than from theories of learning or child psychology. The corpus of research and analysis arising from Shulman's impetus is leading to the acquisition of a formal body of knowledge which bears upon classroom practice but it suffers from limitations identified previously. In particular it does not face the problem that pedagogic knowledge, however relevant to practice, which is articulated as formal knowledge and expressed as recommendations or principles cannot be translated directly into practice, and it fails to appreciate that the class teacher, through her training and experience is already a practising pedagogue. The teacher has a repertoire of pedagogical expertise which she deploys in practice and which 'works' for her within the constraints of her classroom. (For the moment questions about the effectiveness and quality of the teacher's pedagogical expertise and what 'works' are set aside.) Teachers' pedagogic knowledge is embedded in their teaching and this practical pedagogic expertise may be contrasted with the more formal pedagogic knowledge identified and articulated by Shulman.

I define the teacher's practical pedagogical expertise as 'vernacular pedagogy'[9] and I use this term both descriptively and prescriptively to embrace a number of themes, namely:

- That individual teachers working within the particular constraints of their classrooms will, to some degree, work out in practice their own pedagogical strategies in order to encourage children to learn.
- That the teacher's central responsibility is to foster children's learning. This should not be taken to mean that other aspects of the teacher's work should be ignored; these are important for her work but they should not be included within the notion of pedagogic expertise.
- That at the crucial point in the educational process when the teacher seeks to communicate subject matter knowledge to her pupils she must talk with them in commonplace language. It therefore follows that the teacher's pedagogical expertise should be expressed in ordinary language.
- That the teacher's pedagogical expertise will be local and part of her personal knowledge and experience.

I also use the term vernacular to encapsulate the belief that pedagogical practice should extend beyond technical expertise and that teachers should have a sense of conviction or commitment based upon their values and moral principles.[10]

The teacher's professional expertise, as described by the notion of vernacular pedagogy, is central to the teaching and learning process within ordinary classrooms. As such it should form an essential part of the professional base for teaching. A comprehensive knowledge base for teaching should address normative questions and consider (a) alternative views of teaching and learning (b) the nature of the material which is to be learned and (c) practical 'how to' questions which are rooted in pedagogy.[11] It should also address the ends and purposes of education together with the values which inform discussions on these matters.[12] But in addition, knowledge acquired directly from practice must be incorporated within the formal educational knowledge which informs teaching.

A characteristic of the primary teacher's work is that it is often a private and personal affair. The teacher can be a Robinson Crusoe figure who often practises behind the closed door of the classroom.[13] There is little opportunity for contact with other teachers in similar circumstances so as to compare and discuss professional expertise – in so far as it relates to promoting learning. Teaching is conducted without the benefit of an audience of peers[14] and individual teachers may be unfamiliar with the range of pedagogical practices employed by their colleagues and with the ways in which practice may have developed historically and may be developing in other societies.

In so far as it is the class teacher who shapes children's learning it will be her vernacular pedagogic knowledge which is most likely to influence the nature and quality of that learning. We are woefully ignorant about the nature and content of this expertise. An important challenge facing educationists (if not the most important) is to establish teachers' vernacular pedagogy as a corpus of professional knowledge which can be set down, codified, subjected to independent critical analysis, and promoted as a central part of the knowledge base for teaching. Through such a process the professional expertise hard won by individual teachers may become recognised and established as part of the formal professional knowledge of the teaching profession; thereby the teacher may be established as an authoritative professional and her expertise valued and given due credit. In a word the practitioner becomes an acknowledged expert on classroom practice.

The issue, therefore, is how is this endeavour to be undertaken?

ACQUIRING VERNACULAR PEDAGOGY

It is inappropriate to think in conventional terms about engaging in educational research. The notion that educational researchers, who have their own academic agendas to pursue and who judge their work by a certain set of standards, may have a significant part to play in the investigation of vernacular pedagogy must be treated with circumspection. The procedures, rules, criteria, and ways of knowing entailed by conventional modes of research may not be relevant to the enterprise in question.[15] If educational researchers are to contribute they must adopt the approach epitomised by Eisner's comment:

> educational researchers are beginning to go back to schools, not to conduct commando raids, but to work with teaches as colleagues in a common quest and through such collaboration to rediscover the qualities, the complexities, and the richness of life in classrooms. We are beginning to talk with teachers, not only to teachers.[16]

It is essential to listen to the voice of the teacher and recognise her authority[17] if the expertise of class teachers is to be codified and made available to others.

The very notion of vernacular pedagogy carries with it the connotation of subjectivity; of being the personal property of the teacher, of being part of her experience and expertise, and of being tied to the circumstances of her professional domain. As such, vernacular pedagogy is difficult to assess and acquire and also difficult to appraise, judge, and review. No class teacher – or anyone else for that matter – relishes having their own professional practice revealed and opened up for public scrutiny and judgement. The greater the extent to which it is likely that personal expertise is to be evaluated the greater the likelihood that teachers may resist outside inquiry or present a contrived version of their practice which they may think would be approved of. It is necessary to overcome these obstacles if vernacular pedagogy is to become part of the knowledge base for teaching. Practical examples of vernacular pedagogy which are employed by teachers in their daily work must be collected, codified and critically reviewed if professional expertise is to be established as a corpus of knowledge which may make a contribution to formal professional knowledge and, say, be incorporated within initial and in-service training courses. The process necessarily involves the direct observation of teaching.

My proposal is that Karl Popper's[18] distinction between three 'Worlds of Knowledge' provides a useful frame of reference for guiding procedures which can be used to establish teachers' vernacular pedagogy as a body of formal professional knowledge. Popper argues that a major task for philosophers is to develop pictures of the world which are imaginative, critical and of theoretical interest.[19] In his 'Thesis of the Three Worlds' he distinguishes between:

- 'World One' – which is the world of physical states; it includes machines and all living forms.
- 'World Two' – which is the world of mental states or of conscious experiences; it includes our perceptions experiences, memories, imaginings, thoughts, actions, and dispositions.

- 'World Three' – which is the world of ideas in an objective sense; it includes possible objects of thought, theories in themselves, theorems, problems, and critical arguments.

'World Two' is essentially the world of our subjective experiences which can interact with either 'World One' or 'World Three' knowledge. Popper demonstrates that World Three knowledge has an independent existence by means of two 'thought experiments'. In the first, all machines and tools are destroyed as are our subjective memories of science and technology. But libraries and our capacity to learn from them survive. Clearly it would be possible after much effort to recreate our civilisation if 'World Three' knowledge survived. In the second, all 'World One' and 'World Three' knowledge is destroyed. In this case, without the objective knowledge collected in libraries and books our civilisation would be obliterated and we would lack the capacity to recreate it.

Within this frame of reference we may consider vernacular pedagogy as being incorporated within 'World Two' knowledge as part of the teacher's subjective professional expertise. If we take steps to record and codify the subjective experience of 'World Two' vernacular pedagogy this personal knowledge may then pass into the realm of 'World Three' knowledge where it can be treated as what Popper terms 'objective knowledge'. It is objective in the sense that it can be written down and subjected to review and analysis; it is not, of course, objective in the sense that it is 'neutral' or 'true'. 'World Three' is the domain in which we record and store the physical records of human experience and creativity. In our case that professional expertise which has been designated as vernacular pedagogy. This may, at first sight, be regarded as a somewhat superficial procedure to recommend since not much of significance seems to be entailed in transferring professional knowledge from the subjective world of the class teacher to the objective world of the written format. This is not so; it is an important shift for a number of reasons.

First, once subjective knowledge is recorded it becomes detached from the person and – as it were – it ceases to be their personal property. Indeed, there is no reason why authorship need be revealed. Second, it provides a means of ensuring that personal expertise can endure beyond the experience of the individual teacher and be passed on to others. (For instance the passing on of expertise by word-of-mouth is of limited value since only a comparatively small number of colleagues can be reached in this way.) Third, other parties can review, analyse and criticise what has been written down in a way which need not involve the person whose subjective expertise it is. The transcript exists objectively as a record and it can be reviewed and analysed without this critical activity being seen as a personal challenge or threat to the teacher whose vernacular pedagogy is being scrutinised. Indeed there is no reason why the teacher cannot be party to a review of her professional expertise without anyone knowing that she is the focus of critical attention. Fourth, once a large number of transcripts of vernacular pedagogy have been recorded it becomes possible to scrutinise them for consistent patterns, typical ways of proceeding, and alternatives for tackling the same problem etc. We may, by proceeding in this manner, begin to assess whether and to what extent there is a systematic body of professional knowledge embedded in vernacular pedagogy. It also becomes possible, in principle, to scrutinise collected examples of vernacular pedagogy in order to tease out possible theories, principles, assumptions or general reasons which may account for regularities in classroom practice.

Three speculative examples illustrate the potential worth of what is being proposed. First, HMI have compiled and made available in attractive formats examples of good primary practice in their *Aspects of Primary Education Series*.[20] The *Aspects* books offer descriptions of practice together with an account of how the work was planned and executed; what is illustrated is presented as good primary practice. What is missing from the *Aspects* series is the teachers' vernacular pedagogy; namely the teachers' own accounts of how they, within the context of their classrooms, with their children, with their resources were able to achieve good practice. Without the voice of the teacher we lack an essential element in professional knowledge and the one element which is vital if we wish to evaluate and analyse professional expertise and pass on examples of good practice to others. Assume, for instance, to illustrate my point, that the teacher's voice reported that while the science HMI was in the school excessive attention was devoted to science and that other subjects suffered, or that the head teacher has a special interest in science and spent a considerable proportion of the budget on science equipment, or that it was clear that the teacher had a degree in science. This additional background information would colour the interpretation and evaluation of what is presented as examples of good primary science teaching in the HMI *Aspects* book on primary science. Second, assume that a set of transcripts of vernacular pedagogy revealed that when using a certain maths scheme which included many practical activities for children, teachers had a tendency to get the children to pass over specific practical exercises (perhaps because of the possible disruption involved in using sand or water). Thereby practical experiences which were presumably seen by the scheme's author as an important part of pupils' mathematical learning were being avoided. It would be useful to access teachers' vernacular pedagogy on this matter. It is futile for publishers to include practical exercises in schemes of work which are regularly avoided in practice because they create organisational problems. Class teachers, on the basis of their pedagogic expertise, may have sound proposals for alternatives which would be practically acceptable. The third example is taken from the appendix to this chapter (item 3) where the teacher articulates a valid pedagogical case for ignoring children's wrong answers to her questions. This contrasts starkly with the predictable advice found in methods texts and proffered by teacher trainers which is that teachers should check wrong answers and correct the child's error.

THE METHOD

The task is to determine how to acquire examples of that part of teachers' professional expertise which has been identified as vernacular pedagogy and to transfer them from 'World Two' to 'World Three'. This requires the adoption of appropriate methodological procedures. It has to be recognised that the notion of vernacular pedagogy sets the agenda. The selection of appropriate methods therefore, means setting aside conventional notions concerning the canons and criteria by which research may be judged.[21] What cannot be avoided is the presence in the classroom of a 'third party' who is there in order to observe and record the class teacher's vernacular pedagogy in action. The third party may be an educationist or teacher colleague but whoever it is must be a person whose function is to record examples of vernacular pedagogy and as such he may be designated as an amanuensis. The amanuensis must, by training and experience, be someone who is familiar with classroom practice, who is aware of the tensions and dilemmas within teaching and who accepts that the teacher brings her own values and aspirations to the task of teaching. The amanuensis must demonstrate what Eisner calls educational connoisseurship[22] which is the art of perception which makes an appreciation of classroom complexity possible. The educational connoisseur can, for instance, distinguish between the noise of children working and plain noise.[23]

The prescriptive requirement placed upon the amanuensis is that he should focus upon those parts of the teacher's performance which may, at first sight, be loosely defined as those occasions when the teacher deploys her pedagogical skills so as to engage children in learning activities. It must be accepted that this is a loose definition and that what is embraced will, to some degree, be a matter of judgement and discernment. For instance, Hirst[24] in arriving at his definition of teaching (referred to previously in Chapter 3) rules out activities such as opening windows and sharpening pencils as not being central to the enterprise of teaching since they are not teaching acts whose intention it is to bring about learning. Such a claim should not be arrived at by definition. It must be judged within the context of practice, since, from the teacher's point of view, she could, say, open a window as an intentional pedagogic act which she felt would 'blow the cobwebs away' and have an effect upon her children's work rate. The amanuensis must be sensitive to such fine details of classroom practice.

The amanuensis may be unable to record all instances of vernacular pedagogy and there is a need to decide what should be accorded significance and recorded (suggestions are made below). The aim should be to obtain as complete and accurate a record as is possible of examples of the teacher's pedagogical practices. It must be remembered that any account and record of vernacular pedagogy must include not only reference to the teacher and her teaching acts but also reference to the children, their reactions, and their learning. Once the amanuensis has made his record he should, as soon as possible, show it to the teacher and gain her agreement that she is satisfied with the account of her pedagogical performance. He should then engage in discussion with the teacher so that she may add her explanations or accounts to what has been recorded. This must be undertaken with care since the amanuensis should not seek to offer or impose his interpretation. The purpose must be to give the teacher the opportunity to add her gloss so that we have her account of why she taught as she did. (Some illustrative examples are appended to this chapter.)

Once examples of vernacular pedagogy have been written up and supplemented with the teacher's comments they may then become part of an accumulating corpus of 'World Three' knowledge which describes teachers' pedagogical practices. This independent corpus, which has been separated from the individual teachers who generated it, may be subject to scrutiny and interrogation in order to come to some informed judgement about the quality of various examples of vernacular pedagogy and also to see if it is possible to identify regularities in teachers' teaching or preferable ways of proceeding in certain circumstances.

It is necessary to elaborate upon the process sketched out above and offer guidance relating to the collection and interpretation of the transcripts of vernacular pedagogy. It has been suggested that the criteria by which we should judge any well-crafted study of teaching resemble those which we apply to any proposed undertaking be it research, a creative work of art, a surgical operation, or the repair of a broken pipe.[25] These are that it should be rigorous in method, thorough in outlook and part of a cumulative programme. Eisner[26] has addressed the question of what makes a subjective account of classroom practice believable and he adduces three features. 'Coherence' – which is to ask does the story make sense? Does it ring true? Is it corroborated by other sources of evidence? 'Consensus' – are other parties likely to concur that findings and interpretations reported by an investigator are consistent with their own experience? Consensus does not imply truth but it indicates that others are likely to agree that what is recorded is likely to have taken place. 'Instrumental utility' – which is to ask if the account is useful. Does it aid and advance our understanding or comprehension and does it act as a guide for the anticipated understanding of future actions? The problems of acquiring narrative evidence from teachers which is based upon their educational experiences have been addressed by Connelly and Clandinin[27] and they make a number of recommendations. It is important that the recorder listens first to the practitioner's story and that she is given time and space to tell it and is not silenced. Practitioners must be allowed to tell their stories in their own terms using the words they use to reflect upon life and explain themselves to others. Conventional research criteria which have to do with validity, reliability and generalisability should be replaced with more appropriate criteria such as verisimilitude and transferability. Finally, in order to judge the quality of a narrative and assess whether it is a good account, the test is to give it to another participant and to ask her questions such as 'What would she make of it in her teaching situation?' Recommendations[28] for the collection of teachers' craft knowledge include: 'considering its source' which involves making judgements about the teachers from which the information is acquired. Typically it is suggested that only 'good' or exemplary teachers should be included but this is questionable – certainly any selection should not be restricted to teachers who are 'good' people who are easy to get on with and who are affable and articulate; 'considering the chunk' whereby examples of practice recorded reflect and fit into the teacher's usual pattern of behaviour and the routine of classroom events – the example or 'chunk' of practice recorded should not be artificially constrained by what it is convenient to record; 'considering the context' which relates to acquiring examples from within naturally or normally occurring patterns of events – it would be misleading, for instance, to acquire evidence from a specially prepared lesson demonstrated by a 'master teacher'; 'considering the significance' whereby examples collected should have significance for others – trivial examples of practice or minor idiosyncrasies may not have more general significance for other practitioners in other contexts.

As is clear from these suggestions, it is not difficult to nominate criteria or considerations which offer guidance and establish bench-marks for the collection and recording of vernacular pedagogy. But, as is so often the case, it is one thing to nominate the criteria by which to judge the value and worth of an enterprise. It is another matter to decide in practice whether particular examples exemplify or adequately fulfil the nominated criteria; this entails making an assessment with reference to actual cases. For instance, Eisner's criterion of instrumental utility cannot be met in some abstract sense. To ask whether an account is useful will depend upon who asks and who is asked the question, what they understand by useful, and their disposition to make it useful within their circumstances. The criteria indicate questions and issues which should be borne in mind when examples of vernacular pedagogy are being collected but the quality of the examples acquired will depend very much upon the discernment and acumen of the amanuensis.

INTERPRETING VERNACULAR PEDAGOGY

Once examples of vernacular pedagogy have been recorded they exist as independent records of 'objective' information – in the 'World Three' sense. The problem then becomes one of what to do with the information which is collected and which may be expected to steadily increase in amount. How are the particular examples of vernacular pedagogy to contribute to the development of a systematic body of formal knowledge which may be established as part of the knowledge base for teaching? There are various approaches to this problem and one of the advantages of compiling a corpus of objective knowledge in 'World Three' is that we may examine and interrogate the corpus at will and in different ways.

At one level the material can be seen as containing examples of usable information which may be made available to a wider professional audience. These include examples of pedagogical practices which have been found useful and to work for other teachers. As examples of vernacular pedagogy are acquired it will become possible to organise the corpus into categories or arrange it within a typology. As vernacular pedagogy accumulates within various categories which, say, relate to particular teaching and learning situations it will become increasingly useful for teachers. There are, for instance, numerous well-known and predictable pedagogical problems which teachers have to face from time to time such as coping with spelling and pronunciation problems occasioned by the 'silent e' at the end of a word, teaching the seven-times table, or demonstrating that it is possible for wind to erode rock. Primary teachers have a variety of practical pedagogical strategies for coping with these sorts of teaching problems and they need to be made available to a wider audience of professional colleagues. The greater the extent to which pedagogical practices which are actually used by teachers in the classroom can be acquired as objective knowledge then the greater the extent to which the private knowledge of the class teacher may become part of a relevant and usable body of professional knowledge.

This sort of activity should not be regarded as a mere low-level exercise involving little more than the acquisition and recording of examples, akin to stamp collecting. In a number of areas of academic endeavour the accumulation of basic information and material in the field depends to a significant degree upon the enthusiastic involvement of participants who undertake the essential task of reporting examples of specific instances. The compiling of the *Oxford English Dictionary* relies upon numerous contributors who record examples of word usage. The science of ornithology depends upon the efforts of a host of twitchers who, through their reported sightings, make it possible to plot and record the distribution and movement of bird populations. There has been a burgeoning in the numbers of artefacts being made available to archaeologists resulting from the activities of investigators sweeping the countryside with metal detectors. The examination of records of practical cases plays an important part in professional training in fields such as medicine, law, and engineering. What is probably peculiar about teaching is that the vast wealth of professional expertise remains the private property of individual teachers and is not collected together to form a 'data base' for the advancement of professional knowledge. Information which has been recorded and which is characterised as 'descriptive' (rather than theoretical) should not be discredited since it is a potentially valuable source of knowledge for practitioners. Making vernacular pedagogy available to others, as it stands, is a potentially worthwhile activity. There is a sense in which what is involved is an extension of the staff-room conversation. It does not require too great a leap of imagination to envisage a huge corpus of vernacular pedagogy recorded on a compact system and for the class teacher confronted with a pedagogical problem being able to punch a few key words into the classroom micro and obtain a printout of possible pedagogical strategies she could employ in order to cope with her problem.

A more ambitious way in which to use the corpus of vernacular pedagogy is to explore the extent to which it may be employed so as to improve the quality of teaching and learning in schools and by extension to enquire how it may contribute to the initial and continuing education of teachers. Exercises of this type require assessments to be made about (a) the quality of examples of vernacular pedagogy and (b) their suitability and applicability within primary classrooms in general. Judgements of this sort cannot be made in a mental vacuum, they must be set within what is essentially a theoretical context. Teaching and teaching acts are not good in and of themselves and we can never discover by research what constitutes good teaching.[29] Deciding what is competent or effective practice involves making a judgement about quality and this is something which we impose upon teaching, it is not something which emerges without interpretation from observing teaching. From the very outset, via some frame of reference, values and beliefs necessarily inform the judgements which we make about teaching; when scrutinising examples of vernacular pedagogy these should be made explicit. For example, the ways of regarding teaching described in earlier chapters provide frames of reference in terms of which examples of vernacular pedagogy may be appraised. These expositions provide ways of regarding teaching (which necessarily embody values) which offer standards and bench-marks by which teaching may be evaluated. It is important to remember that there are alternatives. Any attempt to appraise teaching should require the judges to articulate their standards, otherwise they remain covert and it should be open to others to challenge them and to offer different frameworks. Whatever frames of reference are adopted they should enable practitioners to make judgements about the worth of examples of vernacular pedagogy with respect to how they may be implemented in classrooms so as to improve the quality of pupils' learning. They should also recognise that there are costs and benefits entailed in making pedagogic choices.

Finally, the corpus of vernacular pedagogical knowledge may be scrutinised in a manner which is more avowedly theoretical. For instance examples may provide evidence which could be adduced by educationists interested in devising more theoretical accounts of teaching and learning such as providing explanations of why some intentional pedagogical acts are more likely to be successful than others in terms of promoting pupil learning. Alternatively, say, examples of vernacular pedagogy acquired from teachers early in their teaching careers and from those with greater experience could be compared and the evidence used to support accounts of how professional expertise develops over time.

VERNACULAR PEDAGOGY BY PROXY

The nature of vernacular pedagogy as it has been explained and defined emphasises practical expertise in the classroom. It thus follows that examples of vernacular pedagogy should be acquired by direct observation in the classroom. This presents a problem in that the collection and recording of information places a burden upon the class teacher and requires the resources to support the time and work of the amanuensis. This will create difficulties for individual teachers who are interested in engaging in personal investigations of vernacular pedagogy within their own schools. A fall-back position which is less demanding in terms of time and expense is to collect examples of vernacular pedagogy by what may be termed proxy methods. These are less satisfactory in that the information acquired does not relate directly to actual practice and refers rather to what practice might be, but they offer a possible alternative for teachers who may wish to undertake small scale studies. These methods include:

- Asking teachers to keep a diary and record a number of nominated examples of their enactment of pedagogical practices each day.
- Asking teachers to identify critical instances where they were faced with getting across to their children something which was difficult to learn and asking them to provide an account of how they coped with the problem in their teaching.
- Selecting a page from a scheme of work which is routinely used in the classroom and going through it with the teacher and discussing with her any teaching problems which are likely to be generated when children are completing that work.

With a little ingenuity it is not difficult to devise other methods which will be appropriate for a particular set of circumstances. Proxy approaches should not be based upon hypothetical situations and should relate as closely as possible to actual practices in classrooms. The information acquired by such means suffers from the limitations which are involved when relying upon memory to make records after the event and when providing conjectural accounts of what teachers would do in nominated circumstances. Nevertheless, such exercises do permit the collection of information which, with due safeguards, may stand proxy for vernacular pedagogy.

SUMMARY

I have sought to define and encapsulate the essence of teachers' practical expertise within the notion of vernacular pedagogy. I have outlined how it is possible to acquire and record examples of vernacular pedagogy and illustrated how a corpus of information directly concerned with professional expertise may become encoded and established as an independent body of objective (in Popper's sense) knowledge. This professional knowledge may then be interrogated in a number of ways with the aim of generating more formal and systematic bodies of knowledge which are usable and which could lead to improvements in the quality of classroom practice. The thrust of the exercise is to provide the means whereby serving teachers become an essential and authoritative source for the acquisition and development of professional knowledge. Teachers must move beyond being the recipients of educational knowledge created and provided by educationists who do not teach; there is no reason why teachers who are central and crucial to the educational process should not help generate and codify professional expertise. Teachers' professional expertise should provide an important part of the formal knowledge base which underpins professional education, practice and development. The manner in which the teacher's professional authority may be recognised and established is considered in more detail in the final chapter.

APPENDIX

In order to illustrate the proposals described in this chapter, examples are provided from an exploratory exercise. They are examples of the vernacular pedagogy of a teacher working in a middle school where pupils of mixed ability spend a substantial proportion of their first year with their class teacher who is responsible for the major part of the curriculum (that is, a situation comparable with the final junior year in a primary school). The examples selected focus upon the teacher's more general pedagogical skills because they are more likely to be accessible to a wide audience. During lessons I, as the amanuensis (A), made longhand notes which included observations and queries and as soon as possible afterwards I talked with the teacher (T) about examples of her teaching which I had recorded. As we talked I made brief notes and afterwards I wrote an account of the conversation. This was given to the teacher to check and amend if necessary and the final record was agreed with her. After each example a number of 'implications' are listed which indicate how it may be possible to develop examples of vernacular pedagogy as part of the more formal knowledge base for teaching. Since they are based upon examples collected from one teacher they are, of course, no more than speculative.

Examples

1 Teacher movement

A   During a 'question and answer' session for some of the time you stood at your desk you also varied your position by walking to different parts of the room. Was this pattern of movement pre-meditated and if so, why?

T   Yes, I knew where I was moving to and why. If I sensed that a child or group were thinking of misbehaving or getting restless I moved to stand close to them to remind them of my presence and to calm them down, without having to disrupt the whole class or interrupt the flow of questions and answers.

Implications

(a) Teacher moving to stand close to children can be a way of controlling their behaviour.
(b) Teacher needs to continually monitor children and take action to control potential misbehaviour.
(c) It is preferable to take action to control behaviour which does not disrupt the flow of learning in the class.

2 Teacher's voice

A   You tend to talk rather quietly but very clearly. When you use your voice to gain children's attention you tend to lower it, rather than talk more loudly. Is the way you use your voice deliberate and if so why?

T   Children pick up the general atmosphere in a classroom and relate to it immediately. If I keep level-headed and calm I am in control and they feel secure and happy. Quiet, firm authority gives a framework for self-discipline and this is my aim (remembering all the time they are children not adults!)

I do occasionally state my opinion in a very loud voice, which I can project so that it hits the end wall of the school corridor. Used once in a while it is very useful.

Noise and chaos give me a headache! I intend to survive.

Implications

(a) The teacher's manner, as expressed through the way she speaks, affects the classroom atmosphere.

(b) Lowering the voice as well as raising it is a ploy for gaining children's attention.

(c) It is preferable to use 'dramatic' gestures or actions to control behaviour only sparingly, if they are to be effective.

(d) An acceptable atmosphere in the classroom is for the teacher's benefit as well as for the children's.

3 Response to children's answers

A   During 'question and answer' sessions children sometimes give wrong or silly answers. You do not deal with these in an abrupt or punitive manner. Rather, you tend to gently point out the error or guide the child to 'see' how he or she was wrong and sometimes you ignore wrong answers.

T   As far as lesson content is concerned I try to make it clear that I want them to speak out and attempt to answer questions (i.e. to make an effort/contribution). It is important that they be encouraged to talk aloud and express themselves in the classroom. Thus all the children must be encouraged and given confidence, even when they give wrong answers.

Also in public children should not be shown up or made to look silly. Wrong responses should not be used by the teacher as an opportunity to demonstrate her superiority or to punish the child. It is important to have the personal maturity to maintain a stable relationship with the children and to treat them reasonably. They know if they give wrong answers. They will give up altogether if I am always telling them so in front of the class.

Implications

(a) 'Question and answer' sessions may have other purposes than establishing what children know etc., they are also used to encourage children to express themselves orally.

(b) The way in which the teacher responds to answers from individual children may have a wider effect upon the children as a whole.

(c) Children need to be encouraged and motivated to talk and answer in public and the problem is more difficult with those children who are likely to give wrong answers.
(d) The way in which the teacher responds to children's answers is an aspect of the way in which she considers it appropriate to treat the children in general and the relationships she develops with them.

4 Response to children's queries

A   When children come to you with queries about the content of their work or ask advice about what they ought to do, a common response is to turn the question back on them (e.g. 'Tell me what you think'). Why do you use this ploy?
T   I teach skills and facts – but my mission in life is to encourage them to think for themselves! Children learn by doing – and that 'doing' should include 'thinking'.

Implications

(a) Children must be encouraged to think for themselves if they are to learn.
(b) Children must be encouraged to be independent and not rely upon the teacher for help and advice.

5 Response to children's completed work

A   When taking project work there was a steady trickle of children coming to present their completed work. Often they thrust it at you without a word but they were all obviously seeking your praise, approval, comment or instructions. In every instance you did more than, say, nod or give a brief response. You indicated your reaction by facial expression and gesture and spoke a few sentences which usually elaborated upon the child's work or made interesting observations or suggestions (i.e. you gave a considered reply to individual children's work). This must have been demanding. How do you cope? Are your responses 'stage managed' as it were, or are they a genuine, sincere reaction?
T   This way of teaching cannot be premeditated or an act. It arises because I enjoy the children very much and have a real interest in them and their work. I know the capabilities of each one and they must be treated as individuals and I must show that I care for what they are doing.

Implications

(a) The teacher must demonstrate that she takes each child seriously and cares about what they do. If the teacher does not care why should the children.
(b) The teacher must know and treat the children as individuals and the manner in which she responds to their work is an aspect of her general relationship with them.
(c) The importance of motivation in affecting children's work.

6 Class tests

A   When you were doing the 'Planets Test' you gave capital letter clues for some of the answers. Why?
T   1 I had been teaching them about the use of capital letters and wanted to remind them.
     2 I was using the test also for teaching, to remind them that the planets were also the names of gods – my next project.
     3 I wanted everyone to get a minimum of 50 per cent, to have some success, otherwise they fail to be motivated for the next project.

Implications

(a) Class tests may be much more than simply tests to grade children and discover what they know, they can have other teaching functions.
(b) Tests can easily demotivate children, therefore tests may be devised with 'built-in' measures of success so that all children have a feeling of achievement. This is especially important in mixed ability classes.
(c) A test is not a one-off event. It is an episode in the life of the class, thus its effect upon certain children's subsequent behaviour and attitudes must be considered.

7 Displaying work

A   Two periods on Monday afternoon and one period on Tuesday afternoon were devoted to writing out and preparing neatly for display purposes work which had already been completed in rough for seasonal biology. Why did you consider this a worthwhile use of so much time?
T   Remember these are children still at top primary stage and thus need to continue primary experiences, etc. The content of the work is important but they also need to practise basic skills such a handwriting and reporting in proper sentences. I need to encourage children to be neat and tidy in presentation. Also children must be

encouraged to produce work which gives them satisfaction and in which they have some pride. The preparation of work for public display encourages these aims. Visitors to school, including parents, look at it and also children from other years!

Implications

(a) The content of a lesson is not always and obviously subject matter. Subject content can be used as a vehicle to teach other competencies such as handwriting and correct use of English.
(b) The preparation of work which children know is to be displayed motivates them to produce good work in a way which is not always possible when it is 'hidden' in their exercise books.
(c) The public display of children's work is a source of satisfaction to children and motivates them. This is especially so when the work is on public display outside the classroom and can be seen by a wider audience of adults and children.

Chapter 9

The professional authority of the teacher

The vital element within the educational system responsible for children's learning is the class teacher. No Act of Parliament, no reform in educational policy, no rhetoric from political platforms, no increase in resources, and no educational research or theory, can have any impact upon the quality of children's learning or lead to improvements in children's educational opportunities unless in some way they enhance or inform the practice of the teacher in the classroom. Within the classroom there is, in the final analysis, only one expert and one person who can be responsible for children's learning – and that is the class teacher. Whatever our opinions about teachers, however much politicians or parents may wish to control them and what they teach and how they teach, we are stuck with and had better accept the fact that once children enter the school we hand over to the teacher responsibility for their learning. The awkward paradox is that while we must necessarily accept this, it is also the case that teachers are increasingly scrutinised by those educational experts in all their political, administrative, inspectorial, and academic guises who legislate for and seek to shape and control class teachers' professional activity. The teachers who hold the chief responsibility for the education of children are (and it is probably by virtue of this fact) being increasingly subjected to outside influence and control. This state of affairs needs to be redressed and the means have to be found whereby class teachers become a major source of educational knowledge, expertise and authority. Teachers must be recognised as professional people who have a distinctive body of expertise and whose authority in matters to do with teaching is acknowledged and respected by those members of the education service who determine policy and allocate resources. Even if politicians and educationists find this hard to accept they may as well do so because once the door of the classroom closes it is the class teacher who is responsible for educating our children.

The pressing issue is to establish teachers' practical expertise as a body of formal knowledge which informs classroom practice. Experienced teachers must become the creators of professional expertise; they should not continue to be the doubtful beneficiaries of knowledge and expertise generated by those who do not practise. In this chapter I develop this theme and suggest how teachers' vernacular pedagogy may become incorporated as an important part of the knowledge base for teaching and through this process help establish teachers as authoritative professionals whose views and expertise must be attended to and taken into account by those who have political and administrative responsibility for the educational system.

PROFESSIONALS AND PROFESSIONAL AUTHORITY

Teachers should aspire to professional status and they should have a stake in the development of professional knowledge. In order to focus upon these goals, a necessary preliminary step is to determine what is entailed by the claim that a group of workers are accepted as professionals and that their practice is based upon professional expertise. All too often the appellation 'professional' seems to mean whatever anyone wants it to mean, although it is usually regarded as 'a good thing' to be seen as a professional. Established high-status occupations such as the law and medicine are accepted as professions without question but how far may the designation be extended? There used to be a television commercial showing infantrymen jumping out of tanks and taking up firing positions with the accompanying invitation to 'come and join the professionals' and sports commentators reserve the term 'professional foul' for conduct which negates everything a professional should stand for. As the twentieth century has progressed increasing numbers of white-collar occupational groups have sought professional status. There have been many studies which have sought to establish the criteria for deciding whether or not particular occupations ought to be considered as 'professions'[1] and then proceeded to identify those which may be accepted as such. These exercises are somewhat academic since the crucial issue is not whether teachers can be defined as professional people according to nominated criteria but whether members of society at large do in practice recognise teachers as professionals. Teachers, of course, consider themselves as professionals[2] and will often defend their actions by an appeal to professional judgement. But it is a moot point as to whether or not the wider public are always ready to recognise teachers' professional status. Politicians, pressure groups, and parents often have no hesitation in criticising teachers and suggesting how they should do their job. This is probably for two reasons. One is that since most people act as teachers from time to time in their daily lives they assume that 'anyone can teach', not recognising that teaching within the particular context of the school (as I have described previously) is what requires distinctive training and expertise. The other is that the body of formal, academic knowledge which should inform teachers' practical expertise is, in part, irrelevant and counter-productive or simply not available (as was demonstrated in earlier sections). In order to illustrate my theme it is instructive to consider differences in the political and public stance on events concerning health and education. If, for example, there is some criticism of the health service because it has been revealed that there has been a fall-off in the quality of patient care due to economic cutbacks or because a surgeon has made a gross error in treatment, the public will be rightly concerned and politicians will call for extra resources and require the medical profession to discipline the perpetrators of surgical malpractice. This is the appropriate reaction; comment will not usually intrude into matters of clinical judgement which are seen as the province of professional medical staff. There is not the same reticence with regard to educational matters. If, for example, there is concern over reading standards or the relevance of school leavers' education to the needs of industry the political and public response will not only involve expressions of concern over the level of provision and quality of teaching; it will extend to prescribing practice. The Secretary of State for Education or heir to the throne will not hesitate to tell teachers how they should teach reading; they take it as self-evident that their lay experience is sufficient to enable them to pronounce upon professional practice.

A plausible response may be that medical staff have a body of distinctive professional expertise and that the situation is quite different in teaching where the outsider's view is as valid as that of the experienced teacher. A serious and considered reply to this challenge requires us to ask what is and where is the established body of knowledge which constitutes the teacher's professional expertise concerning the management and promotion of learning within the particular environment of the classroom. If teachers have a superior claim to be attended to and a special expertise, where is the objective expression of their professional knowledge? This is an awkward question because for the most part teachers' expertise is contained within the minds of the individual teachers as part of their practical experience; it is not formally expressed in written documents.

Consider the issue this way. When we visit the dentist we hope that he has a wider view of his role and is concerned, for instance, about the funding of the health service, that he will treat us with consideration and offer an explanation of the treatment we may require, and that he considers all his patients equally without regard to gender or race. All of this expertise, which is an adjunct to professional practice, will count for nothing if he reduces us to agony while drilling a tooth. When one examines the knowledge base for teaching it seems that too much of it is not essential for professional practice; such knowledge is no doubt important but it is not of the essence of the teacher's task which is to do with promoting learning in the classroom. It addresses matters concerning the history, philosophy, sociology or psychology of education and issues such as social relationships, social justice and equity. These matters have a bearing upon teaching but if they constitute the knowledge base for teaching it is hardly surprising that teachers lack a distinctive and authoritative body of expertise. As with any occupation, all interested parties should have a legitimate interest in the political, social and economic context in which professionals operate and the way in which they treat their clients as people but special knowledge in these areas does not confer professional authority.

This is the central reason why I have been deliberately prescriptive in arguing that the essence of teaching is to promote learning within the particular circumstances of classrooms. There can be no doubt that teachers do possess – in varying degrees – professional expertise which informs their endeavours but it remains as part of their personal knowledge. If we are to develop a more systematic and coherent body of expert knowledge and if teachers are to be attended to as informed professionals a necessary step is to codify their expertise as part of the formal knowledge base for teaching. It must be established as a usable and workable body of information which enables teachers to promote more effectively children's learning in classrooms.

For teachers to be accepted unequivocally as professionals there must be developments on a number of fronts. One of the most important defining characteristics of occupations usually accepted as professions is that they offer a service to the public (as do the clergy or surgeons) which involves an element of trust on the part of those who use the service – a trust which the practitioner must not abuse. Hence the established professions have enshrined in statute the responsibility of the profession to govern its affairs and to be responsible for the conduct of its members. It is the Royal Colleges and the Institutes of Engineers who decide whether medical practitioners and engineers have the qualifications and expertise to offer their services to a wider public and who sit in judgement upon their peers in cases of malpractice, not a department of government. This is not the case for teachers in England and Wales where efforts to found a professional body, the General Teaching Council, have yet to be successful, and where the body responsible for professional training, the Council for the Accreditation of Teacher Education, is subject to ministerial control. It is beyond the scope of this book to contribute to this aspect of the campaign for professional status.

Another important characteristic of occupations accepted as professions is that their members are well-educated and hold degrees and professional qualifications which have been awarded after sustained and advanced study within institutions of higher education. This is because the work which professionals undertake is complex and challenging and a substantial knowledge base is required in order to practice. The decisions taken by professionals are not always clear cut; the professional, before deciding how to act in a particular set of circumstances, must exercise judgement and reflection which is informed by a broad base of relevant professional knowledge acquired in universities and colleges. In regard to this aspect of professional acceptability teachers have won part of the battle. Teaching is now established as an all-graduate profession after many years of struggle.[3] (Although with the introduction of the Licensed Teacher Scheme the Department for Education has established a means of offering school-based teacher training to people who have some experience of higher education but who have not necessarily reached degree level.) Hence, in so far as teachers' professional knowledge includes having advanced qualifications in the subjects they teach, it has been recognised that this must be at graduate level. The vocational training of professionals should also be located within higher education institutions and in this regard also teachers have been successful although it was only in the 1980s that all teachers were required to undertake a formal training programme in an institution of higher education. (This, too, has been undermined by the Department for Education with the introduction of the Articled Teacher Scheme which offers an alternative route into teaching which is predominantly school based and the recent change in policy which will locate two thirds of secondary PGCE training courses in schools.)

The main challenge to the professional training of teaches comes from those who argue[4] that the first degree qualification provides virtually all that is required by way of professional knowledge. Vocational training within higher education institutions, it is claimed, may be dispensed with since there is not a distinctive body of professional knowledge which is directly concerned with the *teaching* of subject matter and the educational knowledge and theory included in training programmes is irrelevant, counter-productive, or ideologically biased. Because teaching expertise is, essentially, practical expertise, so the argument goes, any vocational training can be provided on the job and acquired through practical experience. There are also those[5] who invoke the model of the 'teaching school' based upon teaching hospitals as the appropriate location for school-based teacher training. These criticisms of the established modes of teacher training are wide of the mark in that they fail to acknowledge that a substantial proportion of time is already allocated to school-based practice (typically over half on Post-Graduate Certificate in Education (PGCE) courses). Also they fail to recognise that acquiring knowledge and expertise via experience is not necessarily to be commended; as someone once said, 'any damn fool can learn from experience'. Learning through experience can be an extremely inefficient and potentially dangerous way of learning. First, it takes a long time and tyros must laboriously learn for themselves what generations of other professionals have already established. Second, such learning is limited to particular circumstances and beginners may fail to acquire a wider vision of their work and gain an appreciation of alternative practices; formative learning which is based upon experience of poor or inadequate practice has nothing to commend it. Third, while the novice is learning from experience those who are being experienced upon may suffer. Must succeeding generations of pupils be subjected to the inadequate falterings of untrained novice teachers who work out for themselves how to teach and who, if all training is reduced to learning on the job, may never know whether or when they become effective teachers as judged by any standards beyond those encountered in the school in which experience is acquired? We do not, because we are concerned for our own well-being and safety, expect workers in other walks of life to acquire their professional expertise through experience upon ourselves without prior training. Why should we make an exception for the teachers of our children?

Nevertheless, those who criticise the professional training of teachers do have a telling point to make and it must be recognised and attended to. It is that an important part of what should constitute the knowledge base for professional practice is unavailable. We require a corpus of knowledge which is based upon teachers' classroom experience and which is concerned with how teachers communicate knowledge to children within the classroom environment so as to promote effectively their children's learning. A body of knowledge which will be both practically useful and also promote reflection and analysis about practice. Given this lacuna in professional knowledge educationists resort to shipping in educational theory which is inadequate or counter-productive. Thereby professional training exposes itself to criticism since the body of formal knowledge which is introduced in order to promote professional reflection and analysis is often not up to the task expected of it. If significant progress is to be made in developing a more usable and relevant corpus of formal knowledge which informs thinking about practice it is necessary to consider carefully (a) what is entailed by thinking about practice and (b) the nature of the knowledge base which should underpin that reflection.

THINKING ABOUT THINKING ABOUT TEACHING

There has, in recent years, been a substantial and flourishing body of research which has investigated teachers' thinking.[6] There are, of course, awkward theoretical and methodological issues in attempting to discover what teachers are thinking when they plan or engage in their teaching.[7] How does one ever identify what is actually going on in the teacher's head and how do you know that the teacher's account of what she was thinking about when she was teaching is actually what she was thinking at the time? Despite such problems it is claimed that research into teachers' thinking may be used as a basis for encouraging practitioners to reflect upon their teaching and to set it within a wider theoretical context. This point of view informs those teacher education programmes which seek to develop a stronger association between 'theory' and 'practice' by devising courses which, rather than present theory in a formal manner in the expectation that it will underpin teachers' reflections upon practice, take as their starting point students' practical experience in the classroom and as that develops seek to relate theory to practice.[8] Such solutions seek to make educationists' knowledge and theory drawn from the social sciences more relevant to practice but it is debatable whether they do any more than offer an alternative way of retaining an established body of theory within the system when what is required is a different body of knowledge through which to inform reflection.[9] Barrow[10] has pointed out that the teaching profession has been right to reject this type of educational theory since it is poor and does not work. Devising courses which draw theory into reflective practice are not going to make theory relevant to practice if the theory is inadequate in the first place. The reflective practitioner is not someone who applies theory or scientific findings in a thoughtful way, it is someone who practises in a thoughtful way.

When thinking about thought and practice in the classroom it is salutary to remember a passage from Jackson's report of his conversations with teachers who had been designated as good teachers:

> The personal qualities enabling teachers to withstand the demands of classroom life have never been adequately described but among these qualities is surely the ability to tolerate the enormous amount of ambiguity, unpredictability and occasional chaos created each hour by 25 or 30 not-so-willing learners. What is here called the conceptual simplicity evident in teachers' language may be related to that ability. If teachers sought a more thorough understanding of their world, insisted on greater rationality in their actions, were completely open-minded in their consideration of pedagogical choices, and profound in their views of the human condition, they might well receive greater applause from intellectuals, but it is doubtful that they would perform with greater efficiency in the classroom.[11]

If we wish to claim that teaching is a professional activity characterised by reflection it is necessary to consider how thought and action are associated with each other in practice. Educationists who advocate that practice should be informed by their theories assume an image of the human mind which stands apart from the body,[12] and that when people act their actions are guided by a separate mind – a notion which is often referred to as the 'ghost in the machine'. This is an inappropriate model to apply to teaching where thought and action are inextricably linked together. We need to attend to what Ryle[13] terms the intellectualist legend whereby intelligent action is assumed to require some prior internal operation of planning what to do. He argues that when people act intelligently they are not doing two things, considering and then executing, but one. He claims that efficient action precedes theory and that the proposition that intelligent action requires prior theoretical operation is mistaken since it implies a view of the actor going through a process of regress whereby he is endlessly applying criteria at a mental level before deciding how to act. What distinguishes what Ryle calls sensible from silly operations is their procedure not their parentage. This view is substantiated by those experimental studies which have demonstrated that people find it difficult to access or report upon mental activities such as judging, problem solving and initiating behaviour, but that they are capable of providing fluent accounts of why they behaved as they did in specific situations.[14] Ryle[15] articulates his thesis with respect to teaching by arguing that all teaching is to some purpose and that in order to teach the teacher invokes various methods (telling, showing, demonstrating, etc.) so as to achieve a specific end; teaching involves making use of vehicles to get over information to learners. As such, thinking about teaching is not some independent activity which can be investigated and subsequently taught to intending teachers. Teaching involves acting intelligently in practical situations in order to achieve specific goals, hence thinking about teaching requires teachers to examine how they may better their teaching methods, which are all part of the activity of encouraging people to learn. Intelligent teaching involves trying out promising tacks and thereby improve upon practical activities intended to achieve specific ends; it cannot entail the application of learned rules or theories about the nature of teaching and learning. Although it will require the teacher to test repeatedly her tacit assumptions about how children learn and, via practice and experience, accumulate teaching practices which facilitate learning.

When thinking about thinking it is also necessary to be aware of the danger of outsiders imposing their notions of what constitutes acceptable cerebral activity upon the activities of others. There must be a suspicion that the image of the reflective practitioner which is advocated by educationists is one which requires practising teachers to display precisely those qualities of mind which the academic approves of and to employ, in their thinking about practice, those theories, concepts and languages which educationists have devised and which provide the basis for their own expertise. Outsiders should not press their prescriptions for reflection upon practitioners because they are likely to be inappropriate and counter productive. The imposition of outsiders' theories and views upon teachers' professional practice may, justifiably, alienate teachers. Rorty[16] observes that all human beings have a set of words which they employ to justify their actions, beliefs and lives; these are the words in which we tell the story of our lives and are the language of common sense which we take for granted. Thinking about thinking is likely to foster a style of thought which he terms 'ironic'. Ironists have a self-conscious awareness about the language they use and turn to other vocabularies to enable them to understand their situation, they know that the terms in which they describe themselves and their world are liable to change and they are aware of the power of re-description. This is probably the source of the tension between the thinker and the practitioner. The academic researcher gains power or authority by way of a capacity to re-describe the practical working lives of teachers. For Rorty a generic trait of the intellectual is to redescribe human activity and thereby humiliate actors. As he says in a key passage

> Ironism, as I have defined it, results from awareness of the power of redescription. But most people do not want to be redescribed. They want to be taken on their own terms – taken seriously just as they are and just as they talk. The ironist tells them that the language they speak is up for grabs by her and her kind. There is something potentially very cruel about that claim. For the best way to cause people long-lasting pain is to humiliate them by making the things that seemed most important to them look futile, obsolete and powerless.[17]

This, of course, rings true and the feelings of resentment often expressed by teachers against those educationists who seek to theorise and research teaching without a full appreciation of what the job involves are often justified and understandable.

There is substantial evidence that the available research on teacher thinking can provide no guidance for the content of teacher education and that it merely offers 'food for thought'.[18] If our aim is to ensure that teachers' practice is informed by a body of theory and knowledge which promotes reflection upon practice, we must acknowledge that it is necessary to progress towards a new knowledge base which may provide appropriate and relevant frames of reference for analysis and reflection upon practice.

TOWARDS A PROFESSIONAL KNOWLEDGE BASE

Teaching is not and should not be considered as a merely practical activity. Teachers need to think about their teaching both before and while engaging in practice; it is simply not possible to teach without some thought being given to the task. But, as has been indicated, the relationship between reflection, analysis and action is complex. The imposition of inappropriate frameworks for guiding thought and an expectation that teachers should reflect upon practice in ways which outsiders may commend may not necessarily lead to improvements in practice. Any act of teaching will be accompanied by thought of some kind – however overt or covert this may be – and any teacher's teaching – whatever its quality – is influenced by some sort of knowledge or theory. If the teacher devises an activity in which the children are led to discover information for themselves her planning has been informed by a 'theoretical' assumption that this is the proper way for children to learn in a particular set of circumstances. If the teacher keeps a child in at playtime for misbehaving, her actions are informed by some 'theory' such as it is right to punish bad behaviour and that it will lead to improvements in the child's conduct.

The practice of teaching is steeped in often unarticulated theory or knowledge and therefore any attempt to expunge theory must be resisted since practice is necessarily influenced by 'theory' and value laden assumptions which should be exposed to examination and analysis. Presumably, also, everyone associated with teaching aspires to improve practice, and to make any comment or proposal concerning the quality of teaching is, in effect, to theorise about practice. To advocate, say, that 7-year-old children should be subjected to extensive formal testing is to engage in theoretical speculation about how to enhance children's learning. The problem with teaching is not that practice is informed by theory but that, as I have sought to demonstrate, the theory invoked by educationists to support professional training and reflection is inadequate for the task and that devising novel ways of repackaging the theory is no solution. What is required is a better appreciation of how teachers may reflect upon their practice and the development of an alternative body of professional knowledge which may underpin practice.

It is necessary to consider how the practitioner's reflection upon practice differs from the outsider's. The issue may be illustrated by drawing an analogy from the creative arts.[19] A distinction may be made between the criticism offered by the critic and the critical interpretation provided by the performer. When the artist enacts his performance or creates his artefact he engages in some sort of thought and interpretation.[20] Neither the artist nor the teacher can do their work without thinking about it. Their thought is intimately tied in with their action – at its best it will be concerned with how to improve performance and interpretation and at its worst it may be concerned with how to get by in a routine manner. The critic is in a different position; he stands back from the performance and can reflect upon it at leisure and his own critical review will be judged by his readers and he will seek to inform, entertain and display his own erudition for their benefit. The artist and the critic have different audiences and aspirations. The superb practitioner may never become a half-decent critic while the outstanding critic may be totally incapable of adequate performance. It is never the critic who leads the master class, it is always the performer. This distinction needs to be made with reference to the theory and practice of teaching also. Educationists (as critics of teaching) have their own concerns to pursue besides improving teaching in the classroom. Highly regarded educationists may be able to analyse and theorise upon classroom practice in exquisite detail and to offer valuable insights and interpretations[21] but it does not follow that they themselves could perform well in front of the class. This may, of course, be seen as putting the case unfairly since the critic's job is to interpret and comment for a wider audience and to locate practice within a broader context. This is a valid point but simply to articulate it is to accept the proposition that the critic reflects upon performance in a special way. Since this is the case, it is legitimate for the performer to inquire of the critic, 'Why your reflection rather than mine since I am concerned with the quality of performance?' Teachers must reflect upon practice therefore we should be open to the possibility that it is a special corpus of professional knowledge created by them which should inform their analysis.

There have in recent years been various initiatives to involve teachers more closely in the development of professional knowledge. For instance, many serving teachers now take advanced in-service courses which provide opportunities for them to pursue their own small-scale research and development projects.[22] Such courses typically prepare and assist teachers to undertake action research in their own schools. The research topic is not laid down by the supervisor; it is the teacher who identifies the focus for her investigations and through this process it is hoped that she will improve her own understanding of the issue, set it within the wider context of other research and theory, and make suggestions for improvements in practice. Thereby the teacher may become a more perceptive and reflective practitioner whose practice is enhanced.

Evaluations indicate that teachers find it preferable to take part in their own small-scale projects which relate directly to their own practice rather than become the providers of information and data for educationists[23] and it is involvement with personal research which is likely to affect their practice rather than information derived from large-scale studies conducted by outsiders. It is not only teachers but also head teachers and local authority officers who testify to the value of these programmes for professional development and improving schools.[24] Courses which involve serving teachers in their own investigations which enhance their own professional practice are to be welcomed and encouraged but they are open to two reservations which must be addressed if this type of professional development is to have a wider and more enduring impact upon practice. The first is that these programmes are usually concerned with personal involvement and practice; they are designed so that teachers may focus upon their own practice and their value is judged by what the individual teacher may gain in terms of understanding and professional development.[25] This is an important dimension of in-service education but we also need to ask how experienced teachers may make a wider contribution to professional knowledge and practice which extends beyond the enhancement of their personal expertise. If teachers' professional experience and action research is to have a wider impact upon practice then it must be codified, systematised, and made publicly available through publication. It is at present extremely difficult for teachers to get their work published and when it is it is usually in inaccessible forms such as higher degree theses. The second reservation is linked directly to the problem of the wider dissemination of teachers' knowledge. It is that the genre of published work associated with teachers' action research consists, for the most part, of papers and articles by educationists who advocate the importance of teachers' action research and describe their own role in its promotion. Educationists have appropriated the teachers' professional practice and it is they who are writing about it. What is published often does not tell the reader what teachers may have found out and how it actually influenced their practice. It consists of theoretical and methodological commentaries by educationists.[26] As one commentator has noted[27] we run the risk of turning teachers' knowledge into researchers' knowledge and thereby colonising it and thus silencing the voice of the teacher.

It is necessary to develop strategies which foster established teachers' expertise and reflection upon professional practice in ways which provide for teachers to make a genuine contribution to a wider body of professional knowledge and for that knowledge to be established as part of the formal knowledge base for teaching.[28] I suggest that vernacular pedagogy provides a means for achieving this. (The irony of my position is conceded but I must necessarily write as an outside educationist in order to make prescriptive proposals as to how teachers themselves may contribute to the development of professional expertise!) Vernacular pedagogy provides a means whereby teachers may both focus upon their own professional practice and also make a more general contribution to the development of professional knowledge.

THE ESTABLISHMENT OF TEACHERS' KNOWLEDGE

The claim that vernacular pedagogy provides a means for developing a body of formal knowledge which will contribute to the enhancement of professional practice and offer appropriate frames of reference for teachers' reflection upon practice must be substantiated. It therefore becomes necessary to determine what is required of any theory or knowledge base which could inform professional practice and consider how it could aid teachers when they reflect upon their practice.

The term 'theory' when applied to teaching and indeed to much professional activity seems pretentious and misplaced and, moreover, gives a hostage to fortune to those who criticise teachers' vocational training as being 'too theoretical'. When the physician decides upon alternative courses of treatment he may, in a sense, be 'theorising' but it is more appropriate to say that he is making an informed choice based upon the best available professional knowledge (some of which may be conjectural). Likewise, it is preferable to refer to the 'professional knowledge' which may inform teaching rather than to educational theory. The professional knowledge which provides the basis for teachers' reflection and analysis should be *usable* and *likely to work*. The adoption of these two criteria needs justifying. Consider the case of the general practitioner who diagnoses his patient's malady. He will examine the patient, acquire information, think about the problem and prescribe a cure. The knowledge which informs his reflection is usable because it relates directly to the problem in hand. But in dealing with particular cases the general practitioner does not think like a robot. He must employ his professional knowledge in order to make a clinical judgement because individual cases are slightly different, because there are alternative treatments, and because he may not be able to predict the course of the disease. His professional knowledge allows him to suggest a remedy which is likely to work but he may have to prescribe alternative treatments before he finds a cure and despite his best efforts the patient may not respond to treatment. The knowledge base informing teaching should be considered in a similar manner. We should seek to establish a knowledge base which is usable in that it relates directly to the issue of enhancing the quality of teaching and learning in the classroom and which is likely to work. It cannot be put more strongly than this because learning cannot be legislated for or predicted since it has a contingent relationship with teaching.

If knowledge is to be usable and likely to work we need to consider the contexts within which teachers reflect upon practice. At the outset it is crucial to recognise and value (a) the particular and concrete circumstances within which teachers teach and (b) the ordinary everyday language which they use to describe their practice and which gives meaning to their professional activities. We should start from and recognise the authority of the teacher's situation and experience[29] and ask what are the circumstances of a particular case.[30] This is not an invitation to retreat into solipsism or whim, it is to acknowledge that any formal knowledge which is usable must attend to the context in which the teacher teaches and appreciate practice from her stance.

Within her classroom the teacher does not practice in some general sense, her teaching has a purpose which is to foster children's learning and to establish the classroom order which makes this possible. Consequently the knowledge base must be directly related to the problems and issues which teachers are likely to encounter in their efforts to communicate subject matter to children and foster learning. Such knowledge is unlikely to offer predictable or final solutions to the teacher's pedagogic problems – teachers are presented with new challenges every day and matters which are thought to have been resolved have a habit of re-emerging, probably in different guises. What the knowledge base must offer is possible solutions which are directly related to the teacher's tasks and which are usable in her classroom. The manner in which vernacular pedagogy has been construed and the requirements for the acquisition of examples of vernacular pedagogy and their codification and analysis are such as to lay the foundations for developing a body of professional knowledge which may directly inform and enhance professional practice.

It is not sufficient that teachers as professionals reflect upon their practice *per se*. Thinking of itself has little to commend it; what matters is the quality of teachers' thought and reflection if it is to be accepted as one of the hallmarks of professional authority. Incompetent teachers may be particularly adroit at reflecting upon their practice and offering wordy explanations which justify and defend what others judge to be professional incompetence. Indeed, people may dazzle us with their thoughts and reflection but fail to make it clear precisely where their cogitation may take them or how it may influence their practice.[31] Poor teachers may be good at thinking about their teaching precisely because they are the very people who are likely to be called upon repeatedly to give accounts of their practice. Moreover, there are no neutral or abstract bench-marks for judging the quality of teachers' reflection. Teachers often have firm views about the process of education and how they should teach and relate to children. Unless it is possible to demonstrate that their views and practices are harmful or counter-productive it will be difficult to challenge teachers' convictions. And unless he has something which is demonstrably preferable to put in their pace the outsider should hesitate before seeking to do so. There must be convincing reasons before the educational values and beliefs of the commentator are substituted for those of the practitioner. What can be expected of the teacher, given her educational beliefs and values and given the challenges which she faces in encouraging children's learning in her classroom, is that her teaching and reflection upon practice should advance whatever it is that she aspires to. It is important to remember that as far as teaching is concerned there are often no agreed standards of good practice and that situations and problems can be constructively and viably resolved in different ways. Moreover, reflection upon practice involves not only considering the means of attaining goals but often of determining the goals themselves.[32]

What is needed is a procedure which provides a context for guiding and assessing the quality of teachers' professional reflection. The procedure must accommodate a number of requirements. It must embrace the notion of vernacular pedagogy and focus upon individual teachers' practices while communicating subject matter to children so as to foster their learning. In addition, it must regard the teacher, whatever the quality of her professional knowledge, as someone who must continually seek to reflect upon and resolve pedagogic problems within the classroom. The procedure must be one which has the potential for developing usable professional knowledge which may enhance the quality of practice by offering teachers ways of resolving problems which they encounter during teaching and also offer advice and solutions which may be drawn upon during the planning phase of teaching. Another aspect of Karl Popper's methods for developing objective knowledge offers an appropriate framework. A schema developed by Popper[33] provides a workable procedure which initially addresses the subjective identification of problems and the subsequent attempts made to resolve them and from this starting point offers a way to build up a corpus of objective knowledge. In a word this proposal focuses upon trial and error solutions to practical problems and how a systematic body of knowledge may be generated from the resolution of problems in actual cases. The general form of his scheme is:

$$P_1 \rightarrow TS \rightarrow EE \rightarrow P_2$$

Where P_1 is the original problem
  TS is the trial solution
  EE is the elimination of error brought about by the trial
    solution
  P_2 is the resulting situation which may itself generate new
    problems

The model does not describe a deterministic process. The teacher never achieves that state of professional perfection whereby all problems and difficulties are solved by following this procedure. Popper recognises that the tentative solution to a problem may generate a new set of circumstances which will present the practitioner with new problems to be resolved. The best we can hope for is to make gradual progress through the elimination of error.

The basic form of the schema may be elaborated to reflect that in any one set of circumstances there will be a number of tentative solutions and it can be developed thus:[34]

$$P_1 \rightarrow (TSi/TSii/TSiii) \rightarrow EE \rightarrow P_2$$
Background knowledge

For any problem facing the teacher there will be a number of possible trial solutions (ranging from TSi, TSii, TSiii, etc.), all or some of which may, or may not, resolve the problem. This is a particularly apt model for teaching since, because of the contingent relationship between learning and teaching, any attempt by the teacher to resolve problems associated with learning may involve trial and error using different possible solutions.

These tentative solutions are provided by the teacher's background knowledge which I advocate should be based upon an evolving corpus of professional knowledge founded upon vernacular pedagogy.

The model may be further developed so as to illustrate how trial solutions can be located within formal bodies of knowledge relating to practice.[35] The issue for our purposes is that as professional knowledge develops, possible solutions may become established as more general rules or procedures, which may be regarded as tentative principles derived from the analysis of the evolving corpus of objectively recorded vernacular pedagogy. Thus codified and organised vernacular pedagogy may offer a body of professional knowledge (background knowledge in Popper's schema) from which tentative solutions and tentative principles may be drawn in order to address practical problems concerning teaching and learning in the classroom.

The value of such a model with respect to reflection and practice is that it offers a frame of reference whereby the individual teacher is seen as a thoughtful practitioner who must make decisions concerning teaching and learning. The quality of her reflection and practice may be judged by how successful her pedagogical solutions are in overcoming the original problem and achieving her goals. The model is realistic in that it recognises that there are no final agreed solutions or absolute standards. Whatever the teacher does she is presented with new problems and new challenges within the changing circumstances of her classroom. There is a sense in which professional knowledge and solutions are always provisional but, nevertheless, we must expect professionals to think clearly about the problems which face them and how they may resolve them and then make informed assessments about the relative success of their professional decisions. This is what good teachers routinely do. The advantage of locating sound practice within a frame of reference which is concerned with the objectification of vernacular pedagogy and the development of professional expertise through the trial and error solution of problems is that it offers the means whereby teachers may make a significant contribution to the development of the professional knowledge base for teaching.

TOWARDS PROFESSIONAL AUTHORITY

An important aspect of teachers' quest to establish their professional authority and autonomy must be for them to become more closely implicated in the development of the knowledge base which informs their practice. To a significant degree knowledge confers authority and it is, in part, because educationists generate formal bodies of knowledge which are established in print that they have credibility and authority in educational discussion and decision making. There is a need for the teaching profession to establish a comparable corpus of authoritative knowledge. There is much talk about the empowerment of teachers.[36] This is a pointer to what is required but it is not a particularly helpful notion since to claim to be in a position to offer the means of empowering teachers is to imply that some interested party has either the power to confer empowerment or can offer the means whereby teachers may acquire empowerment. It is akin to taking the dog for a walk on a spring-loaded lead and for the master to play it out so long as Rover behaves himself. From the outset teachers must be regarded as at least equal partners in any educational enterprise and decision making and perhaps it is they who should condescend to permit the empowerment of other parties who share a stake in education.

What teachers can learn from educationists is that educationists see as central to their professional practice the creation of knowledge which is made publicly available and open to scrutiny. They appreciate that advances in knowledge and its accumulation come about, in part, from exposing their theories and research to the wider critical examination of their peers. Individual teachers develop a fund of working expertise but inevitably it remains their personal property and it must be said that they do not always relish exposing their classroom practice to critical inspection by colleagues.[37] My aim has been to suggest how teachers' expertise may enter the public domain and become codified as a body of formal knowledge which informs their practice and establishes their particular professional expertise. Teachers are, and indeed should be, constrained in the sense that they should accept the social mandate that they are responsible for passing on to children knowledge and for fostering their learning. Once that responsibility has been conferred the professional authority of the teacher must be respected. Respect cannot be won if expertise is hidden from the gaze of informed colleagues and interested parties. Teachers' teaching should not remain imprisoned within and constrained by their occupational biographies and the particular circumstances within which they work. To some degree they may develop a wider and better informed vision of their role by having access to educationists' knowledge.[38] More importantly, they should have recourse to and contribute to a corpus of knowledge which has been developed by practitioners and which establishes the basis for primary teachers' professional authority.

Notes and References

INTRODUCTION

1 For example this is the solution which, in essence, is offered by the report of the 'Three wise men', namely: R. Alexander, J. Rose, and C. Woodhead, *Curriculum Organisation and Classroom Practice in Primary Schools: A Discussion Paper* (London: DES, 1992). The report asks teachers to reject dogma and invites teachers to combine selections from methods usually associated with one approach rather than another.

2 Department of Education and Science, *Children and their Primary Schools*, vol. 1 (London: HMSO, 1967), p. 7.

3 By C. Cox, 'The sharp compassion: the costs of caring', lecture, University of Durham, 1991. The phrase comes from:
    Beneath the bleeding hands we feel
    The sharp compassion of the healer's art
'East Coker', *Complete Poems and Plays of T.S. Eliot (London: Faber & Faber, 1969)*, p. 181.

4 For a treatment of the theme see A. Blyth, 'Five aspects of informality in primary education: an historical sketch', in A. Blyth (ed.), *Informal Primary Education Today: Essays and Studies* (Lewes: Falmer Press, 1988), pp. 7–24.

5 G. Steiner, *Real Presences* (London: Faber & Faber, 1989), p. 11.

6 Ibid., p. 9.

7 For a recent exposition on this theme see R. Alexander, *Policy and Practice in Primary Education* (London: Routledge, 1992), ch. 2.

1 ON TEACHING

1 For example H. Loukes, 'Morality and the education of the teacher', *Oxford Review of Education* (1976), 2(2). J. Gathorne-Hardy, *The Public School Phenomenon, 1597–1977* (London: Hodder & Stoughton, 1977). J.R. De S. Honey, *Tom Brown's Universe* (London: Millington Books, 1977). G. Highet, *The Art of Teaching* (London: Methuen, 1951). E.B. Castle, *The Teacher* (Oxford: Oxford University Press, 1970).

2 For an analysis of this particular theme see P. Jackson, *Life in Classrooms* (New York: Holt, Rinehart & Winston, 1966).

3 For example J. Wilson, *Educational Theory and the Preparation of Teachers* (Slough: NFER Publishing Co., 1975). W. Combs *et al.*, *The Professional Education of Teachers* (2nd edn) (Boston: Allyn & Bacon, 1974). R. Catell, 'The assessment of teaching ability', *British Journal of Educational Psychology* (1931), 1(1).

4   J.W. Getzels and P.W. Jackson, 'The teacher's personality and characteristics', in N.L. Gage (ed.), *Handbook of Research on Teaching* (Chicago: Rand McNally, 1963).

5   See for example M.D. Shipman, *Participation and Staff/Student Relations: A Seven Year Study of Social Change in an Expanding College of Education* (London: SRHE, 1969). W. Taylor, *Society and the Education of Teachers* (London: Routledge & Kegan Paul, 1969).

6   Wilson, op. cit.; Combs *et al.*, op. cit.; Taylor, op. cit.

7   University of Waikato, personal communication.

8   J. Kozol, 'A new look at the literacy campaign in Cuba', *Harvard Educational Review* (1978), 48(3), pp. 341–77. A.P. Morales, 'The literacy campaign in Cuba', *Harvard Educational Review* (1981) 51(1), pp. 31–9.

9   J.M. Stephens, *The Process of Schooling: A Psychological Examination* (New York: Holt, Rinehart & Winston, 1968).

10 L.W. Paine, 'The teacher as a virtuoso: a Chinese model for teaching', *Teachers College Record* (1990), 92(1), pp. 49–81.

11 *Introduction to Geography and Astronomy*, 3rd edn (Newcastle: Preston & Heaton). Preface to 2nd edn dated 1805, and Advertisement to the 3rd edn dated 1810.

12 Ibid., p. 391.

13 Ibid., p. xi.

14 J. Raven, 'Parents, education and schooling', in C. Desforges (ed.), *Early Childhood Education* (Edinburgh: Scottish Academic Press, 1989), pp. 47–67.

15 D. McNamara, 'Teaching skills: the question of questioning', *Educational Research* (1981), 23(2), pp. 104–9.

16 For an overview of these issues see P. Gammage, 'Chinese whispers', *Oxford Review of Education* (1987), 13(1), pp. 95–109.

17 Department of Education and Science, *Primary Education in England: A Survey by HM Inspectors of Schools* (London: HMSO, 1978).

18 S.N. Bennett, 'Teaching styles: a typological approach', in G. Chanan and S. Delamont (eds), *Frontiers of Classroom Research* (Slough: NFER, 1975), pp. 89–108.

19 M. Galton *et al.*, *Inside the Primary Classroom* (London: Routledge & Kegan Paul, 1980).

20 J. Barker Lunn, 'Junior school teachers: their methods and practices', *Educational Research* (1982), 26(3), pp. 178–88.

21 N. Bennett *et al.*, *The Quality of Pupil Learning Experiences* (London: Lawrence Erlbaum Associates, 1984).

22 P. Mortimore *et al.*, *School Matters: The Junior Years*, (Wells: Open Books, 1988).

23 R. Alexander, *Primary Education in Leeds* (Leeds: PRINDEP, University of Leeds, 1991).

24 L. Cuban, *How Teachers Taught: Consistency and Change in American Classrooms 1890–1980* (New York: Longman, 1984).

25 K.A. Sirotnik, 'What you see is what you get; consistency, persistency, and mediocrity in classrooms', *Harvard Educational Review* (1983), 53(1), pp. 16–31.

26 C. Richards, 'Demythologising primary education', in C. Richards (ed.), *The Study of Primary Education: A Source Book*, vol. 1 (London: Falmer Press, 1984), p. 59.

27 The literature on this theme is vast but see, for example Jackson, op. cit. C. Desforges and A. Cockburn, *Understanding the Mathematics Teacher: A Study of Practice in First Schools* (Lewes: Falmer Press, 1987), ch. 6. M.W. McLaughlin, *The Rand Change Agent Study Ten Years Later: Macro Perspectives and Micro*

Realities, (Stanford: Center for Research on the Context of Secondary Teaching, Stanford University, 1989).

28 See for example Cuban, op. cit. J. Raths *et al.*, 'A plight of teacher educators: clinical mentalities in a scientific culture', in L.G. Katz and J.D. Raths (eds), *Advances in Teacher Education*, vol. 4 (Norwood, NJ: Ablex, 1991), pp. 37–49.

29 Cuban, op. cit.

30 Raven, op. cit.

31 This and other similar issues are graphically illustrated by Jackson, op. cit.

32 P.V. Gump, *The Classroom Behaviour Setting: Its Nature and Relation to Student Behaviour (Final Report)* (Washington, DC: US Office of Education, Bureau of Research, 1967), quoted by W. Doyle, 'Classroom organisation and management, in M.W. Wittrock (ed.), *Handbook of Research on Teaching*, 3rd edn (New York: Macmillan, 1986), p. 399.

33 Alexander, op. cit., pp. 65–6.

34 J. Dewey, 'The relation of theory to practice in education', *National Society for the Scientific Study of Education*, 3rd yearbook, part 1 (1904), repr. in R.D. Archambault (ed.), *John Dewey on Education: Selected Writings* (Chicago: University of Chicago Press, 1964), p. 318.

35 C. Bereiter, 'Schools without education', *Harvard Educational Review* (1972), 42(3), pp. 390–413.

2 ON LEARNING

1   P. Jackson, *The Practice of Teaching* (New York: Teachers College Press, 1986), pp. 21–2.

2   A rigorous and lucid case for psychology is made by L. Smith, 'Developmental theory in the classroom', *Instructional Science* (1987), 16, pp. 151–7; and 'From psychology to instruction', in J. Harris (ed.), *Child Psychology in Action: Linking Research and Practice* (London: Croom Helm, 1986), pp. 103–25.

3   R.B. Joynson, *Psychology and Common Sense* (London: Routledge & Kegan Paul, 1974).

4   J. Smedslund, 'The invisible obvious: culture in psychology', in K.M.J. Lagerspetz and P. Niemi (eds), *Psychology in the 1990s* (Amsterdam: Elsevier Science, 1984), pp. 443–52.

5   See, for example J. Smedslund, 'Bandura's theory of self-efficacy: a set of common sense theorems, *Scandinavian Journal of Psychology* (1978), 19, p. 14. J. Smedslund, 'Revising explications of common sense through dialogue: thirty-six psychological theorems', *Scandinavian Journal of Psychology* (1982), 23, pp. 299–305. J. Smedslund, 'Between the analytic and the arbitrary: a case of psychological research', *Scandinavian Journal of Psychology* (1979), 20, pp. 129–40.

6   S. Koch, 'The nature and limits of psychological knowledge: lessons of a century qua "science"', *American Psychologist* (1981), 36(3), pp. 257–69.

7   U. Neisser, 'Memory: what are the important questions?', in U. Neisser (ed.), *Memory Observed: Remembering in Natural Contexts* (San Francisco: W.H. Freeman, 1982), pp. 3–19.

8   Ibid., p. 6.

9   J.W. Segal *et al.* (eds), *Thinking and Learning Skills: Vol. 1, Relating Instruction to Research*, and S.F. Chipman, *et al.* (eds), *Thinking and Learning Skills: Vol. 2, Research and Open Questions* (both London: Lawrence Erlbaum Associates, 1985).

10 Chipman *et al.*, op. cit., p. 6.

11 Ibid., p. 7.
12 Ibid., p. 20.
13 R. Glasser, in Segal, op. cit., p. 614.
14 R. Gelman, in Segal op. cit., p. 543.
15 M. Scardamalia and C. Bereiter, in Segal, op. cit., p. 563.
16 J. Bruner, in Segal op. cit., p. 600.
17 E.J. Mason et al., 'Three approaches to teaching and learning in education: behavioural, Piagetian, and information-processing', Instructional Science (1983), 12, pp. 219–41.
18 G.D. Haertel et al., 'Psychological models of educational performance: a theoretical synthesis of constructs', Review of Educational Research (1983), 53(1), pp. 75–91.
19 B. Joyce and M. Weil, Models of Teaching (3rd edn) (Englewood Cliffs, NJ: Prentice Hall, 1986).
20 C. Desforges, 'In place of Piaget: recent research on children's learning', Educational Analysis (1982), 4(2), pp. 27–42.
21 K.A. Strike, 'Towards a coherent constructivism', unpubd manuscript, n.d.
22 See for example G. Brown and C. Desforges, 'Piagetian psychology and education: time for revision', British Journal of Educational Psychology (1977), 47, pp. 7–17. J. Smedslund, 'Piaget's psychology in practice', British Journal of Educational Psychology (1977), 47, pp. 1–6.
23 C. Bereiter, 'Schools without education', Harvard Educational Review (1972), 42(3), pp. 390–413.
24 Ibid., p. 401.
25 L. Webber, The English Infant School and Informal Education (Englewood Cliffs, NJ: Prentice Hall, 1971).
26 C. Desforges, 'Developmental psychology applied to teacher training', in J. Harris (ed.), Child Psychology in Action: Linking Research and Practice (London: Croom Helm, 1986), pp. 208–19.
27 W. James, Talks to Teachers (London: Longmans, Green & Co., 1913), pp. 7, 8.
28 J.S. Bruner, 'Needed: a theory of instruction', Educational Leadership (1963), 20(8), pp. 523–32.
29 W. Doyle, Curriculum in Teacher Education (Tucson: University of Arizona, 1988).
30 For a clear exposition of this argument see D.F. Swift, The Sociology of Education: Introductory Analytical Perspectives (London: Routledge & Kegan Paul, 1969).
31 For an elaboration of this argument see D.R. McNamara, 'A time for change: a reappraisal of sociology of education as a contributing discipline to professional education courses', Educational Studies (1977), 3(3), pp. 179–83.
32 The literature ranges, for example, from A.H. Halsey et al., Education, Economy and Society (New York: Free Press, 1961); through T. Husen, Social Background and Educational Career (Paris: OECD, 1972); to R.B. Ekstrom et al., Education and American Youth (London, Falmer Press, 1988).
33 C. Jencks et al., Inequality: a Reassessment of the Effect of Family and Schooling in America (London: Allen Lane, 1973). S.J. Green, 'Is equality of opportunity a false ideal for society?', British Journal of Sociology (1988), 39(1), pp. 1–27.
34 F. Musgrove, School and the Social Order (Chichester: John Wiley, 1979), pp. 92ff.
35 Ibid., p. 96. For a detailed and penetrating analysis of these issues see J. Murphy, 'A most respectable prejudice: inequality in educational research and policy', British Journal of Sociology (1990), 41(1), pp. 29–54.

36 Department of Education and Science, *Initial Teacher Training: Approval of Courses*, Circular No. 24/89, (London: DES, 1989), p. 10.
37 J. Murphy, 'Race, education and intellectual prejudice', in F. Macleod (ed.), *Parents and Schools: The Contemporary Challenge* (Lewes: Falmer Press, 1989), pp. 11–30.
38 D.J. Smith and S. Tomlinson, *The School Effect: A Study of Multi-racial Comprehensives* (London: Policy Studies Institute, 1989), pp. 6ff.
39 Ibid., p. 305.
40 Ibid., p. 16.
41 Inner London Education Authority, *Differences in Examination Performance*, RS 1277/90 (London: ILEA Research and Statistics Branch, 1990).
42 Ibid., p. 23.
43 Smith and Tomlinson, op. cit., p. 16.
44 Inner London Education Authority, op. cit., p. 9.
45 R. Auld, *William Tindale Junior and Infant Schools Public Enquiry: a Report to the Inner London Education Authority* (London: ILEA, 1976); and T. Ellis *et al.*, *William Tindale: the Teachers' Story* (Tiptree: London Writers and Readers Publishing Co-operative, 1976).
46 For an elaboration of this issue see D.H. Hargreaves, *Interpersonal Relations and Education* (London: Routledge & Kegan Paul, 1972), pp. 65ff.
47 For a detailed discussion with respect to social class and language see H. Rosen, 'Language and class: a critical look at the theories of Basil Bernstein', paper delivered at Ruskin College, Oxford, 1972.
48 J. Korczak, *When I Am Small Again* (Washington, DC: University Press of America, 1990): originally published 1923; for an accessible introduction see L. Brendtro and D. Hinders, 'A saga of Januz Korczak, the king of children', *Harvard Educational Review* (1990), 60(1), pp. 237–46.
49 Jancks *et al.*, op. cit.
50 C. Kamil, *Young Children Reinvent Arithmetic: Implications of Piaget's Theory*, (New York: Teachers College Press, 1985).
51 On the basis of the available research evidence, for example, it has been argued that all curricula and methods have 'equipotentiality' in their capacity to shape learning; see D.C. Berliner and B. Rosenshine, 'The acquisition of knowledge in the classroom', in R.C. Anderson *et al.* (eds), *Schooling and the Acquisition of Knowledge* (London: Lawrence Erlbaum Associates, 1977), pp. 375–96.
52 *The Shorter Oxford Dictionary*.
53 Department of Education and Science: *Children and their Primary Schools*, vol. 1, (London: HMSO, 1967), ch. 20.
54 J.C. Barker Lunn, *Streaming in the Primary School* (Slough: NFER, 1970).
55 Jencks *et al.*, op. cit., pp. 196ff.
56 N. Bennett *et al.*, *Teaching Styles and Pupil Progress* (London: Open Books, 1976).
57 M. Aitken *et al.*, 'Teaching styles and pupil progress: a re-analysis', *British Journal of Educational Psychology* (1981), 51, pp. 170–86.
58 J. Gray and D. Satterley, 'Formal or informal? A re-assessment of the British evidence', *British Journal of Educational Psychology* (1981), 51, pp. 187–96.
59 M. Galton *et al.*, *Inside the Primary School*, (London: Routledge & Kegan Paul, 1980).
60 D.R. McNamara, 'Do the grounds for claiming that school matters matter?', *British Journal of Educational Psychology* (1988), 58(3), pp. 356–630.
61 T.L. Good and J.E. Brophy, 'School effects', in M.C. Wittrock (ed.) *Handbook of*

Research on Teaching (3rd edn) (London and New York: Collier MacMillan, 1986), pp. 570–602.

62 M. Rutter, 'School effects on pupil progress: research findings and policy implications', *Journal of Child Development* (1983), 54, pp. 1–29.

63 P. Mortimore *et al.*, *School Matters: The Junior Years* (Wells: Open Books, 1988).

64 J. Kagan, 'The importance of simply growing older', in J. Oates and S. Sheldon (eds), *Cognitive Development in Infancy* (London: Lawrence Erlbaum Associates, 1987), pp. 285–91.

65 For an elaboration of this view see J.M. Stephens, *The Process of Schooling: A Psychological Examination* (New York: Holt, Rinehart & Winston, 1967).

66 M. Montessori, *The Montessori Method* (London: William Heinemann, 1912), p. 21.

67 J. Lyons, *Chomsky* (London: Fontana, 1970), p. 11.

68 G. Ryle, 'Mowgli in Babel', in G. Ryle, *On Thinking*, edited by K. Kolenda (Oxford: Basil Blackwell, 1979), pp. 95–103.

69 Ibid., p. 102.

70 This thesis is elaborated in various publications by E.W. Eisner such as *The Role of Discipline-based Art Education in American Schools* (Los Angeles: The Getty Center for Education in the Arts, n.d.); 'The celebration of thinking', *National Forum* (1988), 68(2), pp. 30–33; *Cognition and Curriculum: A Basis for Deciding What to Teach* (New York and London: Longman, 1982), ch. 1.

71 T.R.G. Bower, *The Rational Infant: Learning in Infancy* (New York: H. Freeman & Co., 1989).

72 R. Gelman and A.L. Brown, 'Changing views of cognitive competence in the young', in N.J. Smelser and D.R. Gerstein (eds), *Behavioural and Social Science: Fifty Years of Discovery*, (Washington, DC: National Academy Press, 1986), pp. 175–207.

73 C. Desforges, 'Understanding learning for teaching', *Westminster Studies in Education* (1989), 12, pp. 17–29.

74 Stephens, op. cit.

75 Ibid., p. 10.

3 THE TEACHER'S RESPONSIBILITY FOR LEARNING

1 P.H. Hirst, 'What is teaching?', *Journal of Curriculum Studies* (1971), 3(1); repr. as ch. 7, in P.H. Hirst, *Knowledge and the Curriculum* (London: Routledge & Kegan Paul, 1974), pp. 101–15.

2 Ibid., p. 108.

3 Ibid., p. 108.

4 Ibid., p. 110.

5 Ibid., p. 110.

6 For an extended analysis of this issue see D.P. Erickson and F.S. Ellett, 'Taking student responsibility seriously', *Educational Researcher* (1990), 19(9), pp. 3–10.

7 Ibid., p. 6.

8 For an exposition see G. Ryle, 'Thinking and self-teaching', in G. Ryle, *On Thinking*, edited by K. Kolenda (Oxford: Basil Blackwell, 1979), pp. 65–78.

9 For various analytic attempts to do so see, for example, I. Scheffler, *The Language of Education* (Springfield, Ill.: Charles C. Thomas Publisher, 1960). O. Smith, 'A concept of teaching', *Teachers College Record* (1960), 61, pp. 229–41. T.F. Green, *The Activities of Teaching* (New York: McGraw Hill, 1971).

10 P.W. Jackson, 'The way teaching is', *NEA Journal* (1962), 62; repr. in R.T.

Hyman (ed.), *Contemporary Thought on Teaching* (Englewood Cliffs, NJ: Prentice Hall, 1971), pp. 6–12.

11 My argument here is suggested by D.P. Ericson and F.S. Ellet Jr, 'Teacher accountability and the causal theory of teaching', *Educational Theory* (1987), 37(3), pp. 277–93.

12 *Shorter Oxford English Dictionary* and *Longman Dictionary of the English Language.*

13 S.J. Gould, *Wonderful Life: The Burgess Shale and the Nature of History* (London: Hutchinson Radius, 1990); for an extended discussion of the heuristic use of contingency see pp. 282ff.

14 C. Desforges and A. Cockburn, *Understanding the Mathematics Teacher: A Study of Practice in First Schools* (Lewes: Falmer Press, 1987), pp. 95–6.

15 M. Cortazzi, *Primary Teaching As It Is: A Narrative Account* (London: David Fulton Publishers, 1991).

16 Ibid., pp. 50–52.

17 Ibid., p. 50.

18 B. Reed, 'Towards reading?', in R. Webb (ed.), *Practitioner Research in the Primary School* (London: Falmer Press, 1990), pp. 55–76.

19 J.S. Brown, 'Towards a new epistemology for learning', paper presented at the Annual Meeting of the American Educational Research Association, San Francisco, 1989.

20 J.S. Brown *et al.*, *Situated Cognition and the Culture of Learning* (Palo Alto: Institute for Research on Learning, 1988).

4 RELATING TEACHING TO CHILDREN'S APTITUDES

1   W.A. Hart, 'Is teaching what the philosopher understands by it?', *British Journal of Educational Studies* (1976), 24(2), pp. 155–70.

2   Department of Education and Science: *Primary Education in England, A Survey by HM Inspectors of Schools* (London: HMSO, 1978).

3   Ibid., pp. 80ff.

4   N. Bennett *et al.*, *The Quality of Pupil Learning Experiences* (London: Lawrence Erlbaum Associates, 1984).

5   Department of Education and Science, *The New Teacher in School, A Survey by HM Inspectors in England and Wales 1987* (London: HMSO, 1988).

6   R. Alexander, *Primary Education in Leeds* (Leeds: PRINDEP, University of Leeds, 1991).

7   A. Davis, 'Matching and assessment', *Journal of Curriculum Studies*, 25(3), pp. 267–79.

8   Department of Education and Science, *Better Schools*, Cmnd 9469 (London: HMSO, 1985).

9   Ibid., p. 15.

10 Department of Education and Science, *National Curriculum: From Policy to Practice* (London: DES, 1989).

11 See for example C. Desforges and A. Cockburn, *Understanding the Mathematics Teacher: A Study of Practice in First Schools* (Lewes: Falmer Press, 1987).

12 C. Bereiter, 'Schools without education', *Harvard Educational Review* (1972), 42(3), pp. 390–413.

13 M. Galton *et al.*, *Inside the Primary Classroom* (London: Routledge & Kegan Paul, 1980), pp. 155ff.

14 P. Mortimore *et al.*, *School Matters: The Junior Years* (Wells: Open Books, 1988).

15 Ibid., p. 238ff.

16   R. Alexander, op. cit.
17   Bennett *et al.*, op. cit.
18   For a recent attempt to develop a detailed analytical scheme see J. Brophy and
      J. Alleman, 'Activities as instructional tools: a framework for analysis and
      evaluation', *Educational Researcher* (1991), 20(4), pp. 9–23.
19   Davis, op. cit. This paper should be consulted for an extensive treatment of
      the issue.
20   Following an argument in a different context from C. Desforges, 'Develop-
      mental psychology applied to teacher training', in J. Harris (ed.), *Child Psy-
      chology in Action: Linking Research to Practice* (London: Croom Helm, 1986), pp.
      208–19.
21   For the development of this theme see P.W. Jackson, *The Practice of Teaching*
      (New York: Teachers College Press, 1986), pp. 18–19.
22   For a brief overview see W.F. Connell, 'History of teaching methods', in M.J.
      Dunkin (ed.), *The International Encyclopedia of Teaching and Teacher Education*
      (Oxford: Pergamon Press, 1987), pp. 201–14.
23   D.P. Ausubel, *Educational Psychology: A Cognitive View* (New York: Holt,
      Rinehart & Winston, 1968).
24   An up-to-date review pertinent to teaching is C. Desforges, 'Understanding
      learning for teaching, *Westminster Studies in Education* (1989), 12, pp. 17–29.
25   Davis, op. cit.
26   Desforges 1989, op. cit.

5 ORGANISING TEACHING TO PROMOTE LEARNING

1   S.N. Bennett, 'Recent research on teaching: a dream, a belief, and a model',
      British Journal of Educational Psychology (1978), 48, pp. 127–47.
2   D. R. McNamara, 'Time on task and children's learning: research or ideo-
      logy?', *Journal of Education for Teaching* (1981) 7(3), pp. 284–97.
3   For a wider consideration of this theme see P.M. Copa, 'The beginning
      teacher as theory maker', in L.G. Katz and J.D. Raths (eds), *Advances in
      Teacher Education*, vol. 4 (Norwood, NJ: Ablex, 1991), pp. 105–36.
4   C. Bereiter, 'Schools without education', *Harvard Educational Review* (1972),
      42(3), pp. 390–413.
5   R. Alexander, *Primary Education in Leeds* (Leeds: PRINDEP, University of
      Leeds, 1991), p. 61.
6   Ibid., p. 61.
7   R.M. Thomas, 'The individual and the group', in M.J. Dunkin (ed.), *The
      International Encyclopedia of Teaching and Teacher Education* (Oxford: Pergamon
      Press, 1987), pp. 220–24.
8   L.C. Wilkinson, 'Grouping children for learning: implications for kinder-
      garten education', in E.Z. Rothkopf (ed.), *Review of Research in Education*
      (1988–9), 15, pp. 203–23.
9   R. Nash, *Classrooms Observed: The Teacher's Perception and the Pupil's Perform-
      ance* (London: Routledge & Kegan Paul, 1973).
10   J.C. Barker Lunn, *Streaming in the Primary School* (Slough: NFER, 1970).
11   Thomas, op. cit.
12   Thomas, Ibid., and C.M. Evertson, 'Classroom organisation and manage-
      ment', in M.C. Reynolds (ed.), *Knowledge Base for the Beginning Teacher*
      (Oxford: Pergamon Press, 1989), pp. 59–70.
13   R.C. Calfee and D.C. Piontkowski, 'Grouping for teaching', in M.J. Dunkin,
      op. cit., pp. 220–24.

14   M. Galton *et al.*, *Inside the Primary School* (London: Routledge & Kegan Paul, 1980).
15   Wilkinson, op. cit.
16   R.J.A. Alexander *et al.*, *Curriculum Organisation and Classroom Practice in Primary Schools, a Discussion Paper* (London: DES, 1992).
17   D.R. McNamara and D.G. Waugh, 'Classroom organisation: a discussion of grouping strategies in the light of the "Three Wise Men's Report"', *School Organisation* (1993), 13(1), pp. 41–50.
18   Ibid.
19   The framework expounded in the remainder of the chapter draws heavily upon the work of W. Doyle, 'Classroom organisation and management', in M.W. Wittrock (ed.), *Handbook of Research on Teaching*, 3rd edn (New York: Macmillan, 1986), 392–431; W. Doyle, 'Academic work', *Review of Educational Research* (1983), 53(2), pp. 159–99; W. Doyle, 'Content representation in teachers' definitions of academic work', *Journal of Curriculum Studies* (1986), 18(4), pp. 365–79; W. Doyle, *Curriculum in Teacher Education*, (Tucson: University of Arizona, 1988); W. Doyle and K. Carter, 'Academic tasks in classrooms', *Curriculum Inquiry* (1984), 14(2), pp. 129–49; K. Carter and W. Doyle, 'Teachers' knowledge structures and comprehension processes', in J. Calderhead (ed.), *Exploring Teachers' Thinking* (London: Cassell, 1987), pp. 147–60; see also P.C. Blumenfeld *et al.*, 'Task as a heuristic for understanding student learning and motivation', *Journal of Curriculum Studies* (1987), 19(2), pp. 135–48; J. Brophy, 'Educating teachers about managing classrooms and students', *Teaching and Teacher Education* (1983), 4(1), pp. 1–18; P.W. Jackson, 'The way teaching is', in R.T. Hyman (ed.), *Contemporary Thought on Teaching* (Englewood Cliffs, NJ: Prentice Hall, 1971).
20   See for example B. Rosenshine and R. Stevens, 'Teaching functions', in M.C. Wittrock (ed.), *Handbook of Research on Teaching* (3rd edn) (New York: Macmillan, 1986), pp. 376–91. C.M. Evertson, 'Classroom organisation and management', in M.C. Reynolds (ed.), *Knowledge Base for the Beginning Teacher* (Oxford: Pergamon Press), pp. 59–70. J. Brophy (ed.), *Advances in Research on Teaching*, vol. 1 (Greenwich, Conn.: JAI Press, 1989), esp. pp. 6–13, 80–98, 311–23.
21   Rosenshine and Stevens, op. cit., p. 377.
22   For an example from an arts subject see S.W. Button, 'Music and the National Curriculum: the importance of pitch development', *Curriculum* (1991), 12(1), pp. 38–41.
23   Bereiter, op. cit.
24   Carter and Doyle, op. cit., p. 157.
25   Here and in what follows I am basing my exposition on Doyle, 1983, op. cit.; and Doyle and Carter, 1984; op. cit.
26   For an interesting elaboration of this theme see J. Holt, *How Children Fail* (Harmondsworth: Penguin Books, 1965).

6 ORGANISING SUBJECT MATTER FOR LEARNING

1   M. Galton *et al.*, *Inside the Primary Classroom* (London: Routledge & Kegan Paul, 1980).
2   S.S. Stodolsky, *The Subject Matters: Classroom Activity in Maths and Social Studies* (Chicago: University of Chicago Press, 1988). A. Sosniak and C.L. Perlman, 'Secondary education by the book', *Journal of Curriculum Studies* (1990), 22(5), pp. 427–42. T. Wood *et al.*, 'The contextual nature of teaching: mathematics and reading instruction in one second-grade classroom', *Elementary School Journal* (1990), 90(5), pp. 497–513.

3 G.H. Bantock, 'The parochialism of the present: some reflections on the history of educational theory', *Journal of Philosophy of Education* (1979), 13, pp. 41–54.

4 M. Buckman, 'The flight away from content in teacher education and teaching', *Journal of Curriculum Studies* (1982), 14(1), pp. 61–8.

5 M. Warnock, 'The authority of the teacher', *Westminster Studies in Education* (1989), 12, pp. 73–81. M. Buckmann, *The Careful Vision: How Practical is Contemplation in Teaching?* (East Lansing: National Center for Research on Teacher Education, Michigan State University, 1989).

6 S. Lawlor, *Teachers Mistaught: Training in Theories or Education in Subjects?* (London: Centre for Policy Studies, 1990).

7 L.S. Shulman, 'Those who understand: knowledge growth in teaching', *Educational Researcher* (1986), 15(2), pp. 4–14.

8 Department of Education and Science, *Standards in Education 1989–90, The Annual Report of HM Senior Chief Inspector of Schools* (London: DES, 1991), pp. 2 and 16.

9 P.L. Grossman *et al.*, 'Teachers of substance: subject matter knowledge in teaching', in M.C. Reynolds (ed.), *Knowledge Base for the Beginning Teacher* (Oxford: Pergamon Press, 1989), pp. 23–36.

10 Department of Education and Science, *Primary Education in England, a Survey by HM Inspectors of Schools* (London: HMSO, 1978).

11 For example, Department of Education and Science, *Teaching Quality*, Cmnd 8836 (London: HMSO, 1983).

12 W. Taylor, 'The control of teacher education: The council for the accreditation of teacher education', in N.J. Graves (ed.), *Initial Teacher Education: Policies and Progress* (London: Kogan Page, 1990), pp. 109–23.

13 D.R. McNamara, 'Subject knowledge and its application: problems and possibilities for teacher educators', *Journal of Teacher Education* (1991), 17(2), pp. 113–28.

14 Department of Education and Science, *Children and their Primary Schools*, vol. 1 (London: HMSO, 1967).

15 Ibid., p. 198.

16 Ibid., p. 198.

17 Ibid., p. 199.

18 See Ibid., p. 189, for Plowden's acknowledgement.

19 The following exposition is based upon L.N. Tanner, 'The meaning of curriculum in Dewey's laboratory school (1896–1904)', *Journal of Curriculum Studies* (1991), 23(2), pp. 101–17.

20 Quoted in Ibid.

21 With reference to history, geography, and science see Her Majesty's Inspectorate, *Aspects of Primary Education: The Teaching and Learning of History and Geography* (London: HMSO, 1989); Her Majesty's Inspectorate, *Aspects of Primary Education: The Teaching and Learning of Science* (London: HMSO, 1989).

22 Based on L. Cohen and L. Manion, *A Guide to Teaching Practice* (London: Methuen, 1977), p. 122.

23 Based on Schools Council Working Paper 75, *Primary Practice: A Sequel to the Practical Curriculum* (London: Methuen Educational, 1983), p. 109.

24 Department of Education and Science 1991, op. cit., p. 6.

25 See for example R.J.A. Alexander *et al.*, *Curriculum Organisation and Classroom Practice in Primary Schools, a Discussion Paper* (London: DES, 1992). National Curriculum Council, *The National Curriculum at Stages 1 and 2: Advice to the Secretary of Education* (York: National Curriculum Council, 1993).

26 Shulman, op. cit.
27 Ibid., p. 8
28 See, for example D.L. Ball, 'The mathematical understandings that pros-
    pective teachers bring to teacher education', *The Elementary School Journal*
    (1990), 90(4), pp. 449–66. T.P. Carpenter *et al.*, 'Teachers' pedagogical content
    knowledge of students' problem solving in elementary arithmetic', *Journal of
    Research in Mathematics Education* (1988), 19(5), pp. 385–401. P.L. Grossman,
    'A study in contrast: sources of pedagogical content knowledge for secondary
    English', *Journal of Teacher Education* (1989), 30(5), pp. 24–31. R. Marks, 'Peda-
    gogical content knowledge: from a mathematical case to a modified con-
    ception', *Journal of Teacher Education* (1990), 41(3), pp. 3–11. P.L. Peterson *et al.*,
    'Teachers' pedagogical content beliefs in mathematics', *Cognition and Instruc-
    tion* (1989), 6(1), pp. 1–40. S.M. Wilson *et al.*, '150 different ways of knowing:
    representations of knowledge in teaching', in J. Calderhead (ed.), *Exploring
    Teachers' Thinking* (London: Cassell, 1987), pp. 104–24. P. Tamir, 'Subject
    matter and related pedagogical knowledge in teacher education', *Teaching
    and Teacher Education* (1988), 4(2), pp. 99–110.
29 C. Kruger *et al.*, 'A survey of primary teachers' conceptions of force and
    motion', *Educational Research* (1990), 32(2), pp. 83–94. C. Kruger *et al.*, 'An
    investigation of some English primary school teachers' understanding of the
    concepts of force and gravity', *British Educational Research Journal* (1990),
    16(41), pp. 383–97. D.C. Smith and D.C. Neale, 'The construction of subject
    matter knowledge in primary science teaching', *Teaching and Teacher Edu-
    cation* (1989), 5(1), pp. 1–20.
30 D.R. McNamara, 'Subject study in teacher education', in P. Hodkinson and G.
    Harvard (eds), *Action and Reflection in Teacher Education* (Norwood, NJ: Ablex,
    1993).
31 For a discussion see H. McEwan, 'Teaching as pedagogic interpretation',
    Journal of Philosophy of Education (1989), 23(1), pp. 61–71.
32 From Marks, op. cit.
33 These issues are discussed in more detail with reference to the research
    evidence in McNamara (1991), op. cit.
34 See for example Shulman, op. cit.; Marks, op. cit.; Ball, op. cit.; and parti-
    cularly G.W. McDiarmid, 'Why staying one chapter ahead doesn't really
    work: subject-specific pedagogy', in M.C. Reynolds (ed.), *Knowledge Base for
    Beginning Teachers* (Oxford: Pergamon Press, 1989), pp. 193–205.
35 Ball, op. cit.
36 For an illustration of this theme see C. Desforges and A. Cockburn, *Under-
    standing the Mathematics Teacher: a Study of Practice in First Schools*, (Lewes,
    Falmer Press, 1987), pp. 90ff.
37 H. McEwan and B. Bull, 'The pedagogic nature of subject matter knowledge',
    American Educational Research Journal (1991), 28(2), pp. 316–34.
38 Department of Education and Science, *Mathematics Key Stages 1 and 3: A
    Report by HM Inspectorate on the First Year, 1989–90* (London: HMSO, 1991), p.
    16.
39 Grossman *et al.*, op. cit.
40 S. Feiman-Nemser and M.B. Parker, 'Making subject matter part of the con-
    versation in learning to teach', *Journal of Teacher Education* (1990), 41(3), pp.
    32–43.
41 For a discussion see P.L. Grossman, 'When teaching what you know doesn't
    work: a re-analysis of methods and findings', paper presented at the annual
    meeting of the American Educational Research Association, Boston, 1990.

42 E. Eisner, *The Enlightened Eye: Qualitative Inquiry and the Enhancement of Educational Practice* (New York: Macmillan, 1991), pp. 76ff.

7 PEDAGOGY IN PRACTICE: THE CASE OF SUBTRACTION

1 For this issue see W.H. Cockcroft, *Mathematics Counts* (London: HMSO, 1982). M. Lampert, 'Knowing, doing and teaching multiplication', *Cognition and Instruction* (1986), 3(4), pp. 305–42.
2 See for example M. Hughes, *Children and Number* (Oxford: Basil Blackwell, 1985), ch. 2. N. Bennett *et al.*, *The Quality of Pupil Learning Experiences* (London: Lawrence Earlbaum Associates, 1984).
3 Department of Education and Science, *Mathematics in the National Curriculum* (London: HMSO, 1989).
4 For discussion of the notion of tacit skills see M. Polanyi, *Knowing and Being* (London: Routledge & Kegan Paul, 1969).
5 C. Desforges and A. Cockburn, *Understanding the Mathematics Teacher: A Study of Practice in First Schools* (Lewes: Falmer Press, 1987).
6 G. Leinhardt, 'Situated knowledge and expertise in teaching', in J. Calderhead (ed.), *Teachers' Professional Learning* (London: Falmer Press, 1988), pp. 146–68.
7 T.A. Romberg and T.P. Carpenter, 'Research on teaching and learning mathematics: two disciplines of scientific enquiry', in M.W. Wittrock (ed.), *Handbook of Research on Teaching* (3rd edn) (New York: Macmillan, 1986), pp. 850–73.
8 K. Van Lehn, 'Bugs are not enough: empirical studies of bugs, impasses and repairs in procedural skills', *Journal of Mathematical Behaviour* (1982), 3(2), pp. 3–71.
9 J. Confrey, 'Bridging research and practice', *Educational Theory* (1987), 37(4), pp. 383–94.
10 Desforges and Cockburn, op. cit.
11 Hughes, op. cit.
12 For an illustration of the limited and somewhat uninformed manner in which the research makes assumptions about how subtraction is taught and how children approach learning subtraction see K. Van Lehn, *Mind Bugs: The Origins of Procedural Misconceptions* (London: Batsford Books, 1990), pp. 24–38.
13 Van Lehn, 1982, op. cit.
14 Van Lehn, 1990, op. cit.
15 For a full glossary see Ibid., pp. 219–33.
16 Ibid., p. 16.
17 Ibid., ch. 2.
18 R. Penrose, *The Emperor's New Mind: Concerning Computers, Minds, and the Laws of Physics* (Oxford: Oxford University Press, 1989).
19 G. Ryle, 'Thinking and self-teaching', in G. Ryle, *On Thinking*, edited by K. Kolenda (Oxford: Basil Blackwell, 1979).
20 For an example see T.N. Carraher *et al.*, 'Mathematics in the streets and in schools', *British Journal of Developmental Psychology* (1985), 3, pp. 21–9.
21 K. Hart, 'There is little connection', in P. Ernest (ed.), *Mathematics Teaching: The State of the Art* (Lewes: Falmer Press, 1989).
22 For an elaboration on this theme see J. Smedslund, 'Revising explications of common sense through dialogue: thirty-six psychological theorems', *Scandinavian Journal of Psychology* (1982), 23, pp. 299–305.

23 See, for example Department of Education and Science, *Primary Education in England: A Survey by HM Inspectors of Schools* (London: HMSO, 1978). J. Barker Lunn, 'Junior school teachers: their methods of practices', *Educational Research* (1982), 26(3), pp. 178–88. P. Mortimore *et al.*, *School Matters: The Junior Years* (Wells: Open Books, 1988).
24 There are a number of discussions on this issue; see for example R. Rorty, *Contingency, Irony, and Solidarity* (Cambridge: Cambridge University Press, 1989). G. Ryle, 'Knowing how and knowing that', in G. Ryle, *The Concept of Mind*, (London: Hutchinson, 1949).
25 See the discussion in Desforges and Cockburn, op. cit.
26 P. Jackson, 'The way teaching is', in R.T. Hyman (ed.), *Contemporary Thought on Teaching* (Englewood Cliffs, NJ: Prentice Hall, 1971).

8 TEACHERS' PEDAGOGIC EXPERTISE

1   G. Leinhardt, 'Capturing craft knowledge in teaching', *Educational Researcher* (1990), 19(2), pp. 18–25.
2   R.J. Sternberg and D.R. Caruso, 'Practical modes of learning', in E. Eisner (ed.), *Learning and Teaching and Ways of Knowing, Eighty-fourth Year-book of the National Society for the Study of Education* (Chicago: University of Chicago Press, 1985), pp. 133–57.
3   M. Polanyi, 'Personal knowledge', in M. Polanyi and H. Prosch, *Meaning* (Chicago: University of Chicago Press, 1975), pp. 22–45.
4   G. Leinhardt, 'Situated knowledge and expertise in teaching', in J. Calderhead (ed.), *Teachers' Professional Learning* (London, Falmer Press, 1988), pp. 146–67.
5   L. Rubin, 'The thinking teacher: cultivating pedagogical intelligence', *Journal of Teacher Education* (1989), 40(6), pp. 31–4.
6   L.S. Shulman, 'Knowledge and teaching: foundations of the new reform', *Harvard Educational Review* (1987), 57(1), pp. 1–22.
7   J. Schuab, 'The practical: arts of eclectic', *School Review* (1971), 79, pp. 495–542.
8   D.R. McNamara, 'Sir Karl Popper and education', *British Journal of Educational Studies* (1978), 26(1), pp. 24–39.
9   D.R. McNamara, 'Vernacular pedagogy', *British Journal of Educational Studies* (1991), 39(3), pp. 297–310.
10 For an examination of this theme see P. Ashton, 'A teacher education paradigm to empower teachers and students', in L.G. Katz and J.D. Raths (eds), *Advances in Teacher Education*, vol. 4, (Norwood, NJ: Ablex, 1991), pp. 82–104.
11 L. Valli and A.R. Tom, 'How adequate are the knowledge base frameworks in teacher education?', *Journal of Teacher Education* (1988), 39(5), pp. 5–12. J. Henderson, 'A curriculum response to the knowledge base reform movement', *Journal of Teacher Education* (1988), 39(5), pp. 13–17.
12 For a discussion see for example Shulman, op. cit.
13 D.C. Lortie, *Schoolteacher: A Sociological Study* (Chicago: University of Chicago Press, 1975).
14 Shulman, op. cit.
15 See for example M. Cochran-Smith and S.L. Lyttle, 'Research on teaching and teacher research: the issues that divide', *Educational Researcher* 1990), 19(2), pp. 2–11. G. Leinhardt, 1990, op. cit. F.M. Connelly and D.J. Clandinin, 'Stories of experience and narrative inquiry', *Educational Researcher* (1990), 19(5), pp. 2–14. P.W. Jackson, 'The functions of educational research', *Educational Researcher* (1990), 19(7), pp. 3–9.

16 E. Eisner, 'The primacy of experience and the politics of method', *Educational Researcher* (1988), 17(5), pp. 15–20. See also the more extensive exposition in E. Eisner, *The Enlightened Eye: Qualitative Inquiry and the Enhancement of Educational Practice* (New York: Macmillan, 1991).

17 J. Connelly and Clandinin, op. cit.

18 K. Popper, *Objective Knowledge: An Evolutionary Approach* (Oxford: Clarendon Press, 1972).

19 Ibid., pp. 153ff.

20 See for example Department of Education and Science, *The Teaching and Learning of Mathematics* (London: HMSO, 1989). Department of Education and Science, *The Teaching and Learning of Science* (London: HMSO, 1989). Department of Education and Science, *The Teaching and Learning of Language and Literacy* (London: HMSO, 1990).

21 For a technical and extended discussion of these issues see Cochran-Smith and Lyttle, op. cit.; Connelly and Clandinin, op. cit.; Eisner, 1988, op. cit.; Jackson, op. cit.

22 E. Eisner, 'On the uses of educational connoisseurship and criticism for evaluating classroom life', *Teachers College Record* (1977), 78(3), pp. 345–58.

23 Eisner's work and his approach to educational research contain many insights and suggestions which may be useful to those interested in acquiring vernacular pedagogy. It must be remembered, though, that however sympathetic the educational connoisseur may be to classroom life he is envisaged by Eisner as an 'outsider' and someone who offers a critical account and review of schooling and education in a manner comparable with the way in which the critic may evaluate a work of art. The educational connoisseur is, as it were, concerned with engaging in good critical connoisseurship according to the principles of that endeavour.

24 P. Hirst, *Knowledge and the Curriculum* (London: Routledge & Kegan Paul, 1974), ch. 7.

25 Jackson, op. cit.

26 Eisner, 1991, op. cit., pp. 53ff.

27 Connelly and Clandinin, op. cit.

28 Leinhardt, 1990, op. cit.

29 W. Rabinowitz and R.M.W. Travers, 'Problems of defining and assessing teacher effectiveness', in R.T. Hyman (ed.), *Contemporary Thought on Teaching* (Englewood Cliffs, NJ: Prentice Hall, 1971), pp. 213–20.

9 THE PROFESSIONAL AUTHORITY OF THE TEACHER

1 See for example R. Dreeben, *The Nature of Teaching* (Glenview: Scott Foresman & Co., 1970). A. Etzioni, *The Semi-Professions and their Organisation: Teachers, Nurses and Social Workers* (New York: Free Press, 1969). V. Burke, *Teachers in Turmoil* (Harmondsworth: Penguin Books, 1971). S. Cole, *The Unionization of Teachers: A Case Study of the UFT* (Glenview: Praeger, 1969). J. Purvis, 'Schooling as a professional career', *British Journal of Sociology* (1973), 24(1), pp. 43–57. J.T. Ozga and M.A. Lawn, *Teachers, Professionalism and Class: A Study of Organised Teachers* (London: Falmer Press, 1981).

2 Consider, for example, the evidence collected for the Houghton Committee: HMSO, *The Report of the Committee of Inquiry into the Pay of Non University Teachers*, Cmnd 5848 (London: HMSO, 1974). For a wide-ranging discussion of the issues see M. Sudlack, and S. Schlossman, *Who Will Teach? Historical Perspectives on the Changing Appeal of Teaching as a Profession* (Santa Monica:

Rand Corporation, Center for the Study of the Teaching Profession, 1986). M. Warwick, *A Common Policy for Education* (Oxford: Oxford University Press, 1988), ch. 4. International Labour Organization, *The Status of Teachers* (Geneva: ILO, UNESCO, 1984).

3   H.C. Dent, *The Training of Teachers in England and Wales 1800–1975* (London: Hodder & Stoughton, 1977).

4   For example see S. Lawlor, *Teachers Mistaught: Training in Theories or Education in Subjects* (London: Centre for Policy Studies, 1990). D.J. O'Keeffe, *The Wayward Elite, A Critique of British Teacher-Education* (London: Adam Smith Institute, 1990). A. O'Hear, *Who Teaches the Teachers?* (London: Social Affairs Unit, 1988).

5   Such as D. Hargreaves, 'Another radical approach to the reform of initial teacher training', *Westminster Studies in Education* (1990), 13, pp. 5–11.

6   For a review see D. McNamara, 'Research on teachers' thinking: its contribution to educating student teachers to think critically', *Journal of Education for Teaching* (1990), 16(2), pp. 147–60. Much of the discussion on teacher thinking in what follows is drawn from this paper.

7   Ibid.

8   See particularly V.J. Furlong *et al.*, *Initial Teacher Training and the Role of the School* (Milton Keynes: Open University Press, 1988). P. Benton (ed.), *The Oxford Internship Scheme: Integration + Partnership in Initial Teacher Education* (London: Calouste Gulbenkian Foundation, 1990).

9   For a detailed discussion see R. Barrow, 'Teacher education: theory and practice', *British Journal of Educational Studies* (1990), 28(4), pp. 308–18.

10   Ibid.

11   P. Jackson, *Life in Classrooms* (New York: Holt, Rinehart & Winston, 1968), p. 149.

12   For a discussion see for example H. Gardner, *The Mind's New Science: A History of the Cognitive Revolution* (New York: Basic Books, 1987).

13   G. Ryle, *The Concept of Mind* (London: Hutchinson, 1949), pp. 22ff. See also M. Oakeshot, 'The idea of a university', in T. Fuller (ed.), *The Voice of Liberal Learning: Michael Oakeshot on Education* (New Haven, Conn.: Yale University Press, 1989), p. 95.

14   For an extended account see R.E. Nisbett and T.D. Wilson, 'Telling more than we can know, verbal reports on mental processes', *Psychological Review* (1977), 84(3), pp. 231–59.

15   G. Ryle, *On Thinking* (Oxford: Basil Blackwell, 1979), ch. 4.

16   R. Rorty, *Contingency, Irony and Solidarity* (Cambridge: Cambridge University Press, 1989), pp. 73ff.

17   Ibid., p. 89.

18   R.E. Floden and H.G. Klinzing, 'What can research on teacher thinking contribute to teacher preparation? A second opinion', *Educational Researcher* (1990), 19(5), pp. 15–20.

19   There is, of course, the view that teaching should be regarded as an art, see for example E.W. Eisner, 'The art and craft of teaching', in J. Abruscato, *Introduction to Teaching and the Study of Education* (Englewood Cliffs, NJ: Prentice Hall, 1985), pp. 16–25.

20   G. Steiner, *Real Presences: Is There Anything in What We Say?* (London: Faber & Faber, 1989), part 1.

21   For an extensive illustration of this point see E.W. Eisner, *The Enlightened Eye: Qualitative Inquiry and the Enhancement of Educational Practice* (New York: Macmillan, 1991), pp. 129–49.

22 For example J. Nias and S. Groundwater-Smith (eds), *The Enquiring Teacher: Supporting and Sustaining Teacher Research* (London: Falmer Press, 1988). J. Ruddock, 'Practitioner research and programmes of initial teacher education', *Westminster Studies in Education* (1989), 12, pp. 61–72.

23 M. Huberman, 'The professional life cycle of teachers', *Teachers College Record* (1989), 91(1), pp. 31–57.

24 V. Makins, 'The new seekers after truth', *Times Educational Supplement*, 22 March 1991, p. 10.

25 For an example see S. Rowland, 'My body of knowledge', in J. Nias and S. Groundwater-Smith (eds), *The Enquiring Teacher: Supporting and Sustaining Teacher Research* (London: Falmer Press, 1988), pp. 54–65.

26 J. Whitehead, 'How can I improve my contribution to practitioner research in teacher education? A response to Jean Ruddock', *Westminster Studies in Education* (1990), 13, pp. 27–36.

27 F. Elbaz, 'Research on teacher's knowledge: the evaluation of a discourse', *Journal of Curriculum Studies* (1991), 23(1), pp. 1–19.

28 As is exemplified, for example, by the work being encouraged and promoted by the National Primary Centre, (Westminster College, Oxford) and the Association for the Study of Primary Education (Education Office, Peterborough).

29 This theme has been explored by commentators from different disciplinary bases, for example D. Edwards and N. Mercer, *Curriculum Knowledge: The Development of Understanding in the Classroom* (London: Methuen, 1987). J.S. Brown *et al.*, *Situated Cognition and the Culture of Learning* (Palo Alto: Institute for Research on Learning, 1988). Rorty, op. cit.

30 P.W. Jackson, *The Practice of Teaching* (New York: Teachers College Press, 1989), pp. 97ff.

31 For a discussion with reference to education see E. Duckworth, *The Having of Wonderful Ideas and Other Essays on Teaching and Learning* (New York: Teachers College Press, 1987), pp. 16ff.

32 M.M. Kennedy, 'Reflection and the problem of professional standards', *Colloquy* (1989), 2(2), pp. 1–61 (East Lansing: National Center for Research on Teacher Education, Michigan State University).

33 K.R. Popper, *Objective Knowledge: An Evolutionary Approach* (Oxford: Oxford University Press, 1972). K.R. Popper, *Unended Quest: An Intellectual Autobiography* (London: Fontana, 1976).

34 Popper, 1972, op. cit., pp. 241ff.

35 Ibid., pp. 287ff; and Popper, 1976, op. cit., pp. 132–35.

36 A particularly worthwhile discussion is provided by P.W. Jackson, 'The functions of educational research', *Educational Researcher* (1990), 19(7), pp. 3–9.

37 See for example D.C. Lortie, *School Teacher: A Sociological Portrait* (Chicago: University of Chicago Press, 1975). J.W. Little, 'The persistence of privacy: autonomy and initiative in teachers' professional relations', paper presented at the annual meeting of the American Educational Research Association, San Francisco, 1989.

38 See for example P. Tamir, 'Professional and personal knowledge of teachers and teacher educators', *Teaching and Teacher Education* (1991), 7(3), pp. 263–68.

Index

ability grouping 64–7
academic work (nature of) 68–70
action research 140
active instruction 71–2
active learner 19–20, 44–5
adult illiteracy (Cuba) 10–11
'advanced organisers' 12
amanuensis (in vernacular
    pedagogy) 117–18, 119, 122, 123
aptitudes, children's (relating
    teaching to) 46–62
Articled Teacher Scheme 133
artist analogy 138–9
'associationism' 56
attainment targets 51, 83, 89
Ausubel, D.P. 56
authority, see professional authority

Barrow, R. 135
basic skills 16–17, 24, 41, 48, 51, 85
Bereiter, C. 27, 72
Better Schools (1985) 50
blame/criticism 22, 77
breakthroughs/jumps (learning) 43
Bruner, J. 26, 28
'bug migration' 103
'buggy algorithms' 100–5
burn-out 64

centres of interest 80, 83–4, 86, 96–7
child-centred approach 1, 3, 16, 18,
    19–20, 27, 31, 52, 53–4
children: demonstrating importance
    of work to 71–2; disposition to
    learn 32–7; grouping policy 64–7;
    as practical learners 78;
    responsibility to learn 39–40
children's aptitudes, relating

teaching to 46; match closeness
    54–9; matching evidence 47–51;
    matching evidence assessed 51–4;
    subject content 59–61; summary
    61–2
Chinese model (teaching) 11–12
Chomsky, Noam 35
Clandinin, D.J. 119
class tests 17, 127
classroom context 18–19, 21–3, 45, 100
close matching 54–9, 61–2
cognitive structures 56–7
coherence 118
completed work (response to) 126–7
completing work (in classroom) 70
Connelly, F.M. 119
consensus 118
constructivism 27, 33, 34
content 69–70; continuity and 68;
    knowledge 90–1, 93–6; see also
    subject matter; subject matter,
    organising (for learning)
contingency approach 41, 44, 78, 107,
    108, 143
Cortazzi, M. 43
Council for the Accreditation of
    Teacher Education (CATE) 30, 132
craft knowledge 110, 119
criticism/blame 22, 77
cross-curricular themes 87, 89
Cuba (adult illiteracy) 10–11
cultural environment 29
curriculum knowledge 90, 93, 96
curriculum materials 96

Davis, A. 54–5
de-streaming 34
decomposition method 102

delivery model 20, 92
DES 48, 133
descriptive information 121
desk arrangements 66–7
Dewey, J. 23, 84–5
didactic approach 1, 16, 18
differentiated learning activities 46, 51, 65, 82
direct instruction 71
discipline 70
discovery-orientated teaching 3, 20, 21, 49, 50, 52, 66
displaying work 127–8
'domain of knowledge' 90

Education Act (1944) 15
Education Reform Act (1988) 82
educational connoisseur 117–18
Eisner, E.W. 35, 114, 117, 118, 119
empowerment 144–5
energy (teacher) 64
enrichment tasks 49
equivalence method 101–2, 106, 107
ethnic minorities 30–1, 32
expertise 131–2; and its application 89–91; teachers' pedagogic 109–28

'facilitator' role 18, 20
feedback 53, 71, 72
flow charts 85–8
formal approach 1
frames of reference 21, 45, 79, 91, 93, 99, 115, 121, 137, 140, 144

gender 30, 31
General Teaching Council proposal 132
'ghost in the machine' 135
Gould, Stephen 41
grammar schools 30
grouping policy 64–7
Herbart, J.F. 56
Hirst, Paul 38–9, 40, 46–7, 117
HMI 16, 47–8, 50, 81, 87, 96, 116
homogeneous ability groups 65–6

ILEA 30, 52
illiteracy, adult (Cuba) 10–11
incremental tasks 49–50
'inert ideas' 84
infant classrooms (matching in) 48–9
informal approach 1

Inner London Education Authority 30, 52
instrumental utility 118, 119
intelligent action 136
interpreting vernacular pedagogy 120–2
'ironic' thought 137

Jackson, Philip 24, 40, 135
James, William 27–8

knowledge 11–12; application of 92–7; content 90–1, 93–6; craft 110, 119; curriculum 90, 93, 96; objective 115, 120, 143; organisation of 82–9; personal 91–3, 97, 102, 107, 110–12, 132; professional, see professional knowledge; schemata theory 56–8, 59–60, 143; structures 56–8; situated 109; of subject matter 80–1, 89–91; subjective 115; teacher's (acquisition) 91–2; teacher's (establishment) 140–4; vernacular pedagogic 112–28; worlds of 114–15, 117, 118, 120
Korczak, J. 32

language 13, 16–17, 29, 35, 48, 58
learning 24; child's disposition to 32–7; classroom context 18–19, 21–3, 45, 100; failure 103–4, 105; matching teaching to 46–62; 'natural' 32–7, 44; organising subject matter for 80–98; organising teaching to promote 63–79; as practical activity 43–5; psychological contribution 25–8; sociological contribution 28–32; teacher's responsibility 38–45; as work 72–8
Leeds study 50, 53
lesson content, see content; subject matter; subject matter, organising (for learning)
lesson plans, 15
Licensed Teacher Scheme 133

maintaining order 22–3, 67–70, 77, 79
Maori-speaking teachers (New Zealand) 10
master teachers 11–12, 119

matching teaching to learning 46; close
    matching 54–9; evidence 47–51;
    evidence assessed 51–4; subject
    content 59–61; summary 61–2
mathematics 16, 17, 41, 42–3, 48, 58,
    94–5, 99–108
'meaningful learning' 56
memory 26
mismatching 52, 55, 59
'missing paradigm' 81
mixed-ability classes 46, 63, 65, 123
Montessori method 35
motivation 49, 53, 59, 62, 107

National Curriculum 17, 51, 57–8,
    81–3, 85, 87, 89, 91–2, 94, 96, 99, 105
National Curriculum Council 5
'natural' learning 32–7, 44
'natural' teaching 9–14
NFER survey 16
Non-Statutory guidance 87

objective knowledge 115, 120, 143
one-to-one teaching 21
opportunity-maximisation 63–4
ORACLE survey 16, 52
organisation of knowledge 82–9

parents 21, 35
passive learner 19, 20
pedagogic expertise: acquiring
    vernacular pedagogy 113–17;
    interpreting vernacular pedagogy
    120–2; method 117–19; summary
    123; teachers' practical pedagogy
    109–13; vernacular pedagogy
    examples 123–8; vernacular
    pedagogy by proxy 122–3
pedagogic knowledge 90, 93–6, 109–13
pedagogical intelligence 110
pedagogy: definition 6; in practice
    99–108; teaching as practical 67–71
personal knowledge 91–3, 97, 102,
    107, 110–12, 132
Piaget, J. 27, 33
'pick and mix' approach 87
Plowden Report 2–3, 33–4, 52, 83–4, 85
Popper, Karl 114–15, 143
Post-Graduate Certificate in
    Education 133
'practical knowledge' 109–10
practical learner, child as 78

practical learning 43–5
practical pedagogy, teaching as 67–71
practice tasks 49–50
praise (and reward) 76–7
primary education debate 1–7
'primary school revolution' 18
problem-solving strategies 102–3
procedures (learning as work) 77–8
product (of work tasks) 75
production process (work tasks) 75
professional authority 5, 109, 129;
    empowerment 144–5; knowledge
    base 137–40; professional and
    130–4; teachers' knowledge 140–4;
    teachers' thinking 134–7
professional judgement 130
professional knowledge 2, 19,
    110–11; base 4–5, 131–2, 137–40;
    establishment of 140–4; vernacular
    113–14, 116, 121, 123, 140, 142, 144
progressive approach 1, 17–21, 33–4,
    52, 53, 84
project work 80, 83–4, 85–9
proxy methods (vernacular
    pedagogy) 122–3
psychological contribution (to
    learning) 25–8

qualifications (of professionals) 132–3
'question and answer' sessions 124–6
questioning skills 13

race/racial groups 30–1, 32
reading 16, 17, 33, 43, 48, 58
'reflective practitioner' 99, 135–40,
    141–4
religion 30
'repair theory' 102–3
research evidence (pedagogy in
    practice) 100–5
resource use 75
resources 77–8, 96
restructuring tasks 49–50
revision tasks 49
reward (learning as work) 76–7
Richards, C. 18
Rorty, R. 136–7
routine work 68–9
Ryle, G. 35, 136

schemata theory 56–8, 59–60, 143
school (environment) 15–16

School Examination and Assessment Council 5
Schools Council 86
'sea' project 85–6, 87
'sharp compassion' 3
Shulman, L.S. 89–90, 91, 93, 96, 110, 111–12
significance (of work tasks) 75
single-subject lessons 17
situated knowledge 109
skills 59; basic 16–17, 24, 41, 48, 51, 85; motivational 62; questioning 13; tacit 99
social arrangements 68
social class 29–30, 31, 32
social environment 28–32
sociological contribution to learning 28–32
specialist subject teaching 81, 82, 83, 85
stage theory 26
Steiner, George 5
Stephens, J.M. 11, 35
streaming 33–4, 65
subject-centred approach 1, 3
subject matter 14, 15, 23, 67; matching child and 59–61
subject matter, organising (for learning) 80–81; application of knowledge 92–7; knowledge and its application 89–91; organisation of knowledge 82–9; summary 97–8; teacher's knowledge (acquisition) 91–2
subject teaching 81, 82, 83, 85
subjective knowledge 115
subtraction (pedagogy in practice) 41, 99–108
systematic errors 100–5

tacit knowledge 110
tacit skills 99
tasks: learning as work 74–8; matching activities 49–53
teacher-centred approach 2–4, 17, 18–19, 54
teacher research 140
teachers: knowledge acquisition 91–2; knowledge establishment 140–4; pedagogic expertise 109–28; pedagogical choices 67–71; professional authority 129–45; responsibility for learning 38–45; thinking 134–7, 142
Teachers' Centre 96
teaching 8; classroom context 21–3; definitions 38–43; as familiar activity 9–14; inherent stability 14–21; 'natural' 9–14; organised (to promote learning) 53–79; as practical pedagogy 67–71; related to child's aptitudes 46–62
teaching, organising (to promote learning) 63–4; demonstrating importance of work 71–2; grouping policy 64–7; learning as work 72–8; maximising time/opportunity 63–4; summary 78–9; teaching as practical pedagogy 67–71
'teaching school' 133
tests 17, 127
theory 135–6, 137–9, 140–1
thinking, teachers' 134–7, 142
'third party' amanuensis 117
thought experiments 115
time-maximisation 63–4
topic work 80, 83–4, 85–9, 96–7
traditional approach 1, 19–21, 34, 54
training 9, 10, 14, 32, 82; CATE 30, 132; knowledge acquisition 91–3, 114; for professional authority 133–4, 135, 139, 140–1
trust 132

universities 19
vernacular pedagogy 112, 130, 140, 142, 144; acquisition (and method) 113–19; examples 123–8; interpretation 120–2; by proxy 122–3

whole class teaching 18, 19, 66
'William Tindale Affair' 31
Wilson, Harold 30
'wisdom in practice' 110
work: demonstrating importance of 71–2; learning as 72–8
'Worlds of Knowledge' 114–15, 117, 118, 120
wrong answers (response to) 105–6, 117, 125–6